Design and Deploy Microsoft Azure Virtual Desktop

An Essential Guide for Architects and Administrators

Puthiyavan Udayakumar

Apress®

Design and Deploy Microsoft Azure Virtual Desktop: An Essential Guide for Architects and Administrators

Puthiyavan Udayakumar
Abu Dhabi, United Arab Emirates

ISBN-13 (pbk): 978-1-4842-7795-9
https://doi.org/10.1007/978-1-4842-7796-6

ISBN-13 (electronic): 978-1-4842-7796-6

Managing Director, Apress Media LLC: Welmoed Spahr
Acquisitions Editor: Smriti Srivastava
Development Editor: Laura Berendson
Coordinating Editor: Shrikant Vishwakarma
Copyeditor: Brendan D. Frost

Cover designed by eStudioCalamar

Cover image designed by Pexels

Distributed to the book trade worldwide by Springer Science+Business Media LLC, 1 New York Plaza, Suite 4600, New York, NY 10004. Phone 1-800-SPRINGER, fax (201) 348-4505, e-mail orders-ny@springer-sbm. com, or visit www.springeronline.com. Apress Media, LLC is a California LLC and the sole member (owner) is Springer Science + Business Media Finance Inc (SSBM Finance Inc). SSBM Finance Inc is a **Delaware** corporation.

For information on translations, please e-mail booktranslations@springernature.com; for reprint, paperback, or audio rights, please e-mail bookpermissions@springernature.com, or visit http://www.apress.com/rights-permissions.

Apress titles may be purchased in bulk for academic, corporate, or promotional use. eBook versions and licenses are also available for most titles. For more information, reference our Print and eBook Bulk Sales web page at http://www.apress.com/bulk-sales.

Any source code or other supplementary material referenced by the author in this book is available to readers on GitHub via the book's product page, located at www.apress.com/978-1-4842-7795-9. For more detailed information, please visit http://www.apress.com/source-code.

Printed on acid-free paper

To My Mother, Father, Brother, My Spouse
&
You Readers

Table of Contents

About the Author

Puthiyavan Udayakumar is a proficient cloud infrastructure architect/senior infrastructure consultant with more than 14 years' experience in the information technology industry. He is Microsoft certified Azure virtual desktop specialty and Microsoft certified Azure solutions architect expert. He has worked as an infrastructure solution architect/senior engineer in designing, deploying, and rolling out complex virtual and cloud infrastructure. He has more than 13 years of hands-on experience with products such as Citrix/ VMware/Microsoft Virtualization and cloud technologies. Puthiyavan has strong knowledge of cloud solution design and deployment, managed cloud services, cloud migration, and multi-cloud infrastructure management services.

About the Technical Reviewer

Bhadresh Shiyal is an Azure data architect and Azure data engineer and for past 7+ years, he has been working with a big IT MNC as a solutions architect. Prior to that, he has spent almost a decade in private and public sector banks in India in various IT positions working on various Microsoft technologies. He has a total of 18+ years of IT experience, out of which for two years, he worked on an international assignment from London. He has very rich experience in application design, development, and deployment.

He has worked on various technologies which includes Visual Basic, SQL Server, SharePoint Technologies, .NET MVC, O365, Azure Data Factory, Azure Databricks, Azure Synapse Analytics, Azure Data Lake Storage Gen1/Gen2, Azure SQL Data Warehouse, Power BI, Spark SQL, Scala, Delta Lake, Azure Machine Learning, Azure Information Protection, Azure .NET SDK, Azure DevOps, and so on.

Bhadresh holds multiple Azure certifications that include Microsoft certified Azure solutions architect expert, Microsoft certified Azure data engineer associate, Microsoft certified Azure data scientist associate, and Microsoft certified Azure data analyst associate. He has worked as solutions architect in a large-scale Azure data lake implementation project as well as a data transformation project along with large-scale customized content management systems. He has authored the book *Beginning Azure Synapse Analytics* with Apress, and has also reviewed the book titled *Data Science using Azure*.

Acknowledgments

Great thanks to Smriti Srivastava, acquisitions editor from Apress, for continuously shaping this book proposal from day 1. Special thanks to Shrikant Vishwakarma for tireless efforts in materializing the book. Thanks to all Apress production team members.

Introduction

The Microsoft Azure Virtual Desktop (AVD) is a desktop-as-a-service, which can be deployed to any device, is easily managed, and is incredibly secure. After covering AVD essentials, the book turns to the planning and method of preparing for AVD. Subsequent chapters deal with defining requirements and assessing the application, network, and security requirements. Following that, you will learn about the layers of Microsoft AVD, including the access layer, control layer, resource layer, hosting layer, and user layer. Additionally, you will read about deploying the desktop and hosting pool of the AVD services. A modern approach to managing and securing AVD components will be described toward the end of the book.

In this book, we will explain each essential skill to perform the design and deployment. This book aims to offer IT professionals the following:

- The book helps AVD administrators and Azure cloud architects upskill with a broader understanding of AVD services with real-world case studies and best practices.

- Standard DaaS framework and design methodology to be applied in the design workshops in the Microsoft AVD solution.

- The right blend of knowledge and skills required to plan, prepare, and run Microsoft AVD desktops, applications, data, and networking.

- Enabling readers with a method to analyze and assess end users' needs, define requirements, and define migration methodologies for a well-defined AVD service.

- Enabling readers with a method to monitor with golden signals, including KPIs such as speed, calculation, interfaces, and alerts as results help to maintain the reliability of AVD services in production.

- A comprehensive practical guide to managing and securing an AVD environment via site reliability engineering practices along with real examples to automate AVD tasks using Azure PowerShell, Azure CLI, Azure resource templates, and Terraform.

CHAPTER 1

Microsoft AVD Essentials

Azure Virtual Desktop (AVD) integrates virtual desktop infrastructure (VDI) and the cloud. AVD is Microsoft Azure's platform-as-a-service (PaaS) offering from Microsoft. It enables small to large cloud consumers to provide remote applications and full desktops from Microsoft cloud to their end users.

This chapter provides the fundamentals, getting started with desktop-as-a-service (DaaS), key terminologies, and foundations needed for AVD.

By the end of this chapter, you should be able to understand the following:

- Fundamentals of cloud computing and Microsoft Azure,

- Getting started with DaaS,

- Key Microsoft AVD terminologies,

- Foundation for Microsoft AVD.

Introduction to Cloud Computing and Microsoft Azure

In this section, let us get started by understanding what cloud computing is.

Cloud computing is all about delivering computing services such as compute, network, storage, database, software, analytics, artificial intelligence, and other IT functions through the secured network to cloud consumer end users to achieve innovation via economies of scale.

Cloud computing very strongly evolved from a confusing and highly insecure concept to a great IT strategy that every IT consumer consumes. Regardless of size, small, medium, and large organizations can start adapting the overall cloud computing as a key enablement in their IT strategy.

© Puthiyavan Udayakumar 2022
P. Udayakumar, *Design and Deploy Microsoft Azure Virtual Desktop*,
https://doi.org/10.1007/978-1-4842-7796-6_1

A cloud services platform such as Microsoft Azure, Amazon Web Services (AWS), Google cloud (GCP), and other service providers owns and manages the network-connected device required for cloud services while implementing and allowing cloud consumers to obtain what is needed.

Figure 1-1 illustrates the key characteristics of cloud computing.

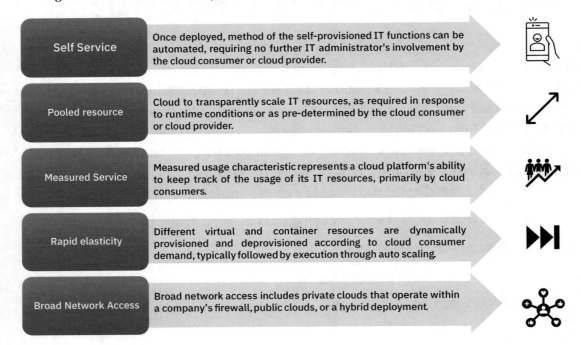

Figure 1-1. *Characteristics of cloud computing*

Cloud computing architecture combines virtualization, service orientation, grid computing, utility computing, and event-driven architecture.

Top Five Benefits of Cloud Computing

Both small and large organizations use cloud computing technology to store information in the cloud and access it from anywhere using the Internet connection.

Figure 1-2 depicts the top five benefits of cloud computing.

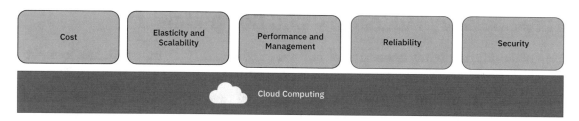

Figure 1-2. *Benfits of cloud computing*

The first benefit is the cost - cloud computing eliminates the need for capital expenditures (CAPEX) such as hardware and software running in on prem data centers (DCs), around-the-clock power and cooling, and subject matter experts in managing complex components 24/7.

Cloud service providers run on a consumption-based model means no upfront cost or no CAPEX and only operating expenditures (OPEX). This approach provides the ability to pay for additional resources only when needed and stop the same when no longer needed.

The second benefit is reachability. Cloud computing is available in both global or local availability to meet security, regulation, and compliance requirements.

The third benefit is performance and management. Cloud computing runs on a worldwide network that is highly secured and frequently patched and upgraded to the latest and greatest computing systems. Cloud computing offers excellent benefits compared with on-premises traditional DCs.

The fourth benefit is reliability. Cloud computing makes data backup, business continuity, and disaster recovery significantly less expensive due to the elimination of the old limiting factor, namely, availability zones. Cloud computing has site-level redundancy. Application and data are replicated and mirrored across the redundant sites as per subscription.

The fifth benefit is security: modern-day cloud service providers offer unlimited security components, controls, policies, compliance needs, and regulation standards, which heavily increases posture end to end. As a result, application infrastructure data are highly secure, and potential vulnerabilities and threats are controlled.

Three Delivery Models of Cloud Computing

Organizations frequently encounter abnormal weight on their IT infrastructure to meet growing client expectations for speedy, secure, and stable services. As they strive to develop their IT systems' processing compute and storage abilities, these organizations often find that improving and managing a hardy, scalable, and secure IT foundation is prohibitively high-priced.

Cloud computing equips DevOps, DevSecOp, and SRE engineers with the ability to converge on what matters most and withdraw undifferentiated trade such as procurement, support, and retention planning. As cloud computing has increased in prevalence, numerous distinct models and deployment strategies have emerged to improve the fit to the specific needs of other users. Each cloud service and deployment organization provides consumers with diverse levels of control, flexibility, and management.

The cloud delivery model depicts a specific flow of IT resources offered by a cloud provider. This terminology is typically linked with cloud computing and is commonly used to represent a remote environment and administration level. As depicted in Figure 1-3, cloud computing has three distinct delivery models: infrastructure-as-a-service (IaaS), PaaS, and software-as-a-service (SaaS).

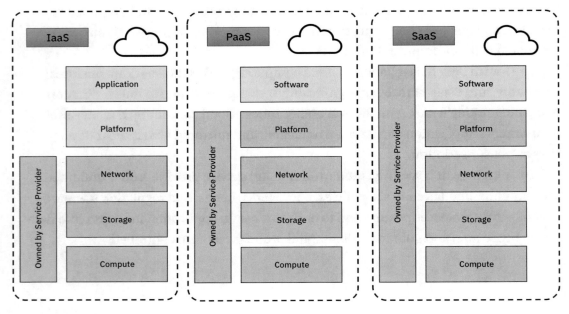

Figure 1-3. *Cloud computing deployment models*

IaaS is about delivering compute, network, storage, and backup as a service can be consumed on a yearly, monthly, or hourly basis. Resource units and their prices are provided as a catalogue.

PaaS is all about IaaS with an integrated set of middleware functions. Software development and deployment tools allow having a constant way to create, modify, update, and deploy an application on the cloud environment.

SaaS is all about the application hosted on top of PaaS or IaaS, either dedicated or shared. In this deployment model, cloud consumers only pay according to the app's consumption. The cloud service provider fully manages the underlying infrastructure and platform. Now, let us explore Azure cloud.

Are you planning to appear for AVD certification or build skills for AVD?

If the answer is "yes," as per the Microsoft exam, candidates appearing for the AVD exam should have proficiency in Azure technologies, including virtualization, networking, identity, storage, backups, resilience, and disaster recovery. Hence, I would like to get started with a high-level overview of Azure.

Microsoft Azure Overview

Azure provides 200-plus IT services online that enable the business to do almost everything required for modern digital needs.

Large businesses approach Azure by moving their existing lower environments to Azure. Migrating workloads to the cloud is a great start; however, the cloud is more than that with constant improvement and new updates.

A cloud consumer consumes Azure services via a web-based approach, namely, a unified console with an alternative to command-line tools. With the Azure portal, a business can manage Azure tenant subscriptions by using a graphical user interface. IT can deploy, manage, and monitor all subscribed IT services. The Azure portal allows creating custom IT dashboards for a structured view of IT services consumed by the cloud consumer. The Azure portal also allows IT users to configure accessibility choices for a better experience.

The first key concept is to broadly understand the foundation of Azure cloud. Azure cloud mainly offers cloud high availability, scalability, reliability, elasticity, agility, geo-distribution, resiliency, security, and Edge to provide the end users maximum uptime.

- **High availability**: Azure offers a wide variety of service-level agreements (SLAs) to choose from; cloud consumer cloud-based applications can implement continuous user action without possible downtime.

- **Reliability**: Azure is in a stable position; Azure offers an IT services workload to perform its intended function accurately and consistently when demanded. It offers a wide variety of autorecovery from failure.

- **Scalability**: Application in the cloud can scale both formats vertically and horizontally:

  - Scaling vertically adds compute capacity by adding vCPU or vRAM to a virtual machine (VM).

  - Scaling horizontally adds compute capacity by adding instances of resources, such as adding VMs.

- **Elasticity**: Cloud consumers can configure cloud-based applications to take advantage of autoscaling, so cloud consumers' applications always have the resources on demand.

- **Agility**: Deploy and configure cloud-based resources promptly as cloud consumers' app requirements demand.

- **Geo-distribution**: Cloud consumers can deploy applications and data to regional DCs around the globe. Efficiently deploy cloud consumer applications in multiple regions throughout the world.

- **Resiliency**: By taking advantage of cloud-based backup services, data replication, and geo-distribution, cloud consumers have a fallback solution whenever disaster kicks in.

- **Security:** Azure security is the highest priority. Azure cloud consumers benefit from a cloud architecture developed to meet the obligations of the standard security-sensitive businesses.

- **Edge**: Azure Internet of Things (IoT) Edge is a fully managed Microsoft service built on the Azure IoT hub. Deploy cloud consumers' workloads, artificial intelligence, Azure services, third-party services, and cloud consumer business logic to operate on IoT Edge devices.

The second key concept to understand Azure global infrastructure can be developed with two key elements. One is physical infrastructure, and the other is connective network components. The physical infrastructure comprises 200+ physical DCs, organized into regions and connected by one of the most extensive interconnected networks.

Azure global infrastructure (Figure 1-4) is classified into the following: Azure regions, Azure geography, Azure availability zones, and availability sets.

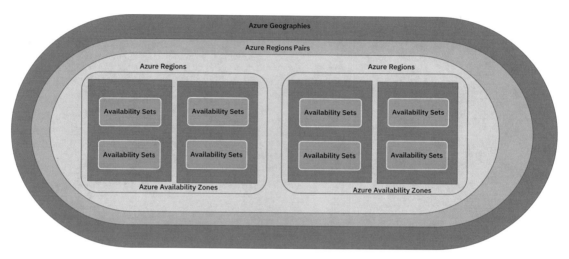

Figure 1-4. *Azure global infrastructure logical view*

Azure Region

An Azure region is a set of physical datacenters installed within a security and latency-defined network perimeter and connected via a dedicated in-part-secured low-latency network.

Microsoft Azure enables cloud consumers the freedom of choice to install and configure applications on demand. An Azure region is equipped with discrete pricing and IT service availability.

Azure developed regions with logical boundaries called a regional pair. Each regional zone contains two regions within the geographically defined boundaries.

An Azure region is a specific geographical boundary, and each region is typically hundreds of miles apart.

Azure Geography

Azure geography is defined with at least one or more regions fulfilling the data residency and compliance requirements demanded by cloud consumers. Azure geography enables the cloud consumers with data residency and compliance to keep their apps and data close to business as much as possible.

Azure geography (Figure 1-5) is fault-tolerant to withstand region failure via dedicated high-capacity networking elements of Azure.

Figure 1-5. *Azure geography*

In Azure cloud, the fact is that each geography holds at least two regions segregated by a considerable physical distance is vital. As a result of this pattern, Azure can achieve disaster recovery in the region.

Azure cloud consumers are encouraged to replicate data in multiple regions. Microsoft guarantees round-trip network performance of 2 milliseconds or less between regions.

Azure Availability Zones

Microsoft Azure developed a cloud pattern named availability zones to achieve maximum availability for IT services that demand maximum uptime.

In Microsoft Azure, a minimum of three availability zones is enabled within each region wherever they exist.

Availability zones enable the cloud to consume with high availability and fault tolerance. They are not designed to allow for disaster recovery because of floods or any other natural disaster if the country or geo is affected. Availability zones apply only to the available services and not to all services offered by Azure.

By deploying IT services to two or more availability zones, the business achieves maximum availability. Microsoft Azure offers an SLA of 99.99% uptime for VMs provided that two or more VMs are deployed into two or more zones.

For the first-time learner, it isn't easy to differentiate between availability zones and availability sets. Availability sets allow IT service to create two or more VMs in different physical server racks in an Azure DC. Microsoft Azure offers an SLA of 99.95% with an availability set, whereas Microsoft Azure provides an SLA of 99.99% with availability zones (Figure 1-6).

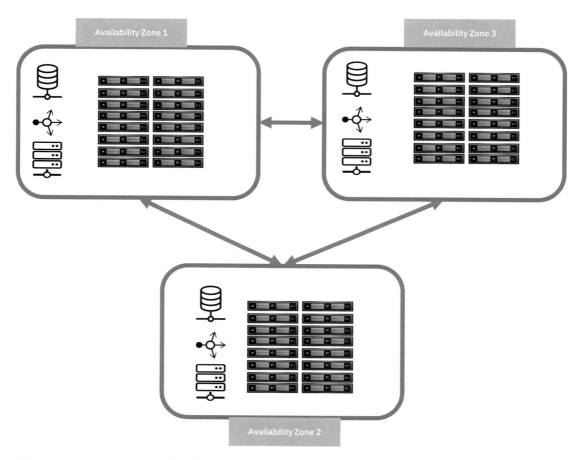

Figure 1-6. *Azure availability zone*

Microsoft Azure offers three types of availability zones: zonal services, zone-redundant services, and zone non-regional services.

Microsoft Azure zonal services are IT services such as VMs, managed disks used in VMs, and public IP addresses used in VMs. To achieve the High Availability (HA) design pattern, the IT function must explicitly install zonal services into two or more zones.

Microsoft Azure zone-redundant services are services such as zone-redundant storage (ZRS) and SQL databases. To use the availability zones with ZRS and SQL DB services, We need to specify the option to make them zone redundant during the deployment.

Microsoft Azure non-regional services: Azure services are constantly ready from Azure geographies and are resilient to zone-wide blackouts and region-wide blackouts. Non-regional services are deployed to two or more regions, and if there is a regional failure, the service instance in another region continues servicing cloud consumers.

Azure Resource Group

For an Azure solution, resource groups serve as containers for resources that are related. Resources for the solution can be included in the resource group or only those you want to manage together. By creating all Azure services integrated with a specific app in a single group, the enterprise Azure admin can then deploy and run all of those services as a single group. This resolves the problem of maintaining an enterprise array of services in the silo.

An Azure resource only exists in a single resource group and cannot be attached to two different resource groups. However, you can move resources from one group to another resource group whenever you want. Deleting the resource group deletes all the resources associated with the group.

Azure Subscriptions

An Azure subscription is automatically initiated as soon as a user signs up for Azure cloud kick start and all the resources created within the subscription. However, an enterprise or business can create additional subscriptions that are tied to its Azure account. Other subscription use cases are applicable whenever companies want to have logical groupings for Azure resources, especially for reports on resources consumed by departments.

Microsoft Azure subscriptions are offered in the following three categories.

- Free Trial – Completely free access for a limited time per account for limited resources; expired accounts cannot be reused.

- Pay-As-You-Go - Pay only for resources consumed in Azure. No CAPEX is involved, and cancellation is possible at any time.

- Pay-As-You-Go Dev/Test - A subscription for Visual Studio that can be used for dev and testing. No production usage.

Each Microsoft Azure subscription has a unique identifier named as a subscription ID. Microsoft recommends using the subscription ID to recognize the subscription.

Management Groups

Management groups are an efficient method to enforce policies and privilege control to Azure cloud resources. An almost identical approach to a resource group, a management group, is a logical container for structuring Azure subscriptions. However, management groups can withhold more than one group and Azure subscription or nested management group. The Azure management group hierarchy supports up to six levels only and it is impossible to have multiple parents on a single management group or a single subscription.

Azure Resource Manager

Azure Resource Manager (ARM) is a crucial component to manage underlying IT resources, in order to avoid operational overhead in managing all Azure services separately. To quickly deploy and manage Azure services, Microsoft developed a solution named ARM.

ARM is a deployment and management service that runs in Azure, and it interacts with almost all Azure services.

Both the Azure portal and the Azure command-line tools work by using ARM, which permits cloud consumers to deploy multiple Azure resources on the go quickly.

ARM makes it possible to reproduce any redeployment with a consistent outcome at the failure of the existing build.

Here is a glance at the most popular Azure services:

- Azure VMs are an IaaS from Microsoft, and Microsoft manages underlying physical compute, network, and storage. Cloud consumers manage the operating system, apps, and data run on top of the VM.

- Availability sets protect VMs with fault domains. Fault domains protect VMs from a hardware failure in a hardware rack.

- Scale sets allow the business to set up autoscale rules to scale horizontally when needed.

- Azure app service makes it easy to host web apps in the cloud because it's a PaaS service that removes the management burden from the user.

- App service apps run inside an app service plan that specifies the number of VMs and the configuration of those VMs.

- Containers allow cloud consumers to create an image of an application, and everything needed to run it.

- Azure container instances (ACI) allow cloud consumers to run containers for minimal cost.

- Azure Kubernetes service (AKS) is a managed service that makes it easy to host Kubernetes clusters in the cloud.

- Azure Cosmos DB is a NoSQL database for unstructured data.

- Azure SQL database is a Microsoft-managed relational database.

- Azure Database for MySQL is a Microsoft-managed MySQL.

- An Azure virtual network provides Azure services to communicate with several others and the Internet.

- Azure load balancer can distribute traffic from the Internet across various VMs in a dedicated VNet.

- ExpressRoute allows cloud consumers to have a high-bandwidth connection to Azure of up to 10 Gbps by attaching to a Microsoft Enterprise Edge router.

- Azure DNS accommodates fast DNS responses and high domain availability.

- Azure disk storage is virtual disk storage specific to Azure VMs. Managed disks remove the operation burden of disks.

- Azure files allows cloud consumers to have disk space in the cloud to map to a drive on-premises.

- Azure blob storage offers hot, cool, and archive storage tiers based on how long cloud consumers intend to store the data, whereby usually the data is accessed frequently.

- Azure DevOps uses development collaboration tools such as pipelines, Kanban boards, Git repositories, and comprehensive automated and cloud-based nonfunctional testing.

- AVD makes apps and desktop readily available to multiple users from almost any device from anywhere.

Azure Management Offerings

Management in Azure is the foundational building block for deployment and supporting the resources in Azure.

Management refers to the assignments and methods required to maintain IT applications and the resources supporting businesses. Azure has several services and tools that operate together to give complete management for cloud consumers (Figure 1-7).

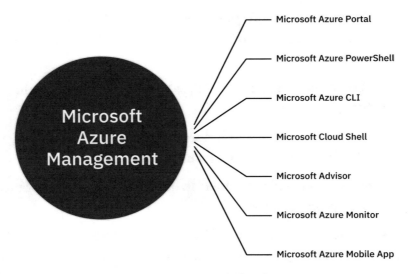

Figure 1-7. Microsoft Azure management methods

Microsoft Azure Portal: Deploy, run, and monitor everything via a single management plane from web apps, databases, VMs, virtual networks, storage, Visual Studio team projects to the aggregate cloud-native application from a unified console.

The first time you sign up for the Azure portal, you'll be given a choice to take a tour of the Azure portal. In case you aren't familiar with the portal, taking the tour will help you understand how Azure portal works.

The original view in Azure is as depicted in Figure 1-8.

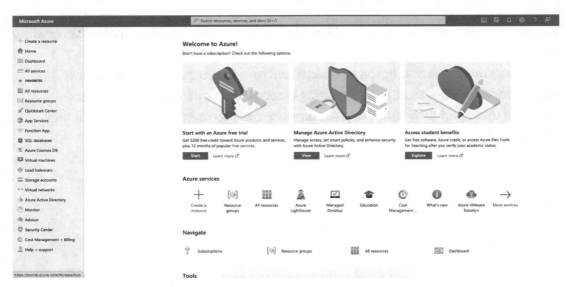

Figure 1-8. Microsoft Azure portal

Microsoft Azure PowerShell: Azure PowerShell is a kit of cmdlets for operating Azure resources immediately from the PowerShell command-line interface (CLI). Microsoft developed Azure PowerShell to make it easy to read, write, and execute the codes to provide powerful automation features for IT support functions. AVD administrators can use Azure PowerShell when they want to automate.

Microsoft PowerShell 7.x and higher are the Microsoft Azure Az PowerShell module's recommended PowerShell module on all platforms.

Use the following command to check PowerShell version:

```
$PSVersionTable.PSVersion
```

Use the following command to install Azure PowerShell module (Az PowerShell module):

```
Install-Module -Name Az -Scope CurrentUser -Repository PSGallery -Force
```

Use the following command to connect Azure account (Az PowerShell module):

```
Connect-AzAccount
```

Microsoft Azure CLI: The Azure CLI is convenient to deploy in Windows, macOS, and Linux environments. Azure CLI is an excellent option; the most straightforward way to begin with Azure PowerShell is by trying it out in an Azure cloud shell environment.

The following command is to install Azure CLI on Windows by downloading and deploying the latest release of the Azure CLI:

```
Invoke-WebRequest -Uri https://aka.ms/installazurecliwindows -OutFile
.\AzureCLI.msi; Start-Process msiexec.exe -Wait -ArgumentList '/I AzureCLI.
msi /quiet'; rm .\AzureCLI.msi
```

The following command is to log in and post install sign in with cloud consumer account credentials in the browser.

```
az login
```

Microsoft Azure Cloud Shell: Azure cloud shell is completely online version; there is no need for any deployment, Azure cloud shell is an interactive, authenticated, browser-accessible shell for managing Azure resources. At the first launch of cloud shell, choose the environment to be used. Cloud shell is presented with two choices, such as Bash and PowerShell; cloud consumers can change it when it is required.

To reach Azure cloud shell, click the cloud shell button (Figure 1-9) in the Microsoft Azure portal.

Figure 1-9. *Azure cloud shell*

Upon clicking, following console loads, once the bash or PowerShell environment is selected, the next step is to create an Azure storage account; however, you need an active subscription (see Figure 1-10).

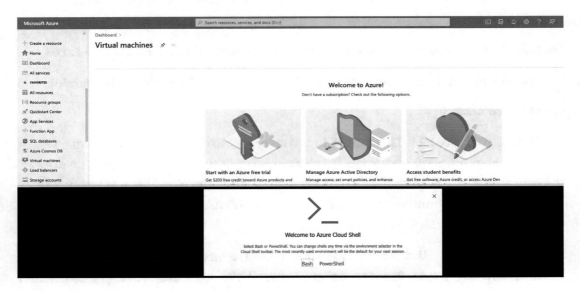

Figure 1-10. *Azure cloud shell bash and PowerShell*

Type following command is to get knowledge about PowerShell in Azure cloud shell.

Get-Help

Microsoft Azure Monitor: Azure Monitor promotes cloud consumers to maximize the functional and nonfunctional key performance indicators (KPIs) of applications and services. It gives an end-to-end solution for gathering, interpreting, and acting on data feed from the Azure tenant cloud and integrating with on-premises environments. In addition, it offers golden signals to identify issues affecting KPIs proactively.

Azure Monitor can perform tasks such as metrics gathering, storing logs, and providing insights.

- Metrics: Azure service automatically gathers metrics (defined KPIs) into Azure Monitor metrics.

- Logs: Azure service maintains diagnostic configuration, collecting platform logs and KPIs to Azure Monitor logs.

- Insight: Azure insight available for the cloud consumer subscribed service, which presents a well-defined monitoring experience for the consuming service.

- Service health: Microsoft runs an Azure Status web page where cloud consumers can observe Azure services' status in each region where Azure runs. While it is an important aspect of overall Azure health, the immense range of the web page doesn't make it the powerful way to get an overview of the health of cloud consumer-specific services. Instead, Azure service health can provide cloud consumers with a picture of consumed resources.

To reach Azure Monitor services, click the Monitor button in the Microsoft Azure portal (Figure 1-11).

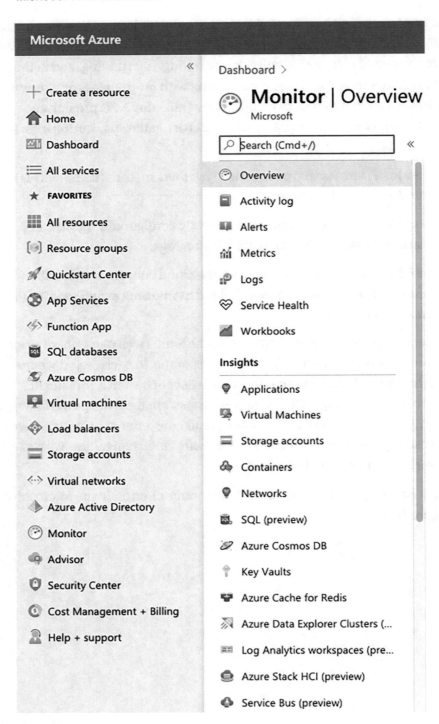

Figure 1-11. *Azure Monitor*

Azure Monitor dashboard provides an overview (Figure 1-12).

Figure 1-12. *Azure Monitor dashboard*

Microsoft Azure Advisor: Microsoft Azure Advisor offers recommendations and impacts of services against cost, security, reliability, performance, and operational excellence. It also suggests guaranteeing that cloud consumer resources are configured accurately for availability and efficiency. In addition, Microsoft Azure Advisor can inform cloud consumers about best practices in Azure services configuration to avoid trouble.

To reach Azure Advisor services, click the Advisor button in the Microsoft Azure portal (Figure 1-13).

Figure 1-13. *Azure Advisor*

Azure Advisor dashboard provides an overview (Figure 1-14).

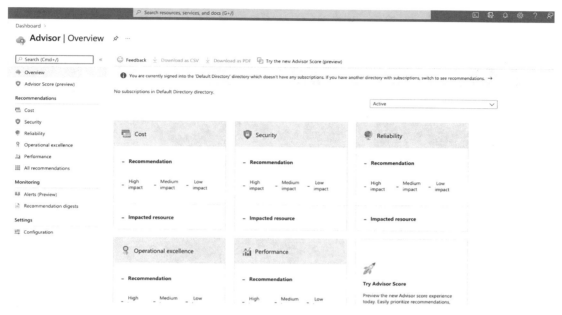

Figure 1-14. *Azure Advisor overview*

Azure Security and Compliance Offerings

Security is one of the several critical aspects of any design. Assuring cloud consumers that business applications and data are secure is indispensable. A data compromise can destroy an organization's reputation and create vital financial wickedness.

When end users, end-user devices, and organization data all continued inside the organization's firewall, it was assumed to be trusted. This implicit trust allowed for an easy oblique move after a malicious hacker compromised an endpoint device.

Study critical defense concepts in depth and identify key security technologies and methods to bring forth a defense-in-depth strategy into reality.

Identities, devices, infrastructure security, network protection, application security, and data encryption are essential and integral to any security design, and securing cloud consumers' networks from attacks and unauthorized access is vital.

Microsoft uses a layered path to security, both in DCs and across Azure services. Together, the key components to know comprise defense-in-depth. The zero-trust model drives security researchers, engineers, and architects to design thinking on applied security approaches and uses layered maneuvering to guard their resources provisioned across the cloud and on-premises with shared responsibility.

Defense in depth: Defense in depth is an approach that applies a series of tools to slow the advancement of an attack to acquire unapproved access to information. Each layer gets protected so that a subsequent layer is already in place to prevent further exposure if one layer is compromised (see Figure 1-15).

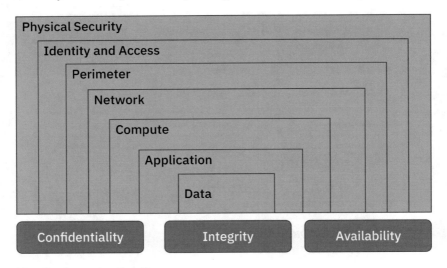

Figure 1-15. *Defense in depth*

Microsoft Azure offers a wide variety of security functionality via three security integrated services:

- Protect against security threats via Microsoft Azure Security Center

- Detect and respond to security threats via Microsoft Azure Sentinel

- Store and manage secrets via Microsoft Azure Key Vault

Azure Security Center: Azure Security Center is a consolidated infrastructure security control system that extends the security posture. It provides exceptional threat protection across hybrid workloads running in the multicloud, including the cloud consumer's private cloud.

Keeping cloud consumers' IT resources protected is a collective work between cloud service provider Microsoft Azure and cloud consumers. Cloud consumers have to make sure data and apps workloads are securely running in Microsoft cloud. At the same time, when you move to IaaS, there is more customer responsibility than there was in PaaS and SaaS. Azure Security Center provides cloud consumers with the rich set of tools demanded to strengthen cloud consumers' networks and secure cloud consumers' benefits.

Azure Security Center addresses the three most common critical security difficulties:

- Swiftly changing workloads: Azure Security Center can address both a strength and a challenge of the cloud.

- Frequently complex attacks: Cloud consumers have to secure workloads in public cloud workloads.

- Security skills are a small number: The number of security alerts and alerting rules is far higher than the number of security professionals with the required knowledge and practice to ensure cloud consumers' environments are protected.

To reach Azure Security Center services, click the Security Center button in the Microsoft Azure portal (Figure 1-16):

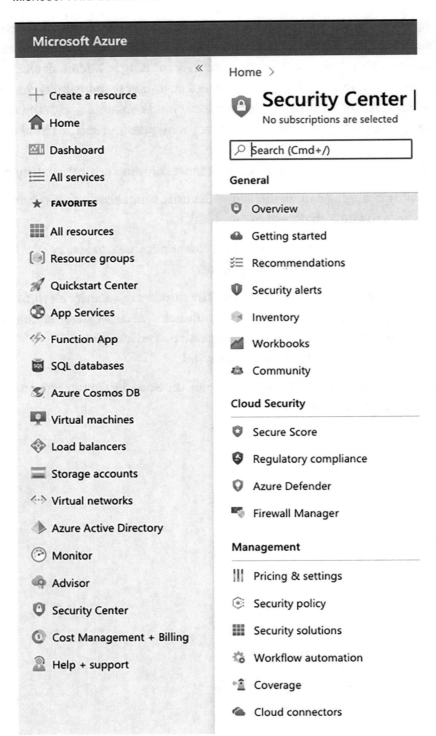

Figure 1-16. *Azure Security Center*

Azure Security Center dashboard provides an overview (Figure 1-17).

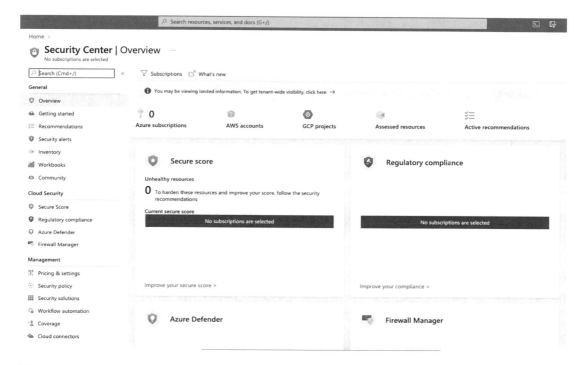

Figure 1-17. *Azure Security Center dashboard*

Azure Key Vault: Azure Key Vault is a cloud-native service for securely saving and reaching secrets (keys). A key is anything cloud consumers want to control access to, such as API keys, passwords, certificates, or cryptographic keys.

Key Vault service supports two types such as vaults and managed hardware security module (HSM) pools. Azure Key Vault strengthens the Transport Layer Security protocol to guard data when moving among Azure Key Vault and clients.

Azure Sentinel: Azure Sentinel is Microsoft's cloud-native Security Information and Event Management (SIEM), which presents exceptional security analytics for the entire cloud enterprise at a cloud scale.

Microsoft's cloud-native SIEM solution is designed as a cloud-native security-monitoring platform that uses the power of the cloud for analytics and detections.

Microsoft's cloud-native SIEM Sentinel provides straightforward amalgamation with flags and statistics from security solutions despite Microsoft Azure or any other cloud, inclusive of private cloud.

Azure Sentinel combines machine learning algorithms, global security investigation, and the extent and intensity of the essential security data available to Microsoft as a significant enterprise vendor.

Azure Sentinel helps cloud consumers discover known and unknown attack vectors, recognizing threats across all steps.

Azure Compliance: Azure compliance has 90+ certifications, including covering 50 distinct global regions and countries, the US, the European Union, Germany, Japan, the United Kingdom, India, and China, along with more than 35 compliance offerings particular to the requirements of critical industries, including government, education, finance, manufacturing, health, and media.

Regulatory compliance in Azure policy presents built-in action representations to observe a listing of the controls and compliance domains based on obligation (cloud consumers, Microsoft, shared).

Microsoft Azure is globally covered with Center for Internet Security (CIS) Benchmarks, Cloud Security Alliance (CSA) STAR Attestation, Cloud Security Alliance (CSA) STAR Certification, Cloud Security Alliance (CSA) STAR Self-Assessment, ISO/IEC 20000-1:2018, ISO 22301:2019, ISO/IEC 27001:2013, ISO/IEC 27017:2015, ISO/IEC 27018:2019, ISO/IEC 27701:2019, ISO 9001:2015, System and Organization Controls (SOC) 1 Type 2, System SOC 2 Type 2, SOC 3, and Web Content Accessibility Guidelines.

Getting Started with DaaS

In this section, let us get started by learning what DaaS is.

The global digital workplace is revamping the workspace around the world constantly to adopt continuous improvements to increase productivity.

DaaS securely delivers virtual apps and desktops from the cloud to anywhere and any device. Using DaaS, businesses gain instant access to resources worldwide, including onboarding remote work from anywhere at any time, enabling workforces with mobility and business continuity.

DaaS provides two departments of an organization, namely, IT and Finance, granular control. It uses a predictable and straightforward pay-as-you-go subscription model, making it easy to scale up or down on demand based on user requirements. Best of all, with DaaS, a managed service provider can improve to manage the day-to-day operations and security of organization end-user requirements (Figure 1-18).

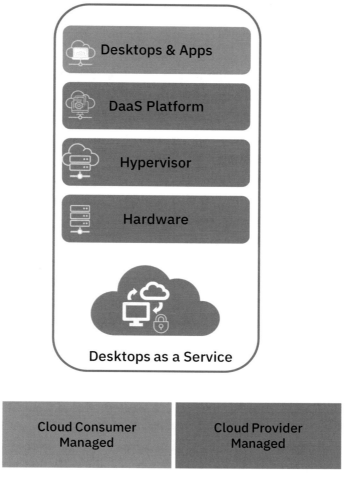

Figure 1-18. *DaaS*

The DaaS solution enables companies of any scope to deliver cloud-hosted virtual desktops and apps to any device from anywhere via any network. Any VDI standard for the cloud is subscription-based with foreseen per-user pricing and is easy to manage because the cloud provides the latest software updates and security patches for VDI systems.

DaaS quickly delivers virtual desktop environments, including operating systems, applications, user preferences, home drive, and context awareness.

By moving desktop and apps to cloud-based DaaS, preferably a privately deployed and managed DC, companies can accomplish all the promises offered by traditional VDI plus the following benefits.

What Are Traditional Workplace Challenges and DaaS Value Proposition?

Desktops are pretty challenging to standardize because of the diversity of the PC hardware and users' requirements to modify the desktop environments. Centralizing desktop management is a challenging task in the face of a widely distributed computing environment and the corporate workforce, which progressively needs secure on-demand access to their desktop environments from any place.

The system needs to protect corporate and consumer information at all times from evolving cyber threats, and the cloud service provider takes care of the host's back-end infrastructure (data storage, network, backup, and upgrades).

Traditionally, IT support functions are enabled with system and security administrators to run complex on-premises infrastructure in line with security standards and compliance demands. However, on-prem infrastructure started to evolve as a cloud offering. In the modern day, the fact is that private and public are current but the hybrid cloud is the future. The way of working is demanding the adoption of an agile approach. Agile methodology is demanding features that remove unnecessary burdens on time, effort, and cost. It is time to move from on prem to DaaS to meet the needs of the digital era.

The cloud service provider takes care of deployment and operations risk-free for a business run in DC facilities, and extended cloud managed services provide managed end-user VDI. Cloud capabilities such as HA pattern can act as leverage in the design to maintain continuous operation of the virtual environment and provide uninterrupted user access to the virtual desktops, with the ability to add a DR solution from two regions of the cloud supplied and scaled to the per-user level.

Cloud-based DaaS architecture is multitenant, and companies acquire the service through a subscription model. They are typically based on the number of virtual desktop resources consumed per month.

The following are several business benefits when DaaS is enabled:

- Assist businesses with strained IT staff and smaller budget

- Enable businesses looking to work remotely securely,

- Allow and manage bringing your own device at scale,

- Reduce costs of delivering desktops in-house,

- Scale up and down desktops to meet dynamic demands,

- Stop spending on specialist computers and GPU processors.

How Does DaaS Work?

DaaS delivers virtual desktops through a cloud service. Cost varies based on a cloud consumption service, which in turn varies based on virtual desktop resource demands.

DaaS cloud computing has opened many new boulevards and converted the way organizations execute their end users' workloads. There are many intrinsic benefits of a cloud-based DaaS solution, including ease of access, flexibility, scalability, business continuity, security, and cost savings.

DaaS delivers virtual applications and desktop services via a public cloud service. Business end users can access VDI resources via an Internet connection using an HTML-based web browser or a secure client application deployed to a device such as a laptop, desktop, thin client, mobile, or tablet.

DaaS is a sort of VDI hosted in the cloud. With VDI, a company deploys from its own on-premises DCs. IT teams are responsible for deploying the virtual desktops and purchasing, managing, and upgrading the hosting and management layer of infrastructure (see Figure 1-19).

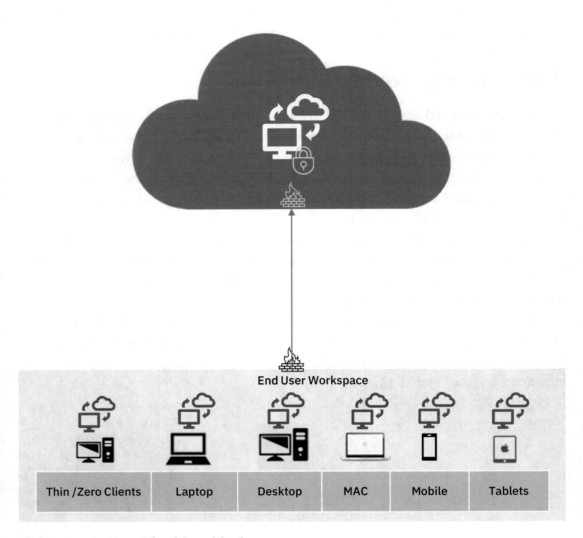

Figure 1-19. *DaaS building block*

DaaS is essentially the same as VDI, but the infrastructure is cloud-based. The company that subscribes to a DaaS solution doesn't need to manage its underlying resources.

DaaS is offered as a subscription service and can extend with multitenant. The core VDI, including the VDI that runs desktop operating systems, is hosted by a cloud provider and managed by the managed service provider in specific cases or by cloud consumer teams by themselves.

The DaaS provider then flows the virtual desktops to a cloud consumer's end-user devices.

DaaS providers manage the VDI core infrastructure deployment and the maintenance, security, upgrades, data backup, and storage. And the managed service provider in the specific case or the cloud consumer teams maintain the run functions of the apps, data, and desktop images. DaaS is a good choice for companies that don't want to expend a great deal of time and resources to accomplish their individual on-premises VDI systems and solutions.

IT administrators securely log in to their cloud management console from any HTML browser and use simple workflows to deploy their first catalog of desktops and apps in just minutes.

End users can access a catalog of apps and desktops from any device using a browser or the DaaS client app, and end users get a genuine Windows 10 experience that IT administrators can easily connect Microsoft 365 apps, SaaS apps, and even Linux apps directly into the virtual desktop.

Apps and data are stored in the cloud, not on the device, excluding the risk of jeopardized end-user devices. The enables IT to control corporate data and the enabled DaaS environment is continuously modernized with the latest Windows 10 version, keeping everything harmless and contemporary.

Benefits of DaaS

- Access DaaS from any device

- Delivers a great user experience

- Centralized and uncomplicated application delivery

- Enhanced security and compliance

- Usage-based billing on a subscription model

Access DaaS from Any Device

- DaaS is accessible from any HTML5-capable browser or a mobile app, enabling end users to work from any device, such as iOS, Android, laptop, desktop, or thin client.

- End users get the same experience across all devices, making it seamless to switch devices throughout the day. As a result, DaaS offers flexibility.

Delivers a Great User Experience

- DaaS guarantees a high-definition user experience no matter where work is getting done in the end, users' offices, at home, or on the move.

- Resource-intensive graphics and other demanding apps can be delivered alongside simple task worker desktops, giving end users the right desktop for the right job, all from a single solution.

Centralized and Uncomplicated Application Delivery

- Centrally manage and deliver Windows-based or Linux-based apps/ desktop to the end-user workforce with a straightforward interface, making the life of IT easier. As a result, DaaS offers turnkey service.

Enhanced Security and Compliance

- DaaS offers companies protection from malicious virus attacks, ransomware, and malware because it saves end-user data offsite and continually maintains backups of end-user data.

- DaaS is delivered virtually; sensitive information is stored in the cloud and not on the device, protecting the business against lost, stolen, or compromised device scenarios. It's a great way to move enterprises one step closer to compliance and other data privacy regulations.

Usage-Based Billing on a Subscription Model

- When businesses go for DaaS like AVD, companies no longer have to invest in on-premises DCs and supporting infrastructure, which significantly reduces business CAPEX and moves the business toward OPEX.

- By adopting a DaaS solution such as AVD, companies can drastically reduce their end-user-associated operating costs. Major studies show that savings could even be to the tune of 50% over one year.

- DaaS makes it easy to scale either vertically or horizontally up or down on demand.

Key AVD Terminologies

In this section, let us explore the top ten terminologies used in the Microsoft AVD. Figure 1-20 gives a holistic view of key terms.

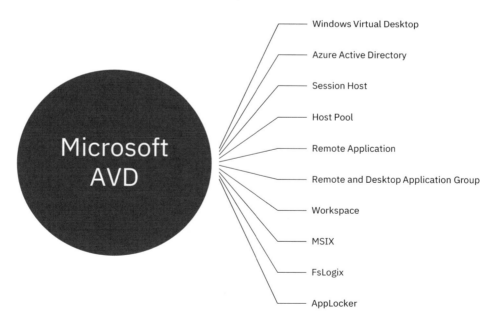

Figure 1-20. *Microsoft AVD terminology*

AVD

AVD from the Azure cloud, desktop virtualization to any device or location. AVD is fast becoming a favored option for authorizing AVD end users to work from anywhere. All end users need is a modern browser to access AVD-hosted experiences.

AVD solutions can protect the organization from high costs, redemption risks, insufficient functionality, mounting administrative jobs, and a user experience that lacks.

The workforce is converting more and more remote. AVD gives end users a way to work from anywhere without developing complexity or exposure as it increases to more places and off-site environments.

AAD

Azure Active Directory (AAD) is Microsoft's enterprise Azure-based identity and access management (IAM) solution. Azure AD is the gist of the Office 365 system, and it syncs with on-premises active directory and grants authentication to hybrid cloud-based systems via OAuth. AAD offers a lightweight directory access protocol (LDAP), Kerberos/NTLM authentication, domain join, group policy; there is no need to manage and patch domain controllers in the Azure cloud.

AAD offers enterprise identity service with single sign-on (SSO) and multifactor authentication (MFA) to protect cloud consumer users from cybersecurity attacks with an SLA of 99.9 %.

AVD Session Host

A session host is a VM that AVD end users interact with for desktop or application sessions. Currently, Microsoft AVD session hosts offered from the gallery are the following:

- Windows 10 Enterprise multisession

- Windows 10 Enterprise

- Windows 7 Enterprise

- Windows Server 2019

- Windows Server 2016

- Windows Server 2012 R2

- Windows 10 Enterprise multisession + Microsoft 365 apps.

- Or Custom image following Bring your own image.

AVD Host Pool

A resource group of session hosts offers up an AVD host pool. Host pools collect one or more identical VMs within AVD environments. Each AVD host pool can include an app group that AVD end users can utilize.

AVD administrators should configure all session AVD hosts in a host pool as identically as possible to gain a better experience as per Microsoft's recommendation.

AVD Remote Applications

A remote application is what gets published to the AVD end users. When an AVD admin publishes an application from a host pool, AVD admin allows an AVD end user to run an application on the VM hosted in Azure. To the end user, using the application resembles working on their local computer.

The end user interacts with the AVD client application, sending their keyboard and mouse input back to the VM hosted in Azure in a secure manner.

AVD Remote Applications and Desktop Groups

A remote application group is a mechanism for grouping remote resources and allocating applications to AVD end users. AVD end users access the AVD-hosted applications; AVD administrators individually publish them to the application group. AVD administrators can build multiple RemoteApp application AD groups to maintain different end-user requirements. Use RemoteApp to virtualize an application that runs on an older generation of Windows operating system, either server or client operating systems or one that needs secured AVD access to AVD resources.

The desktop application group is created by default when the AVD administrator creates a host pool. In this method, AVD end users access the entire desktop.

AVD Workspace

A workspace is a logical grouping of application groups in Microsoft AVD. When AVD end users log in to AVD, they see a workspace with either a desktop or apps published to the application groups assigned to them.

MSIX

MSIX is a Windows application package methodology. It provides a modern packaging experience to all Windows apps. The MSIX package method maintains existing MSI packages, installs files, and converts the new current packaging method and seat features to legacy Win32, new WPF, and Windows Forms apps.

MSIX enables companies to stay modern and ensure their applications remain up to date. MSIX allows AVD admins and on-prem VDI admins to present an end-user-centric solution while still diminishing the cost of purchasing the application by decreasing the need to repackage. AVD applications package working MSIX run in a lightweight application container.

FSLogix

FSLogix is a next-generation application deployment platform that decreases the hardware, administrator, time, and effort required to support AVDs. FSLogix reserves a complete user profile in a single container. At AVD, the user login, the FSLogix container is dynamically attached to the remote desktop service host (RDSH) or client OS environment using natively supported virtual hard disk (VHD) or VHDX format. The user profile is instantly usable and appears in the AVD precisely like a local user profile.

FSLogix solutions include user profile container, Office 365 container, One Drive cloud cache, application masking, and Java version control.

AppLocker

AppLocker is an application whitelisting technology introduced with Windows operating system. It concedes that executable end users can perform based on the program's path, publisher, or hash. AppLocker improves the app control characteristics and features of program restriction defense-in-depth policies.

AppLocker embraces new inclinations and additions that permit AVD administrators to generate rules to allow or disallow programs from running based on the file's unique identities and define which AD users or AD groups can run that authorized program and scripts.

Foundation for Microsoft AVD

Organizations are intended to transform end-user computing to deliver a better end-user experience, and AVD expedites transformation to the digital workplace and the journey to the cloud; AVD is expected to leverage automation, analytics, and AI for competitive advantage offered by Microsoft cloud.

For Enterprise, AVD enables delivery of modern workspaces through fast and automated rollout that enhances user experience and simplifies adoption, provisioning, and administration of digital workspaces

With Microsoft DaaS, organizations can set up AVD to deliver virtual desktop and remote apps to any device. AVD is a desktop and app virtualization service that runs on Microsoft Azure. AVD works across any device from anywhere via modern browsers to access AVD.

With Microsoft DaaS, users can connect to AVD with any device over the Internet safely and securely using multifactor authentication.

With Microsoft DaaS, organizations can deliver two modes of VDI session to end users. One is AVD based out of Windows 10 Enterprise multisession, and the second method is AVD based out of Windows server operating systems.

With Microsoft DaaS, organizations can deliver the AVD at no additional cost if they already consume Microsoft 365. However, organizations need to pay for the Azure resources consumed by AVD.

If you are already working with Microsoft Azure, you might know the benefits of a concept known as resource reservation. The same services are applicable to AVD; buy one year or three years of Azure reserved VM compute instances to preserve up to 72% versus a recurring pay-as-you-go pricing model. Organizations can pay for a reservation upfront or for monthly consumption with proactive planning.

With Microsoft DaaS, organizations can perform the following:

- Organizations can design and deploy virtualize desktops and apps.

- Organizations can design and deploy multisession Windows 10 along with scalability.

- Organizations can design and deploy Microsoft 365 apps for enterprises and optimize them to run multiuser virtual environment scenarios.

- Organizations can design and deploy extended Windows 7 virtual desktops with free comprehensive security updates.

- Organizations can design and deploy Windows client OS- and Windows server OS-based desktops and apps with a unified management experience.

- Organizations can plan to replace their existing aging VDI with vendor-enabled DaaS.

- Organizations can respond to the end of life (EOL) through a combination of hardware refreshes, transitioning to VDI models.

- Organizations are turning to DaaS for performance, security, compliance, and sovereignty requirements.

The foundation of Microsoft AVD is broadly classified into five building blocks as depicted in Figure 1-21.

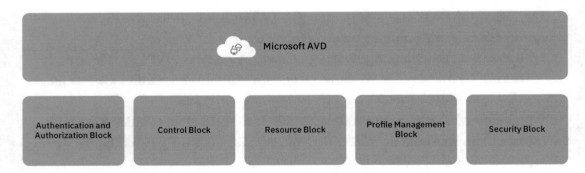

Figure 1-21. *Microsoft AVD building block*

Authentication and Authorization Block

The first building block of the AVD foundation framework is authentication and authorization.

Creating an appropriate design and deployment for the authentication and authorization building block is essential for the AVD process. This block handles end-user validation by authentication and composes access to all elements necessary to establish a safe and secure virtual desktop connection. This block design decision and deployment types based on various requirements such as mobility, endpoint devices, and network connectivity.

Obtaining access to AVD resources is based on the end user's identity. Defining the authentication maneuvering reflects the AVD user's entry point into the Microsoft DaaS environment, and the end user will authenticate.

AVD uses Azure AD as a native authorization and authentication management service. The organization should regulate Azure AD to direct the organization's identity and access management in:

- Microsoft cloud resources include the Azure portal, Azure storage, Azure VM (Linux and Windows), and AVD.

- Cloud consumer organization's resources, such as applications and data on Azure and cloud consumer corporate network resources.

Privileged access is key and makes use of Azure Bastion for administrative tasks; the administrator system needs central management to enforce closed configuration including solid authentication, apps, and resource baselines, restricted logically and isolated by network access.

Control Block

AVD provides virtualization infrastructure as a Microsoft managed service. Microsoft manages the following building block. The foundation of the Microsoft AVD control block is broadly classified into five building blocks as depicted in Figure 1-22.

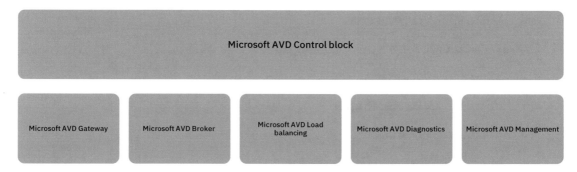

Figure 1-22. *Microsoft AVD control block*

Microsoft AVD Gateway - The Microsoft AVD remote connection gateway service connects end users to AVD apps and desktops from any Internet-connected device running an AVD client. The client connects to a gateway, which then orchestrates a connection from the VDI back to the remote connection gateway.

Microsoft AVD Broker - The Microsoft AVD connection broker service manages user connections to virtual desktops and remote apps. It provides load balancing and reconnection to existing sessions.

Microsoft AVD Load Balancing - The Microsoft AVD remote desktop hosts shared pool load balancing by either vertical or horizontal mechanisms. The broker determines how new incoming sessions' loads are distributed across the VDI VMs in a host pool.

Microsoft AVD Diagnostics - The Microsoft AVD remote desktop diagnostics is an event-based aggregator identifying each user's or administrator's action on the AVD deployment as an audit of success or failure. AVD admin can query the aggregation of events to determine failing elements.

Microsoft AVD Management - Manage Microsoft AVD configurations in the Azure cloud portal. Maintain and publish host pool AVD resources. AVD also covers several extensibility elements. Manage AVD by using Windows PowerShell or with the provided REST APIs, enabling assistance from third-party tools.

Resource Block

AVD provides virtualization infrastructure as a Microsoft-managed service.

Microsoft manages the following building blocks:

- Azure infra services for compute, storage, and networking.

- Microsoft AVD web client.

Cloud consumer manages the following building blocks:

- Microsoft AVD desktop

- Microsoft AVD remote apps

- Microsoft AVD images

- Microsoft AVD networking policies

The foundation of Microsoft AVD resource block is broadly classified into five building blocks as depicted in Figure 1-23.

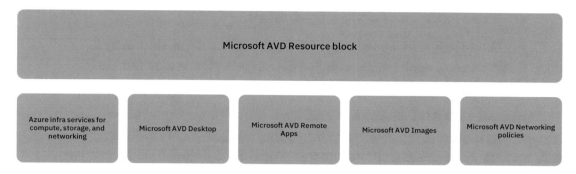

Figure 1-23. *Microsoft AVD resource block*

Azure infra services for compute, storage, and networking: Windows virtual desktop consumes the service from Azure to host virtual desktop pool.

Microsoft AVD Web Client: The web access service lets end users access AVD desktops and remote apps via an HTML5-compatible web browser from anywhere and any device. IT organizations within cloud consumers can secure web access via a multifactor authentication security mechanism.

Microsoft AVD Desktop: Microsoft AVD desktop groups give users access to an entire desktop. The AVD administrator can provide a desktop where the session host VM resources are shared or pooled or personal.

Pooled Stateless Desktops / Pooled Shared or Random Desktops: Desktops that are dynamically assigned to users. When users log off, the desktop becomes free for another user to consume. When rebooted, any changes made to the desktop are destroyed (a nonpersistent environment).

Private Persistent Desktops / Personal Desktops: Desktops that are statically assigned to respective users. When a user logs off, only the given user can access the desktop, regardless of whether the desktop is rebooted. During reboots, any changes made will persist across subsequent restarts (a persistent environment).

The overall benefits of personal and pooled shared desktop deployment models are the following:

- Virtual desktops run on servers in Microsoft Azure

- One-to-one relationship between users and OS instances

- Dedicated compute power per user

- Scalable model

- Cost benefits for increased user volumes

- Suited to resource-intensive applications

- Suited to users who require more flexibility, including the ability to have more applications installed or with persistence requirements beyond the profile.

Microsoft AVD Remote Apps: Remote apps groups provide end users access to the applications individually published to the application group or to individual users. AVD administrators can create multiple remote app groups to accommodate different user requirements.

The overall benefits of the published application deployment model are the following:

- Applications run on servers in the data center

- Many-to-one relationship: High volume of users can share one server

- Scalable model

- Cost benefits for increased user volumes

- Suited to users with a predefined set of applications and limited personalization requirements

- Not suited to resource-intensive applications

Microsoft AVD Image: Image management is offered in multiple different categories, such as bring your image or Windows 10 Enterprise multisession and Office 365 or select from Microsoft Gallery.

Microsoft AVD Networking Policies: Microsoft AVD offers various network topologies to access the virtual desktop and virtual apps based on organizational network requirements. Connect cloud consumer AVD vNET to consumer on-premises network via a virtual private network. Or use Azure ExpressRoute to extend cloud consumer on-premises networks into the Microsoft cloud platform over a personal connection.

Profile Management Block

Microsoft FSLogix is a set of solutions that improve, empower, analyze, and put granular control over nonpersistent AVD environments. FSLogix solutions are suited for virtual desktop environments in both Windows AVD and on-prem VDI. deploying FSLogix with a cloud storage solution like Azure files to containerize user profiles and present a speedy and stateful experiences for VDI end users.

The foundation of the Microsoft AVD profile management block is broadly classified into four building blocks as depicted in Figure 1-24.

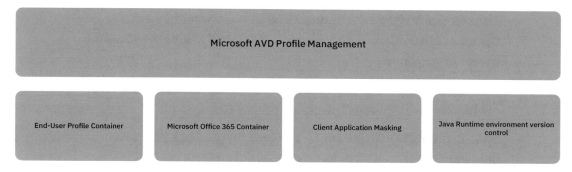

Figure 1-24. *Microsoft AVD profile management block*

Microsoft AVD enabled with FSLogix solutions comprise:

- End-User Profile Container

- Microsoft Office 365 Container

- Client Application Masking

- Java Runtime Environment Version Control

End-User Profile Container- Redirect end-user VDI profiles to a standard network share location using profile container. Profiles are placed in VHDX files and attached at run time.

On demand because existing log-in and log-out times are often unacceptable from a service-level objective standpoint. Mounting and using the standard network share location profile eliminates delays often linked with solutions that copy data.

Microsoft Office 365 Container- Redirect only the division of the profile that includes Office 365 data by using Office 365 container. Office 365 container allows a company to use a temporary profile solution to enhance Office in a nonpersistent environment. This feature is effective with Outlook.OST file.

AVD Client Application Masking- Application masking manages access to an app, font, printer, or other objects deployed in gold image. Access is restricted per user, per group, per IP address range, and according to other criteria. Application masking significantly minimizes the complexity of maintaining large quantities of gold images.

Java Runtime Environment Version Control– AVD Java runtime-based, web-based, or client application can integrate to use only the specific JRE version.

FSLogix with AVD provides profile and personalization solutions:

- Control end AVD user context in nonpersistent AVD circumstances.

- Reduce sign-in times for nonpersistent environments, execute things in the background or whenever required rather than loading everything upfront.

- Optimize file input/output operations between AVD host and AVD client along with remote integrated profile storages.

- Specify the version of Java to be involved by specific web-based application and as well as locally deployed applications.

Security Block

Security requirements for Microsoft AVD are used to define the relevant desktop and policy for each user group.

In case an AVD end-user group requires low security, a hosted pooled desktop inclusive of AVD users is permitted to shift data in and out of the AVD.

In case an AVD end-user group requires medium security, it should secure all AVD resource authentication and session traffic. Users should not install or modify their virtualized environment.

In case an AVD end-user group requires high security and compliance, all AVD addition to session traffic encryption, no data should leave the cloud environment or country it is residing in; should audit all AVD users' access in Azure AVD environment.

Azure AVD should be applied with policies and security control over every component level of AVD and cloud consumer-managed environment and govern the Azure managed components.

Although Microsoft AVD-delegated administration is available, high-security standards may want complete separation between environments to prove compliance with special SLAs.

The foundation of the Microsoft AVD security management block is broadly classified into four building blocks as depicted in Figure 1-25.

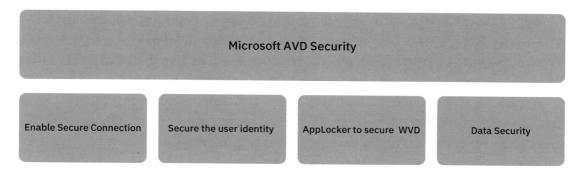

Figure 1-25. *Microsoft AVD security block*

Enable Secure Connection- The gateway acts as an intelligent reverse proxy; the gateway manages all end-user AVD session connectivity, with nothing but pixels reaching the client. Each user must have an active directory account to authenticate and consume AVD services. A token is returned to the remote desktop services client, and the gateway checks the token with the connection broker with successful authentication in AD. AVD admin can also use require multifactor authentication.

AVD admin needs to use service tags in tenant network security group (NSG) rules to allow or deny traffic to a specific Azure service globally or per Azure region.

Secure the User Identity- AVD admin integration with Azure AD is critical in a layered zero-trust security design. The AVD admin should build strong authentication, authorization, and encryption, while also implementing more dependable operational agility.

AVD offers the following user identity security integrations:

- AVD system support using static and dynamic conditional access policies.

- AVD system support using authentication that's improved with multifactor authentication.

- AVD system support subscribing to Azure Security Center or Azure Defender for its combined vulnerability assessment.

- AVD system support using strong credential administration services and policies.

AppLocker to Secure AVD- AppLocker is a defense-in-depth security feature for AVD. AppLocker helps the AVD system control which apps and files users can run inside the AVD. Files include executable, scripts, Windows installer files, dynamic-link libraries, Windows native packaged apps, and Windows packaged app installers.

AppLocker aids reduce AVD admin overhead and support controlling the organization's cost of operating computing resources by limiting the number of service calls that return from AVD end users operating unapproved apps.

Data Security- All files AVD uses in Azure NetApp files are secured via Federal Information Processing Standards Publication (FIPS PUBS) 140-2 encryption standard. The Azure NetApp files service operates all keys and forms an individual XTS-AES-256 data encryption key for all volumes within AVD systems. Also, FSLogix profiles containers with Azure files recommended instead of file shares.

So, the benefits of AVD are moderately extensive and fall into two main sections.

- Management of AVD

- Consumption of AVD

The management of AVD benefits are the following.

The AVD management layer is offered as a service. The management layers manage the end users' global connectivity into their apps and desktop. It is a centralized deployment and orchestration that IT demands.

The management layer is a PaaS service from Azure, and in that, the cloud consumer does not have to deploy or manage it.

The management layer is an evergreen service that cloud consumers consume. No additional cost is involved; the management layer is a service that AVD cloud consumers are entitled to via a license they already hold. Hence, AVD cloud consumers can achieve cost savings by adopting this PaaS service.

Compared with on-prem VDI, it also indicates that AVD cloud consumers do not need to spend time and effort in management, troubleshooting, break-fix, patching, and so on, of their management service. It allows AVD administrators to concentrate on what is considerably more crucial to the business, typically guaranteeing that end users have the best user experience when consuming their applications and data via AVD.

So, the consumption of AVD benefits is the following.

Compared with on-prem VDI, AVD also enables a new feature called Windows 10 Multisession, allowing multiple end users to log on to the exact Windows 10 Enterprise VM. This was not possible before on-prem VDI.

Profile container technology permits the AVD user to switch AVD desktop and apps without missing access to their personalization. Now users may use Microsoft O365 Outlook cache, OneDrive, and indexed search functionality in AVD.

Summary

In this chapter, you read about the fundamentals of cloud computing and Microsoft Azure; we also covered getting started with DaaS, a broad understanding of essential Microsoft AVD terminologies, a well-framed framework for AVD building block.

In the next chapter, you will read about the method of AVD preforming assessment and requirement gathering of Microsoft AVD.

CHAPTER 2

Planning and Preparing for AVD

Azure virtual desktop (AVD) benefits IT by delivering modern workspaces through agile and automated rollout that intensifies the user experience and simplifies adoption, provisioning, and management of virtual workspaces from the Azure cloud.

This chapter provides the planning, preparation, and understanding of the design methodology for AVD, the landscape of AVD with reference use cases, and success criteria for successful AVD design and deployment.

By the end of this chapter, you should be able to understand the following:

- Planning desktop-as-a-service (DaaS).

- Preparing for AVD.

- Design methodology for AVD.

- Architecture of AVD.

Planning DaaS

In this section, let us get started by planning DaaS.

The DaaS initiative is driven by several roles within a business, from IT managers to IT leaders. Even though many positive aspects exist in adapting DaaS for every business, it needs proper planning, assessment, well-defined requirements, and strategic investments.

The first step of planning for DaaS should be with a business case. A business case is essential to explain why an IT organization will invest time, funds, and effort into a project. It is becoming increasingly important for business boards and senior

© Puthiyavan Udayakumar 2022
P. Udayakumar, *Design and Deploy Microsoft Azure Virtual Desktop*,
https://doi.org/10.1007/978-1-4842-7796-6_2

management to focus on investments that produce original business value. To get the business board and senior management to approve a business case, it is required to build a business case that demonstrates why the project is wanted and its benefits.

A well-prepared business case can continuously make the DaaS project stand out amongst the competing preferences within the organization and may be the key to getting approval and finances for the project to enhance end-user experiences.

The DaaS business case is a method to critically explore the possibilities, options, project steps, and financial investment to suggest the best sequence of activities that will produce business value. The DaaS business case should be approached with a five-step process as depicted in Figure 2-1.

Figure 2-1. *Five steps to develop business case for DaaS*

The method of creating a business case is comparable to resolving a problem.

Step 1: Define the scope of business case

To define the scope of the business case that needs to be pursued, the following is critical.

- Recognize a business problem

- Craft a business problem statement

- Classify business aspirations in pursuing the opportunity

- Prioritize business objectives

- Designate metrics to business objectives

The first step in developing a business case is identifying the problem that needs to be solved. The following gives an example:

Consider a company XYZ that wants to evaluate either VDI on-premises or consuming DaaS from a public cloud service provider. The answer depends. All business requirements are unique, so there is no one-stop solution for everyone's business. To recognize a business problem and perform an initial evaluation, making VDI or DaaS a business-wide decision depends on various elements. Identifying the answer to the following question helps to define the business problem statement.

- Is the company seeking a shift from complete IT services to cloud-based services or happy to stay on-prem?

- Is the company comfortable with CAPEX or OPEX?

- Does the company have refreshing infrastructure currently in the business budget as well for the future?

- Does the company have on-prem expertise; is there a cost and headcount to hire VDI skills?

- Does the company want to go global with resiliency and do end users need services available on the move with better performance?

Let us assume that after evaluation, company XYZ wants DaaS based on the following.

Conquering infrastructure requirements is an appealing perk but depends on how the business deploys the VDI. On-prem VDI solutions can be costly, as they want on-staff expertise, specialized infrastructure, and continuous support and administration. Additionally, on-premises infrastructure typically wants to be refreshed every 3 to 5 years and begins to become outdated about as soon as it's working.

The way forward for these business challenges is to replace the deteriorating virtualization foundation with DaaS and expand the capability to scale up/down with DaaS. It can go global with resiliency by achieving better performance by consuming services closest to the end users.

Step 2: Review and develop each choice

To define the review and develop each choice that needs to be pursued, the following is critical.

- Produce a list of choices, a minimum of three choices wherever possible.

- Collect input from business-wide vital stakeholders.

The second step in developing a business case is to establish choices to seize that opportunity; the following gives an example.

Consider a company XYZ wants to evaluate using VDI on-premises or consuming DaaS from a public cloud service provider. The answer depends. All business requirements are unique; let us assume that company XYZ wants to move forward with DaaS based on business requirements and the choices of solutions that comply with organization regulation demands. Also, company XYZ wants to build an agile, long-term remote workplace, using cloud-based services to optimize the end-user experience and offer better performance, security, and compliance. Also to be addressed are various challenging use cases, including streaming audio and video and extensive use of graphics.

Now company XYZ's business case should reflect the choice of DaaS service provider. When trying to decide which DaaS provider to choose, four significant areas need consideration: infrastructure, features, cost, and operational model that fits the organization's demands. Identifying the answer to the following question helps to develop each choice. While it's easy to be persuaded by a charming cost, choosing the most economical DaaS provider could set the DaaS initiative up for collapse because of cheap cloud IaaS, lack of features, or fumbling support. Alternatively, take cost as one factor while accomplishing DaaS due diligence and consider all components, including modern infrastructure, agile features, and aligning to the business operational model.

Company XYZ chooses Vendor 1, Vendor 2, and Vendor 3 as the listed options based on revenue, brand image, current virtual desktop infrastructure solution & service portfolio, R&D expenditure, country reach, new product/service launches, market initiatives, mergers & acquisitions, and other market-related activities.

Step 3: Evaluate the choice

To evaluate each choice that needs to be pursued, the following is critical.

- Combine any choices that could implement logically together.

- Exclude extensive, high-risk decisions.

- Pick the easy-to-implement solution over the complex and challenging.

The third step in evaluating a business case choice is to seize that opportunity; the following gives an example:

Upon receiving various inputs from vendors and internal key stakeholders, it's a point to narrow the list of alternatives down to three options that will best address organizational business objectives and stakeholders' needs. Company XYZ's sample evaluation of pros and cons against each vendor is listed in Tables 2-1 and 2-2.

Table 2-1. *Pros Comparison against Each Vendor*

Pros	Vendor 1	Vendor 2	Vendor 3
Access Anywhere.	X		X
Security and Reliability.		X	X
Uniformity and Control.	X		X
Ability to Switch Environments on the Fly.		X	X

Table 2-2. *Cons Comparison against Each Vendor*

Cons	Vendor 1	Vendor 2	Vendor 3
Need network access.	X		
Single Failure Point.			
Various Use Cases Demand Multiple Images.	X		
Long-term ROI.		X	

One of the most extensive discussions is the cost for company XYZ facing a hardware refresh or DaaS. While evaluating DaaS with a pros-and-cons approach, understanding the total cost of ownership plays a significant role in the final decision of choosing the appropriate vendor.

When evaluating DaaS options, it's easy to get attached to covering costs without recognizing how many KPIs affect the total cost of ownership. Table 2-3 lists all key risks.

Table 2-3. *TCO Planning Sample Worksheet*

TCO Parameters	Inputs
Any value of using existing cloud service (e.g., if client is already using Microsoft 365 or RDS Cals)	$$
Total no of users	$$
Total no of concurrent users	$$
No of endpoint devices with 2- to 3-year working lifespan	$$
No of endpoint devices due to refresh:	$$
No of users with physical desktop	$$
No of users with physical laptop	$$
No of users with thin client	$$
Predictable yearly net new growth:	$$
Software-based cost per desktop:	$$
Average desktop support admin salary:	$$
IT effort to procure, image, and deliver a new PC (hours/PC)	$$
IT efforts to manage existing PCs (hours/year/physical PC)	$$
Electricity consumed by the physical devices	$$
A target percentage of time spends on desktop support:	$$
Helpdesk calls	$$

Step 4: Define high-level deployment strategy

Business requirements and ideas can become real projects, shaping deployment into a project leading to business outcomes.

A critical part of any successful project is careful planning and purpose driven. Without knowing what an organization is trying to achieve, it will be challenging, time-consuming, and frustrating to find the right solution and complete it correctly.

Precise project preparation and expectation setting are significant. Even though DaaS is an elastically scalable service to deliver remote desktop and app experiences without managing the underlying server infrastructure, it needs proper planning.

Ideas can be shaped into an actual project, shaping deployment into a project endeavor leading to business outcomes. Achieving a clear definition of a DaaS project is critical. Three factors go into defining a DaaS project: objective, scope, and requirements.

Defining objective

- Why is a DaaS project necessary and

- When will you finish it?

- What will the business achieve with it?

Defining scope

- How broad are the boundaries of the project?

- How narrow are the edges of the project?

- What are the success criteria for the project?

Defining business requirements

- Time, scope, and cost involved

- Value proposition

- TCO and ROI view.

Cloud-based DaaS architecture demands Agile methodology to achieve design and deployment, continuous integration and development, continuous testing, continuous release and deployment, and continuous monitoring as depicted in Figure 2-2.

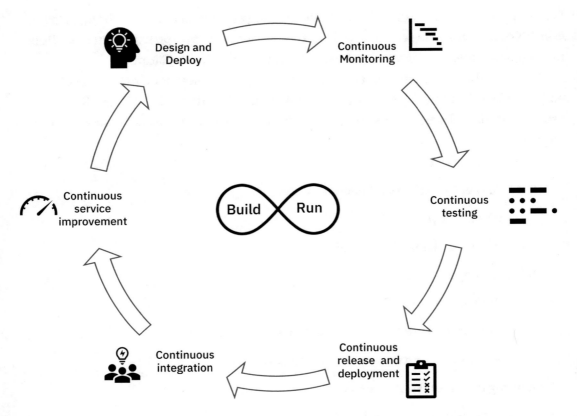

Figure 2-2. *Lifecycle of DaaS management*

Continuous planning aims to plan and deliver business strategy and adopt end-user feedback into the DaaS design and deployment or improvement lifecycle. Ongoing planning provides the tools and practices to help IT function to obtain accurate ideas or features from the DaaS perspective.

Jira and Kanban boards are famous tools used for continuous planning to continuously address the business needs and prioritize them as per IT function product owner needs and take a considerable amount of end-user feedback aligning with business strategy.

Continuous development or improvement facilitates collaboration within IT functions, development, and quality assurance (QA) teams to continuously deliver quality functions and features.

Collaborative improvement or development includes continuous integration, which encourages regular team alliances and automatic implementation. Blending the DaaS and end-user requirements more regularly, issues are recognized earlier and issue upfront before the user raises them.

Continuous testing reduces the expense of testing while boosting the development team's balance of quality and agility. It reduces testing bottlenecks by virtualizing dependent services and interprets the totality of virtualized test conditions that can be effortlessly deployed and refreshed as systems change. These abilities decrease the cost of provisioning and managing test systems and reduce test cycle times by facilitating integration testing beforehand in the lifecycle.

Continuous release and deployment offer a continuous delivery pipeline that automates deployments from Dev, Test, and UAT to production environments. It reduces standard time and effort, resource wait-time, and rewrite by using push-button deployments that facilitate a higher recurrence of releases, reduced mistakes, and fully integrated compliance.

Continuous delivery is a range of methods intended to secure that code can be immediately and carefully deployed to production by delivering each update to production and ensuring that DaaS services function as demanded via rigorous automated testing.

Ansible is a well-known tool for continuous release and deployment.

Continuous monitoring extends industry-standard monitoring and reporting, helping administrators, developers, and testers concede their DaaS performance and availability, even before it is implemented into production. The advanced feedback presented by continuous monitoring is vital to decreasing the cost of errors and updates and steering projects toward successful closure.

As a DaaS consumer, you also need to ensure and understand that the application performs as demanded by end-users and that the environment is stable using continuous monitoring. DevOps principles do recommend that DaaS administrators and engineers also need to monitor the applications. This principle ensures that the DaaS are performing at ideal levels.

Step 5: Define recommendation against outcome

To define the recommendation against outcome needs to pursue, the following is critical.

- Define the success criteria

- Value proposition

The following is an example: Company XYZ has identified that cloud technologies are increasing, enabling companies to benefit from easy access, reduced in-house management, OPEX budgeting, and overall improved efficiency. DaaS has created the perfect storm where businesses can implement high-performing virtual desktops via a cloud solution.

- DaaS service providers take care of the host's backend infrastructure (data storage, network, backup, and upgrades).

- DaaS service providers with managed services also take care of deployment and operations risk-free for cloud consumers.

- DaaS designed with high availability (HA) to maintain the continuous operation of the virtual environment and provide uninterrupted user access to the virtual desktops, adding a DR solution and scale to the per-user level.

- Secure and reliable desktop services provide a security-rich solution designed to adhere to industry standards and leverage has proven cloud infrastructure and services. DaaS comes along with regulation requirements such as Payment Card Industry Data Security Standard (PCI DSS), Health Insurance Portability and Accountability (HIPAA), and much more.

Preparing AVD

Let us say "**hello world**" to Microsoft AVD. The following prerequisites should be taken into consideration as per Microsoft recommendations.

There are a few steps and prerequisites that the AVD administrator needs to address before creating an AVD tenant. The service leverages Azure Active Directory (Azure AD) and Windows Server AD Domain Services (AD DS). Azure networking enables the communication between core AVD virtual machines, Azure storage, directory services, and anything the AVD administrator needs to connect to on-premises. Until all prerequisites are in place, it is nearly impossible to create AVD tenants.

Figure 2-3 depicts the wide range of prerequisites that should be planned prior to design and deployment of Microsoft AVD.

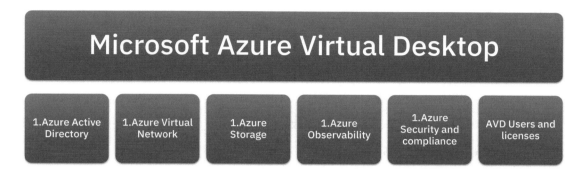

Figure 2-3. *Microsoft prerequisites for AVD deployment*

Azure AD

Microsoft's Azure AD is a cloud-based access and identity management service that maintains an organization's log-in and access resources in external resources, such as Azure portal, Microsoft 365, Microsoft AVD, numerous other SaaS offerings, and internal resources, such as apps hosted within the intranet.

AVD uses Azure AD to manage the users, and the business also needs to connect to the existing directory service into Azure AD. The following are the four types of Azure AD licenses that exist:

a. Azure AD Free with the following offerings:

- Provides user and group management,

- On-premises directory synchronization,

- Basic reports,

- Self-service password change for cloud users,

- Single sign-on across Azure, Microsoft 365, Microsoft AVD, and numerous other SaaS offerings.

b. Azure AD Premium P1 with the following offerings:

- Provides user and group management,

- On-premises directory synchronization,

- Basic reports,

- Self-service password change for cloud users,

- Single sign-on across Azure, Microsoft 365, Microsoft AVD, and numerous other SaaS offerings,

- Hybrid users access both on-premises and cloud resources,

- Dynamic groups,

- Self-service group management,

- Microsoft identity manager,

- Cloud write-back capabilities allow self-service password to reset for on-premises users.

c. Azure AD Premium P2 with the following offerings:

- Provides user and group management,

- On-premises directory synchronization,

- Basic reports,

- Self-service password change for cloud users,

- Single sign-on across Azure, Microsoft 365, Microsoft AVD, and numerous other SaaS offerings,

- Hybrid users access both on-premises and cloud resources,

- Dynamic groups,

- Self-service group management,

- Microsoft identity manager,

- Cloud write-back capabilities allow self-service password reset for on-premises users,

- Azure AD identity protection,

- Privileged identity management.

d. Azure AD Pay as You Go with following offerings:

- Azure AD Business-to-Customer (B2C)

Azure Tenant

Azure tenant is associated with a single identity (personal or business) and can own several subscriptions.

- Azure subscription is related to a payment setup, and individual subscriptions will follow in a separate bill.

- With every Azure subscription, cloud consumers can add virtual resources (VM, storage, network, and many other azure cloud services).

One of the essential requirements for Microsoft AVD is your identity strategy. The following are the options listed by Microsoft for domain controller requirements:

- An Azure AD DS.

- A Windows server AD in sync with Azure AD

- An Azure subscription, fostered to the same Azure AD tenant, includes a virtual network (vNET) containing or connected to Microsoft Windows server AD or Microsoft Azure AD DS instance.

Azure AD domain includes access to remote sessions, privilege administration elements, and AVD end-user provisioning. AVD uses Azure AD to authenticate any service that interacts with services running in Azure.

Azure AD DS is used to authenticate at the AVD service layer. All VMs in AVD are domain-joined, and AD DS is used to authenticate users to the VMs.

For this book, we will use Microsoft cloud-native Azure AD DS. The following ten-step process demonstrates how to perform a primary tenant setup for business.

Step 1: Log in to personal or business account into Azure portal.

The following is the link: `https://portal.azure.com/`.

If you do already have an Azure user login ready to go for Step 2, you can skip the following step (see Figure 2-4).

Figure 2-4. *Microsoft Azure portal login*

For the first-time starter, you need to create an Azure account; you have choice to use your email or phone instead (see Figure 2-5).

Figure 2-5. *Microsoft Azure portal account creation*

Let us choose to get a new email address, and after selecting, enter the preferred email address (Figure 2-6).

Figure 2-6. *Microsoft Azure portal account creation continued*

In the next step, you are prompted to set up password and complete the setup (Figure 2-7).

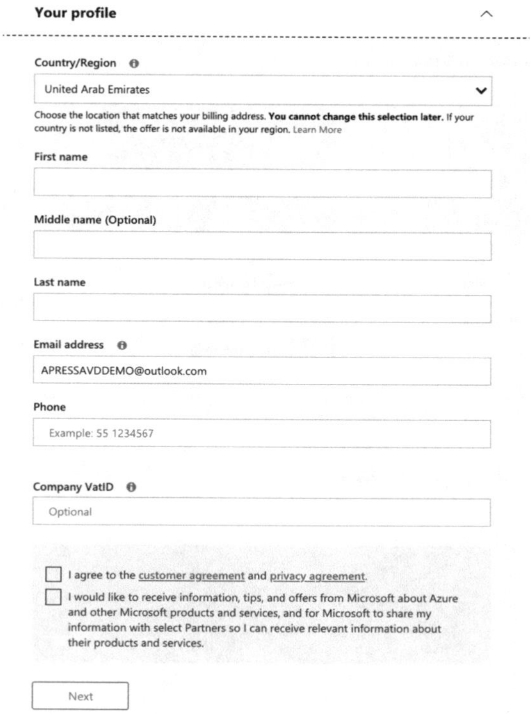

Figure 2-7. *Microsoft Azure portal account creation continued*

Complete verification inclusive of credit card setup (Figure 2-8).

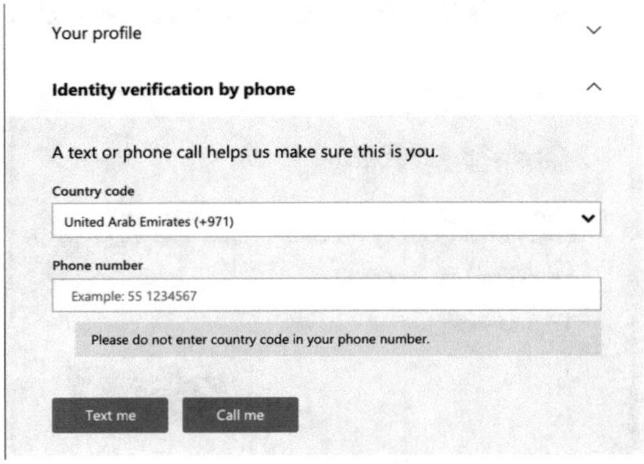

Figure 2-8. *Microsoft Azure portal account validation*

Step 2: From the Azure portal menu, choose **Azure Active Directory** (Figure 2-9).

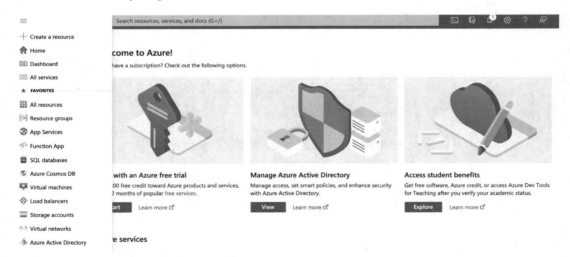

Figure 2-9. *Microsoft Azure AD Setup*

Step 3: Choose to **Create a tenant** (Figure 2-10).

Figure 2-10. *Create an AD tenant*

Step 5: On the Basics tab, choose the kind of tenant you/your organization wants to create; here let us choose **Azure Active Directory** (Figure 2-11)**.**

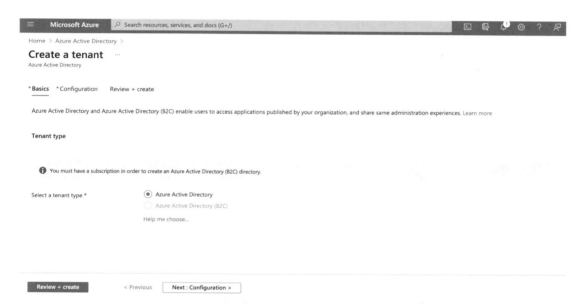

Figure 2-11. *Basic setup*

Step 6: Choose Next: Configuration to move on to the Configuration tab.

Step 7: On the Configuration tab, enter the organization name and domain name and choose the country or region.

- Type APRESSAVD into the organization name box.

- Type AVDLAB into the initial domain name box.

- Choose the United States or your country box (Figure 2-12).

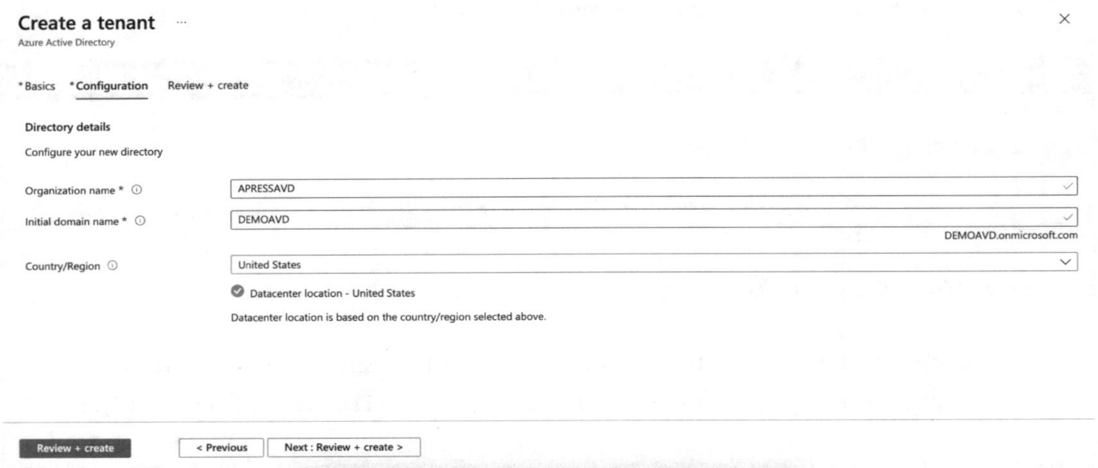

Figure 2-12. *Configuration setup*

Step 8: And then click on **Next: Review + Create**. Evaluate that the data entered is valid and choose to select **create** (Figure 2-13).

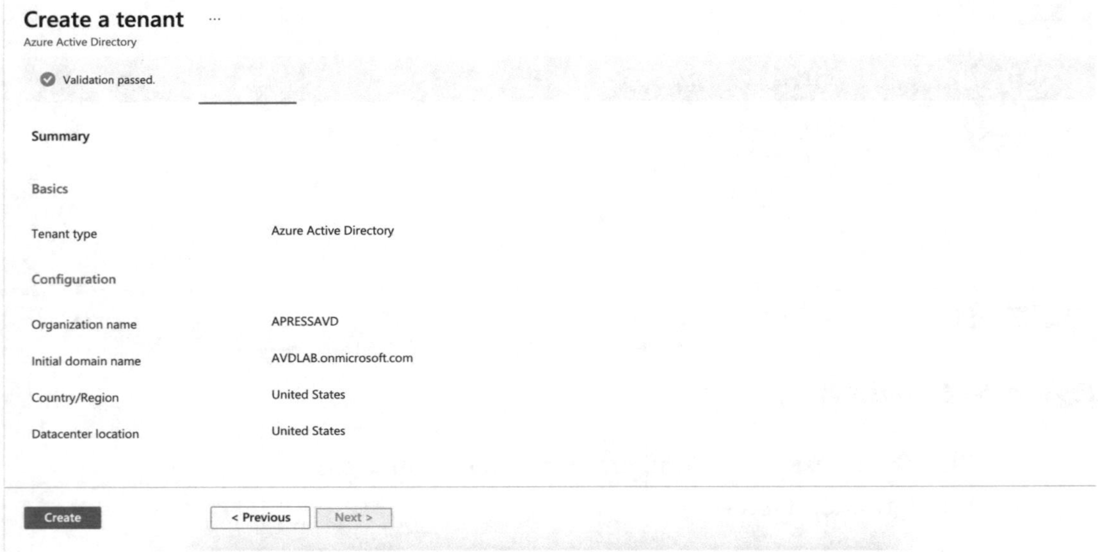

Figure 2-13. *Review and create*

A brand new tenant is now built with the domain; you can validate from Azure portal under Azure AD blade (Figure 2-14).

Figure 2-14. *Validate AD tenant setup*

Step 9: Choose the Azure AD tenant for future details (Figure 2-15).

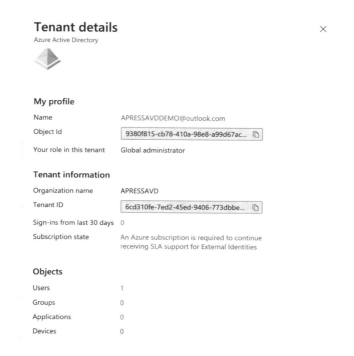

Figure 2-15. *AD tenant detailed view*

When we create a new Azure AD tenant, the creator becomes the first user of the newly created tenant. As the primary user, the creator is automatically assigned the global admin role and becomes the technical point of contact for the tenant.

Azure Virtual Network

Microsoft Azure vNET is the primary building block for the AVD private network in Azure. vNET facilitates many Azure resources, such as AVD, to securely communicate with each other, the Internet, and on-premises networks. vNET is like a legacy network that runs in the legacy data center but delivers extra advantages such as scalability, availability, segmentation, segregation, and isolation. The following are loaded options from the Azure vNET.

- Develop a hybrid infrastructure that cloud consumers control

- Solid cloud consumer connections with an IPsec VPN or Microsoft ExpressRoute

- Develop sophisticated network topologies using virtual appliances

- Follows and implements bring your own IP addresses and DNS servers

- Obtain granular control over traffic between AVD subnets

- Receive an isolated and highly secure environment for cloud consumer applications

For Microsoft AVD, Azure vNET is managed by AVD cloud consumer.

Microsoft AVD offers end-user sessions on the remote session hosts running on Microsoft Azure. Microsoft offers managed services for portions of the services on the cloud consumer's behalf and implements secure endpoints for connecting end users' client sessions and session hosts.

In Azure, an organization needs to create its vNET and subnets. To be accurate, at least for POC or demo environments, you will need the following:

- Subnet 1 for core infrastructure virtual machines that are hosting AVD core components.

- Subnet 2 for end users' remote desktop hosted sharing sessions.

- Subnet 3 for minimum security, and monitoring component deployment.

- Subnet 4 for external connectivity to reach the hosted network.

The vNET in Azure is a design of your tenant network in the cloud. It has logical segregation and isolation within the Azure cloud, and vNET in Azure also provides the opportunity to link vNETs to other vNETs within Azure or in on-premise environments.

The following five-step process demonstrates how to perform a vNET setup for AVD.

Step 1: Log in to personal or business account into Azure portal.

The following is the link: `https://portal.azure.com/`.

Step 2: Choose Virtual networks (Figure 2-16).

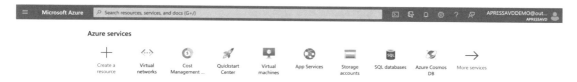

Figure 2-16. *View Virtual network*

Figure 2-17 presents the default view.

Figure 2-17. *Default Virtual networks view*

Step 3: Create vNET, provide instance name and region you want to create (Figure 2-18).

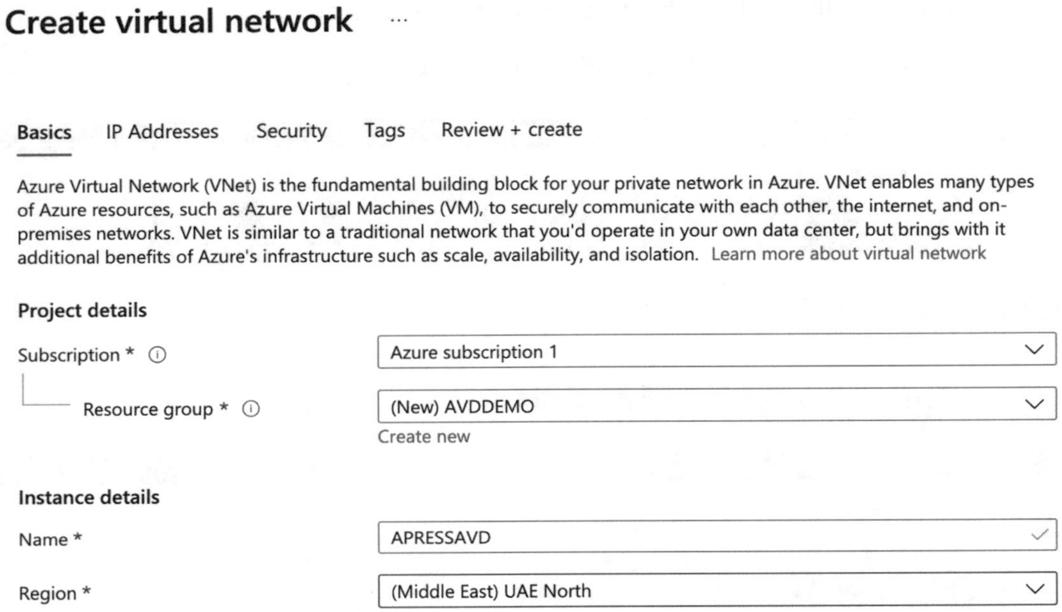

Create virtual network   ⋯

Basics   IP Addresses   Security   Tags   Review + create

Azure Virtual Network (VNet) is the fundamental building block for your private network in Azure. VNet enables many types of Azure resources, such as Azure Virtual Machines (VM), to securely communicate with each other, the internet, and on-premises networks. VNet is similar to a traditional network that you'd operate in your own data center, but brings with it additional benefits of Azure's infrastructure such as scale, availability, and isolation. Learn more about virtual network

Project details

Subscription * ⓘ	Azure subscription 1 ⌄
⌐ Resource group * ⓘ	(New) AVDDEMO ⌄
	Create new

Instance details

Name *	APRESSAVD ✓
Region *	(Middle East) UAE North ⌄

Figure 2-18. *Create vNET Basics tab view*

Step 4: Create vNET in IPV4 address space (see Figure 2-19)

- A subnet for core infrastructure virtual machines that are hosting AVD core components.

  - 10.50.0.0/24 range is created

- B subnet for end users' remote desktop hosted sharing session.

  - 10.51.0.0/24 range is created

- C subnet for minimum security, and monitoring component deployment.

  - 10.53.0.0/24 range is created

- D subnet for external connectivity to reach hosted network.

  - 190.1.0.0/24 range is created

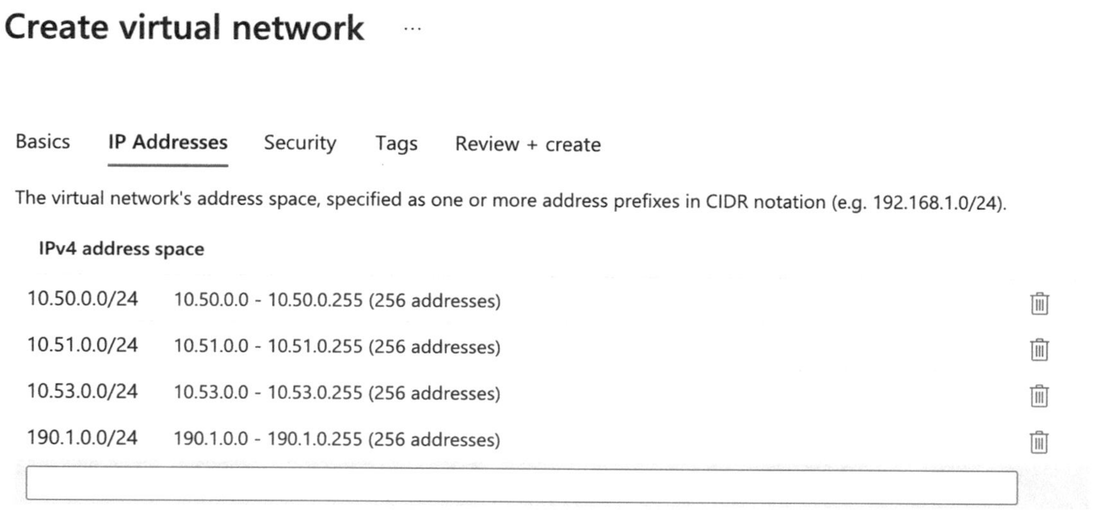

Create virtual network ⋯

Basics   **IP Addresses**   Security   Tags   Review + create

The virtual network's address space, specified as one or more address prefixes in CIDR notation (e.g. 192.168.1.0/24).

IPv4 address space

10.50.0.0/24	10.50.0.0 - 10.50.0.255 (256 addresses)	🗑
10.51.0.0/24	10.51.0.0 - 10.51.0.255 (256 addresses)	🗑
10.53.0.0/24	10.53.0.0 - 10.53.0.255 (256 addresses)	🗑
190.1.0.0/24	190.1.0.0 - 190.1.0.255 (256 addresses)	🗑

Figure 2-19. *Create vNET IP Addresses tab view*

Step 4: Allocate vNET subnet. **+ Add subnet**, then enter (Figure 2-20).

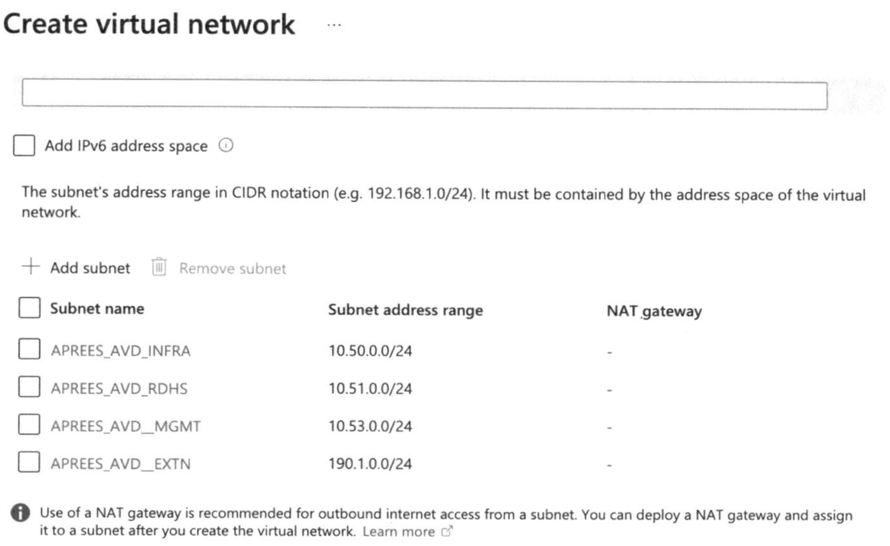

Create virtual network ⋯

☐ Add IPv6 address space ⓘ

The subnet's address range in CIDR notation (e.g. 192.168.1.0/24). It must be contained by the address space of the virtual network.

＋ Add subnet   🗑 Remove subnet

Subnet name	Subnet address range	NAT gateway
☐ APREES_AVD_INFRA	10.50.0.0/24	-
☐ APREES_AVD_RDHS	10.51.0.0/24	-
☐ APREES_AVD__MGMT	10.53.0.0/24	-
☐ APREES_AVD__EXTN	190.1.0.0/24	-

ⓘ Use of a NAT gateway is recommended for outbound internet access from a subnet. You can deploy a NAT gateway and assign it to a subnet after you create the virtual network. Learn more ↗

Figure 2-20. *Create vNET IP Addresses tab view continued*

- APREES_AVD_INFRA subnet for core infrastructure virtual machines that are hosting AVD core components.

  - 10.50.0.0/24 range is created

- APREES_AVD_RDHS subnet for end users' remote desktop hosted sharing session.

  - 10.51.0.0/24 range is created

- APREES_AVD_MGMT subnet for minimum security, and monitoring component deployment.

  - 10.53.0.0/24 range is created

- APREES_AVD_EXTN subnet for external connectivity to reach hosted network.

  - 190.1.0.0/24 range is created

Step 5: Choose the Review & create a tab and click Create (Figure 2-21).

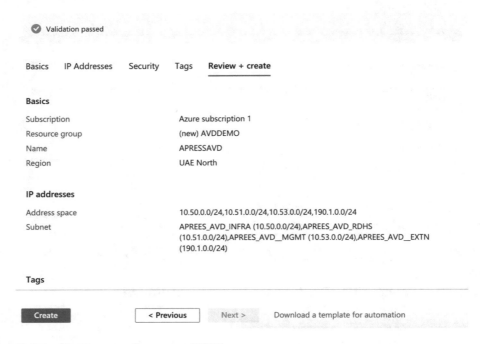

Figure 2-21. Review and create vNET

Azure Storage

Microsoft's Azure cloud storage offers advanced data storage solutions. Core storage services provide a massively scalable, durable, and highly available, secure, managed, and accessible storage solution. The following is an overview of the types of storage.

- Azure Files is a managed file share for cloud deployments as well as for on-premises. Usable for AVD to store profiles and containers.

- Azure Queue is a messaging store for reliable messaging between downstream application components accessed from the AVD.

- Azure Disks are block-level storage volumes for VMs hosted in Azure. Usable for AVD session hosts and pooled or dedicated desktops.

- Azure Table is a NoSQL store for schemaless storage of structured data.

- Azure Blobs is a highly scalable object store for text and binary data. It also includes provision for big data analytics through Data Lake Storage Gen2.

For AVD, AVD end-users can be enabled with home drive, profile, and container stores with the following storage solutions from Azure.

- Build and manage dedicated Azure VM with a file server role deployed in Windows server operating system.

- Azure NetApp Files is an Azure-native setting built on highly possible NetApp technology straight within Microsoft Azure datacenters.

- 'NetApp Files' is a high-performance, metering, enterprise-class file storage service. Azure NetApp files are highly available and support any workload. This service allows you to set performance levels and create snapshots.

- Cloud-native Azure files. Let us explore about cloud-native Azure files.

What are Azure files?

Azure files enable AVD to configure highly available network file shares that can be accessed using the standard server message block (SMB) protocol. Multiple session hosts or pooled desktops can access file share with read and write access. End users or applications can also read the files using the storage client libraries or REST interface.

The principal value adds of Azure files compared over on-prem file shares is that end users can access the files from everywhere globally using a URL with a shared access signature (SAS) token. The IT function can generate SAS tokens; they allow specific access to a personal asset with time expiry.

Before the AVD administrator works with an Azure file share, the AVD administrator must create an Azure storage account. A general-purpose v2 storage account presents the path to all Azure storage services: blobs, files, queues, and tables. The quickstart creates a general-purpose v2 storage account.

One prerequisite for AVD is ensuring that the domain controller is synced with Azure AD and reachable from the Azure vNET where the AVD session hosts exist.

To deploy a general-purpose v2 storage account in the Azure portal, follow these steps (see Figure 2-22):

> **Step 1:** Log in to personal or business account into Azure portal.
>
> The following is the link: `https://portal.azure.com/`.
>
> **Step 2:** Choose Storage account and select + New.

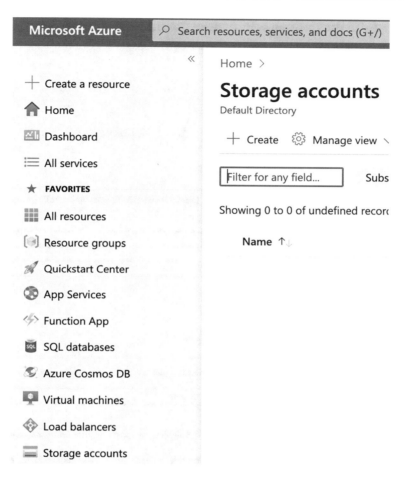

Figure 2-22. *Storage account in Azure Portal*

Step 3: On the Basics blade, choose the subscription to create the storage account (see Figure 2-23).

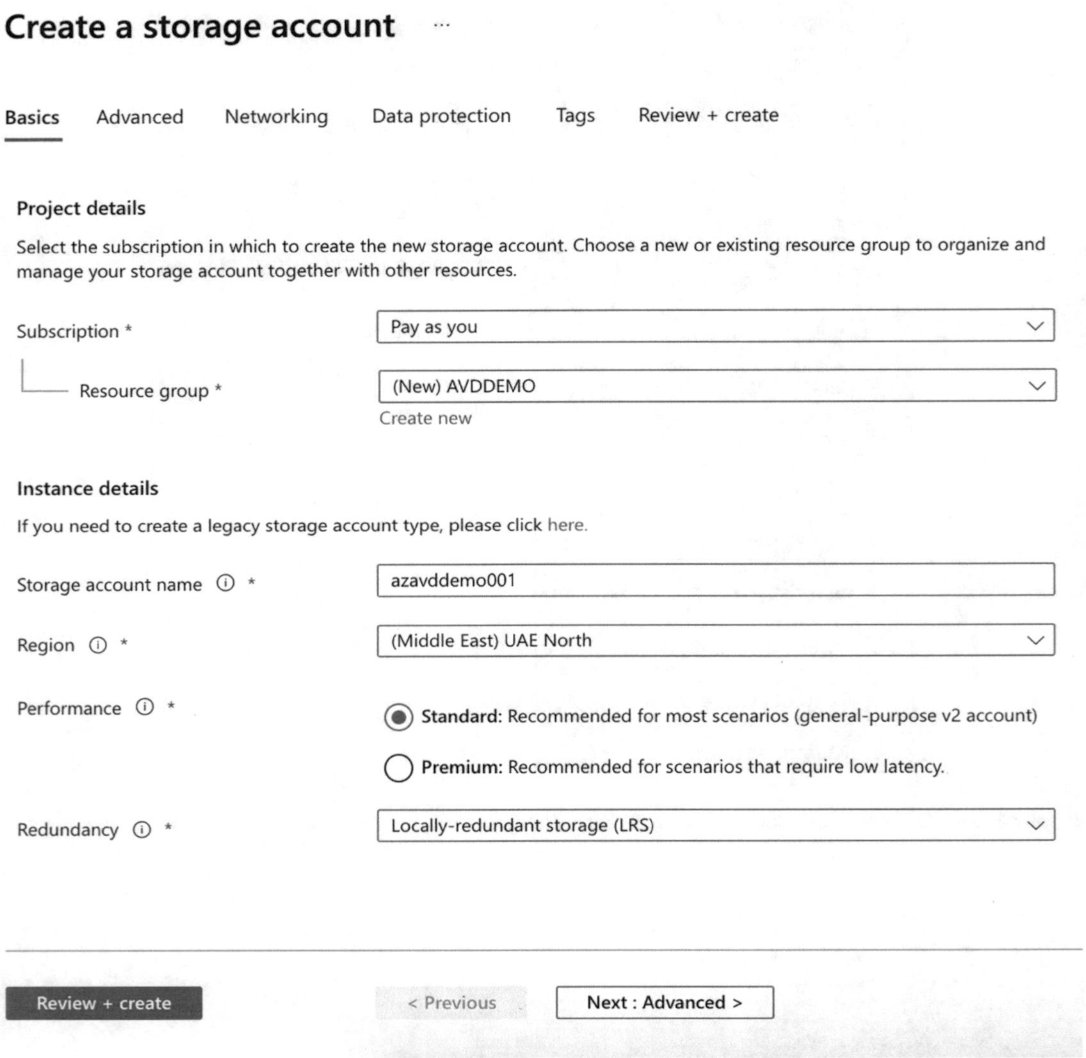

Create a storage account   ...

Basics   Advanced   Networking   Data protection   Tags   Review + create

Project details

Select the subscription in which to create the new storage account. Choose a new or existing resource group to organize and manage your storage account together with other resources.

Subscription *   Pay as you   ⌄

└──── Resource group *   (New) AVDDEMO   ⌄
                                            Create new

Instance details

If you need to create a legacy storage account type, please click here.

Storage account name ⓘ *   azavddemo001

Region ⓘ *   (Middle East) UAE North   ⌄

Performance ⓘ *   ● **Standard:** Recommended for most scenarios (general-purpose v2 account)

                                           ○ **Premium:** Recommended for scenarios that require low latency.

Redundancy ⓘ *   Locally-redundant storage (LRS)   ⌄

[Review + create]   < Previous   [Next : Advanced >]

Figure 2-23. *Storage accounts create basic view*

On the Resource group field, choose the desired resource group.

Next, type the name for a storage account. The name chosen must be unique across Azure.

Choose a region for the storage account or accept the default region.

Choose a performance tier. The default tier is standard.

Choose redundancy: locally redundant storage (LRS), geo-redundant storage (GRS), zone-redundant storage (ZRS), or geo-zone-redundant storage (GZRS).

Step 4: Under the advanced tab, check if there are security requirements specific to in-country data regulation.

Azure storage provides multilayered security to protect cloud consumers' data. Azure storage accounts offer the luxury of multiple security options that protect cloud consumers' data. Azure services such as blob storage, files share, table storage, and data lake store all build on Azure storage. Because of this framework and the azure storage services are built-in from the fine-grained security restrictions.

Microsoft offers the following choices.

- Cloud consumers can protect the data at rest.

- Cloud consumers can protect the data in transit.

- Empower infrastructure encryption for the second level of encryption of data.

- Restrict anonymous unrestricted read access to containers and blobs.

- Block shared key authorization for an Azure storage account (Figure 2-24).

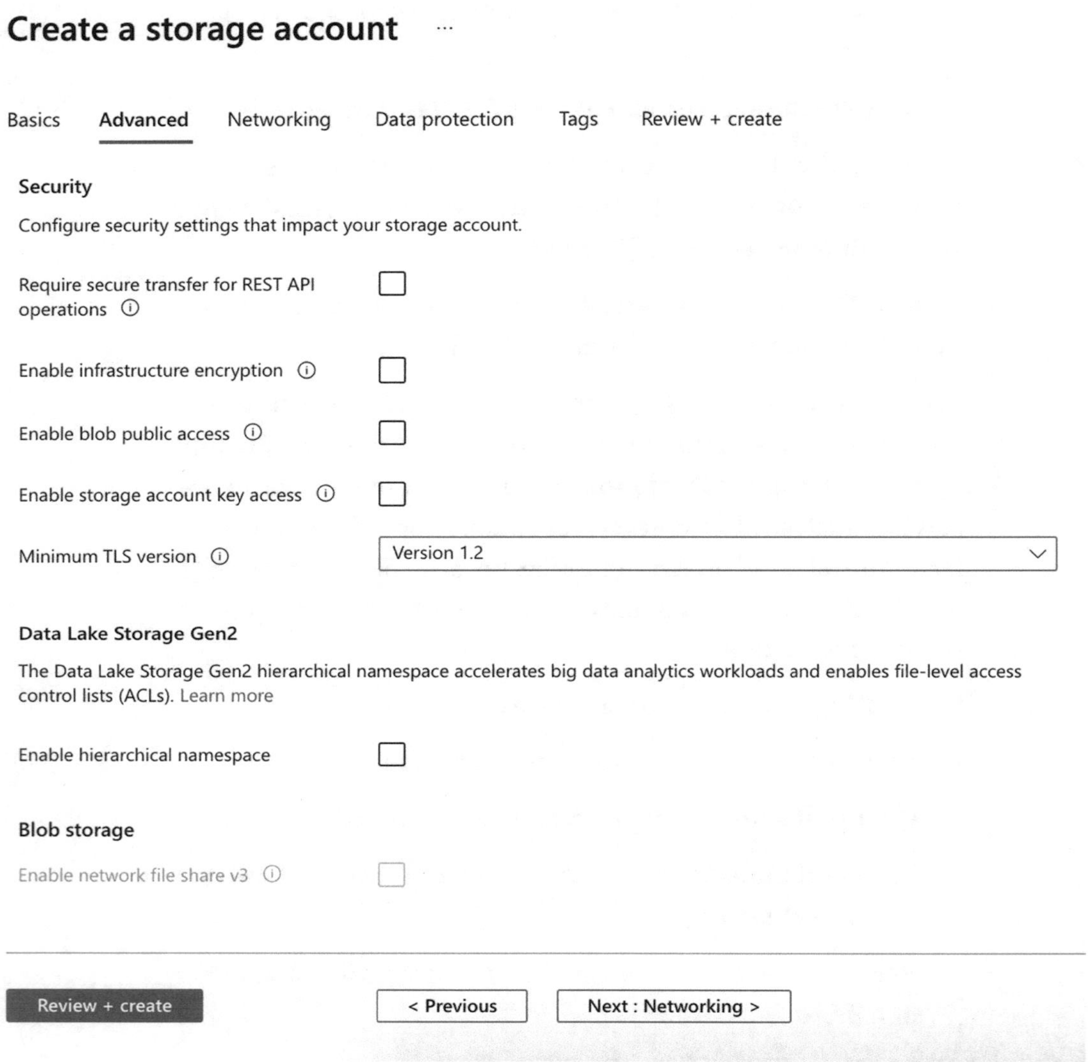

Create a storage account   ...

Basics   **Advanced**   Networking   Data protection   Tags   Review + create

Security

Configure security settings that impact your storage account.

Require secure transfer for REST API
operations ⓘ   ☐

Enable infrastructure encryption ⓘ   ☐

Enable blob public access ⓘ   ☐

Enable storage account key access ⓘ   ☐

Minimum TLS version ⓘ | Version 1.2   ⌄ |

Data Lake Storage Gen2

The Data Lake Storage Gen2 hierarchical namespace accelerates big data analytics workloads and enables file-level access
control lists (ACLs). Learn more

Enable hierarchical namespace   ☐

Blob storage

Enable network file share v3 ⓘ   ☐

| Review + create | | < Previous | | Next : Networking > |

Figure 2-24. Storage accounts create advanced view

When writing the book, the standard Azure file shares with 100
TiB capacity had the following limitations: Azure was supporting
only LRS and ZRS accounts. Also, once AVD administrators enable
large file shares, converting storage accounts to GRS or GZRS accounts is not possible. Once the AVD administrator allows large
file shares choice, the AVD administrator or global administrator
cannot disable it (Figure 2-25).

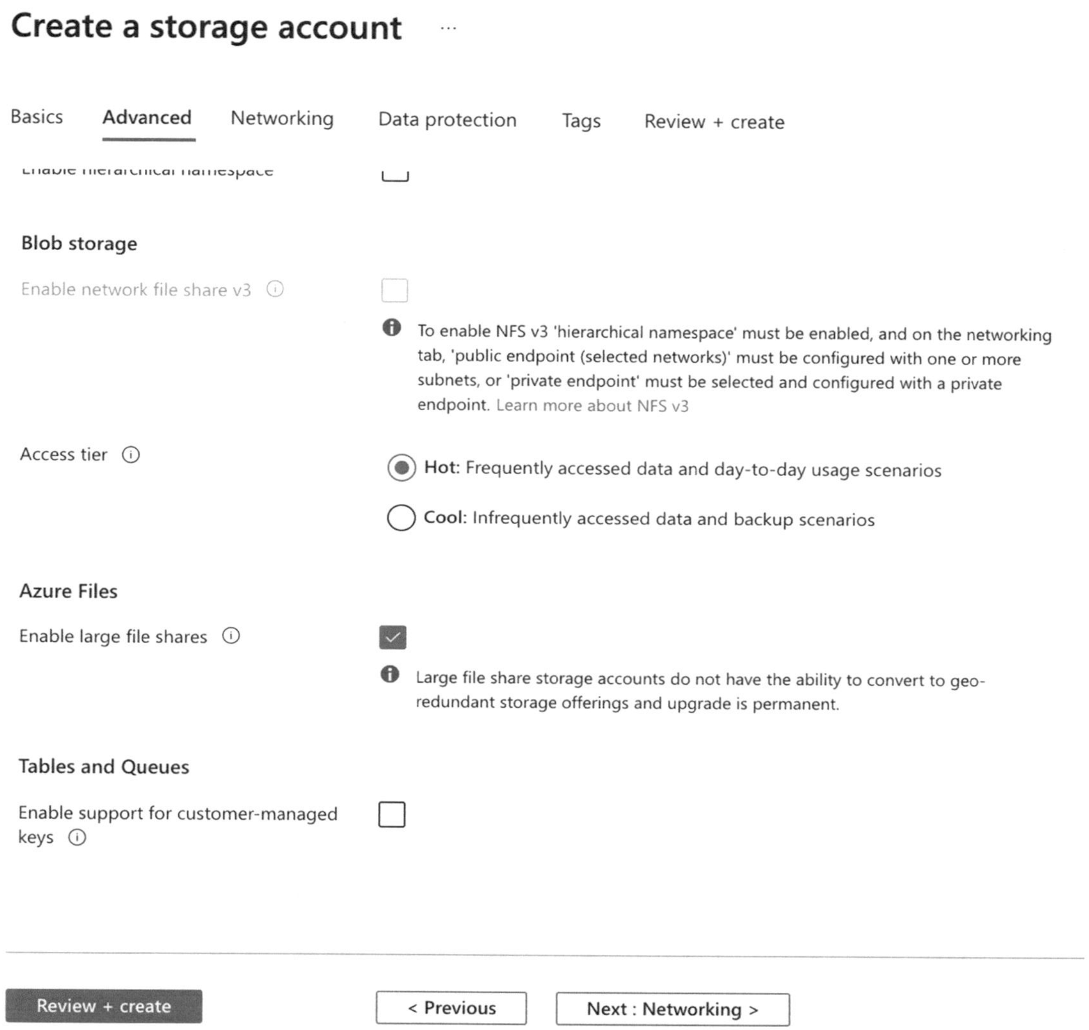

Create a storage account   ⋯

Basics   **Advanced**   Networking   Data protection   Tags   Review + create

~~Enable hierarchical namespace~~   ☐

Blob storage

Enable network file share v3 ⓘ   ☐

ⓘ To enable NFS v3 'hierarchical namespace' must be enabled, and on the networking tab, 'public endpoint (selected networks)' must be configured with one or more subnets, or 'private endpoint' must be selected and configured with a private endpoint. Learn more about NFS v3

Access tier ⓘ   ◉ **Hot:** Frequently accessed data and day-to-day usage scenarios

○ **Cool:** Infrequently accessed data and backup scenarios

Azure Files

Enable large file shares ⓘ   ☑

ⓘ Large file share storage accounts do not have the ability to convert to geo-redundant storage offerings and upgrade is permanent.

Tables and Queues

Enable support for customer-managed keys ⓘ   ☐

[Review + create]   [< Previous]   [Next : Networking >]

Figure 2-25. *Storage accounts create advanced view continued*

Step 5: In the Networking tab, the AVD administrator can define the connectivity. Azure storage provides a layered security model which enables cloud consumers to secure and control the level of access to their storage accounts that AVD environments demand, based on the type and subset of networks or resources AVD is using. For example, AVD administrators can limit access to AVD storage accounts to requests originating from specified IP addresses, IP subnets, subnets in an Azure vNET, or resource instances of some Azure services.

AVD can connect to storage accounts publicly, via public IP addresses or service endpoints, or privately, using a private endpoint (Figure 2-26).

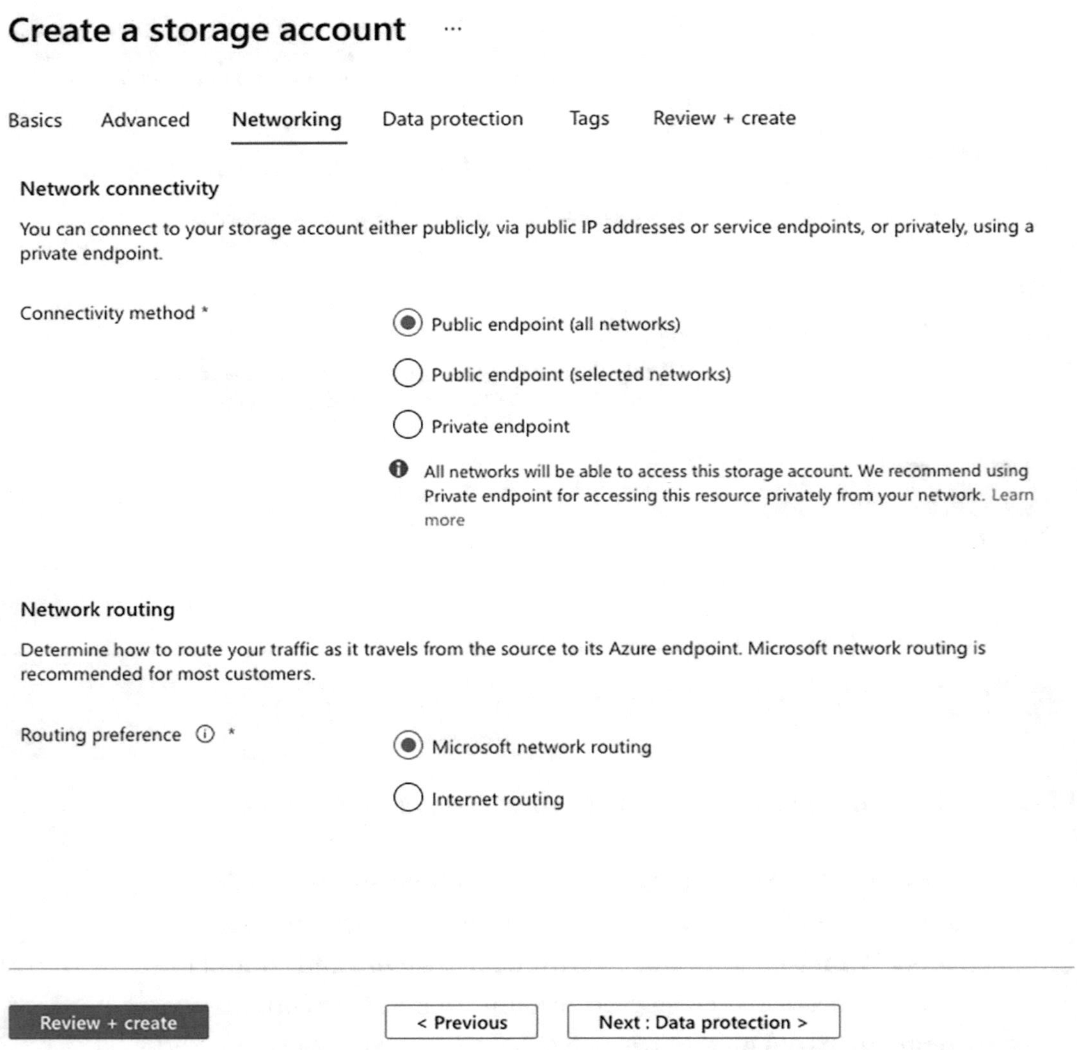

Create a storage account   ⋯

Basics   Advanced   **Networking**   Data protection   Tags   Review + create

Network connectivity

You can connect to your storage account either publicly, via public IP addresses or service endpoints, or privately, using a private endpoint.

Connectivity method *

- ⦿ Public endpoint (all networks)
- ◯ Public endpoint (selected networks)
- ◯ Private endpoint

ⓘ All networks will be able to access this storage account. We recommend using Private endpoint for accessing this resource privately from your network. Learn more

Network routing

Determine how to route your traffic as it travels from the source to its Azure endpoint. Microsoft network routing is recommended for most customers.

Routing preference ⓘ *

- ⦿ Microsoft network routing
- ◯ Internet routing

Review + create   < Previous   Next : Data protection >

Figure 2-26. *Storage accounts create Network view*

Step 6: The Data Protection tab helps cloud consumers to protect data from accidental or wrong deletion or modification.

Microsoft offers the following choices.

- Point-in-time restore protects against accidental deletion or corruption by enabling cloud consumers to restore block blob data to a known good state.

- Point-in-time restore is helpful in scenarios where an AVD home drive user accidentally deletes data or a profile corrupts data.

- Blob soft delete preserves an individual blob, snapshot, or version from accidental deletes or overwrites by keeping the erased data in the system for a particular period; if time is expired, data may be erased.

- Azure files offers soft delete for file shares. A soft delete allows the AVD administrator to recover AVD file share if the share is deleted by an AVD subsystem or other storage account user (Figure 2-27).

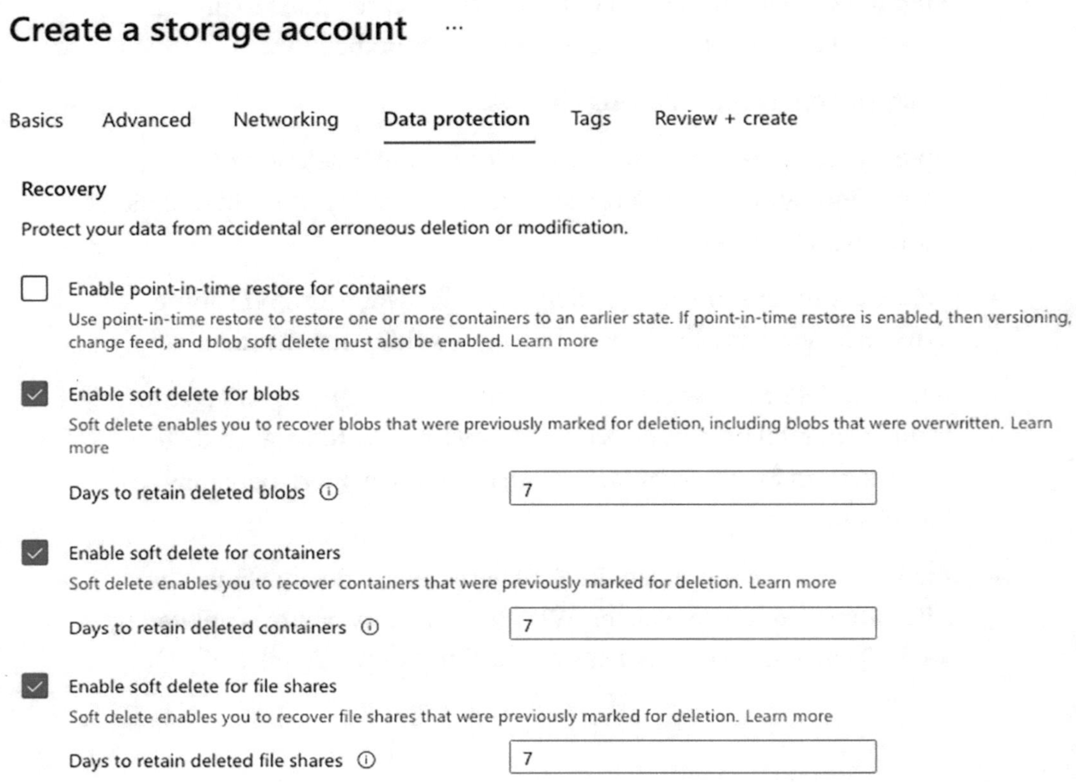

Create a storage account ⋯

Basics   Advanced   Networking   **Data protection**   Tags   Review + create

Recovery

Protect your data from accidental or erroneous deletion or modification.

☐ Enable point-in-time restore for containers
Use point-in-time restore to restore one or more containers to an earlier state. If point-in-time restore is enabled, then versioning, change feed, and blob soft delete must also be enabled. Learn more

☑ Enable soft delete for blobs
Soft delete enables you to recover blobs that were previously marked for deletion, including blobs that were overwritten. Learn more

Days to retain deleted blobs ⓘ

7

☑ Enable soft delete for containers
Soft delete enables you to recover containers that were previously marked for deletion. Learn more

Days to retain deleted containers ⓘ

7

☑ Enable soft delete for file shares
Soft delete enables you to recover file shares that were previously marked for deletion. Learn more

Days to retain deleted file shares ⓘ

7

Figure 2-27. Storage accounts create data protection view

Version control is the method of tracking and runs release management against changes to storage.

Microsoft offers the following choices.

- Blob storage versioning to automatically keep previous versions of an object.

- Changes feed to provide transaction logs of all the changes that occur to the blobs and the blob metadata in your storage account (Figure 2-28).

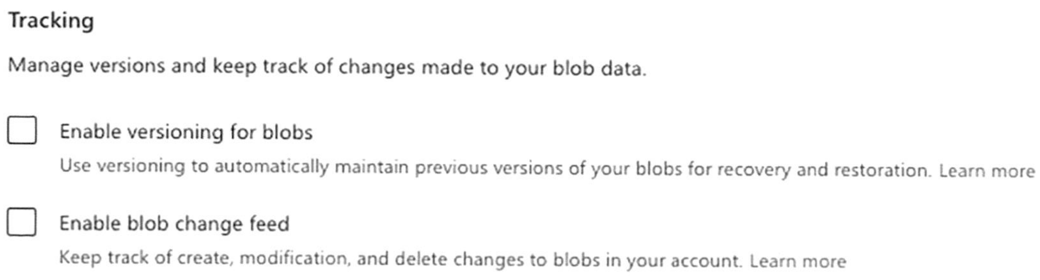

Tracking

Manage versions and keep track of changes made to your blob data.

☐ Enable versioning for blobs
Use versioning to automatically maintain previous versions of your blobs for recovery and restoration. Learn more

☐ Enable blob change feed
Keep track of create, modification, and delete changes to blobs in your account. Learn more

Figure 2-28. *Storage accounts create data protection view continued*

> **Step 7:** In Tags tab,
>
> AVD administrators can use tags against each cloud consumer's Azure resources, resource groups, and subscriptions to rationally make them into a group. Each tag consists of a name and a value pair. So, for example, AVD administrators can use the name environment and the value test, UAT, or production to all the respective environment resources (Figure 2-29).

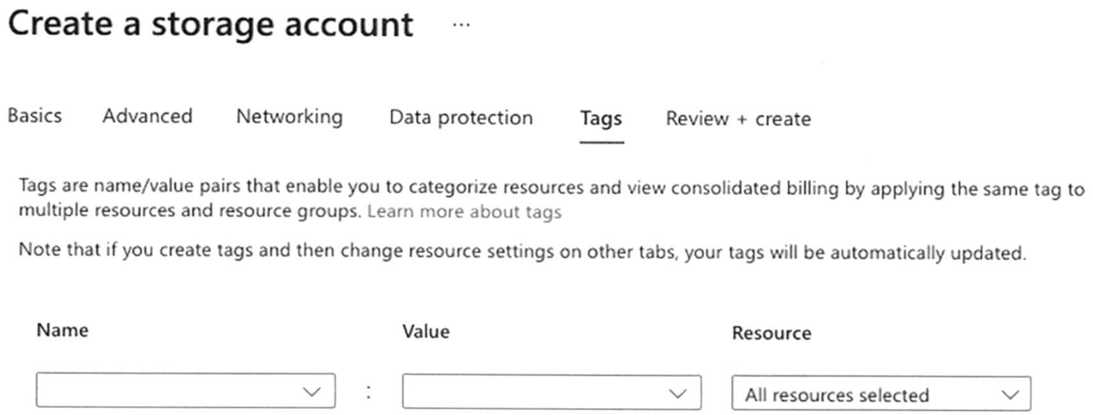

Create a storage account   ...

Basics	Advanced	Networking	Data protection	**Tags**	Review + create

Tags are name/value pairs that enable you to categorize resources and view consolidated billing by applying the same tag to multiple resources and resource groups. Learn more about tags

Note that if you create tags and then change resource settings on other tabs, your tags will be automatically updated.

Name	Value	Resource
⌄	: ⌄	All resources selected ⌄

Figure 2-29. *Storage accounts create Tags view continued*

Step 8: Finally, Review + Create to review storage account settings and create the account (Figure 2-30).

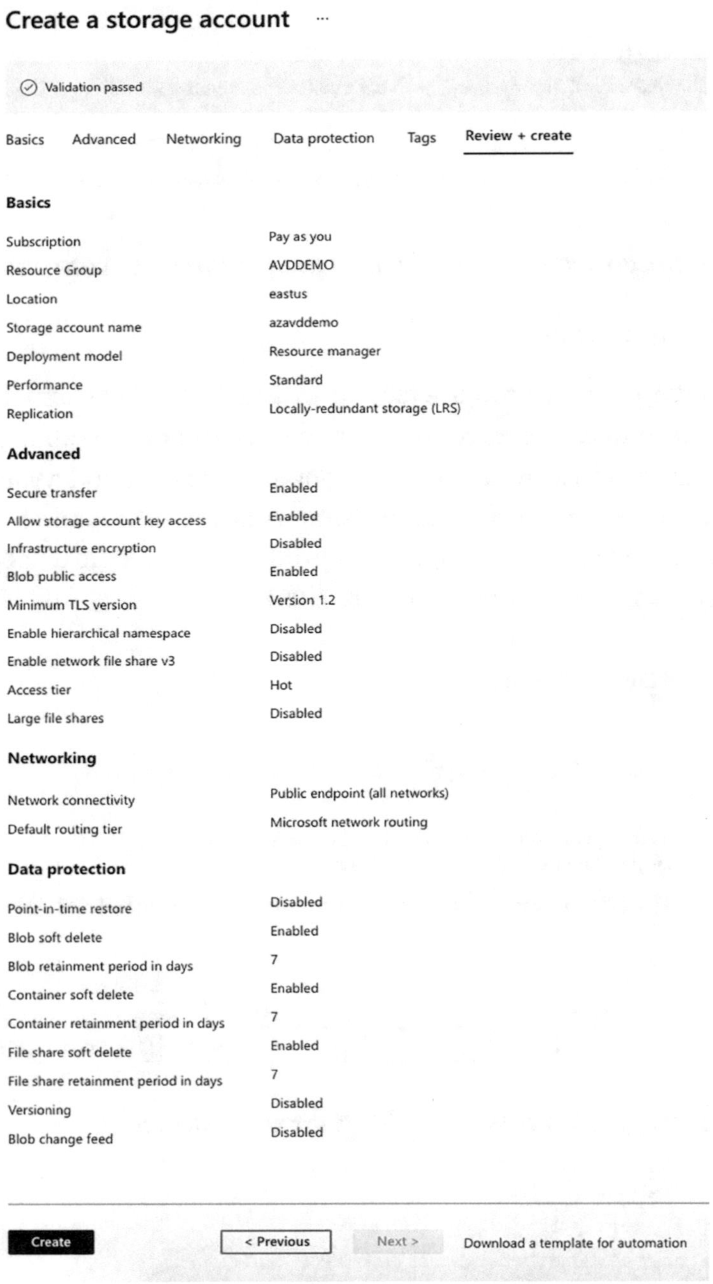

Create a storage account   ...

⊘ Validation passed

Basics   Advanced   Networking   Data protection   Tags   **Review + create**

Basics

Subscription	Pay as you
Resource Group	AVDDEMO
Location	eastus
Storage account name	azavddemo
Deployment model	Resource manager
Performance	Standard
Replication	Locally-redundant storage (LRS)

Advanced

Secure transfer	Enabled
Allow storage account key access	Enabled
Infrastructure encryption	Disabled
Blob public access	Enabled
Minimum TLS version	Version 1.2
Enable hierarchical namespace	Disabled
Enable network file share v3	Disabled
Access tier	Hot
Large file shares	Disabled

Networking

Network connectivity	Public endpoint (all networks)
Default routing tier	Microsoft network routing

Data protection

Point-in-time restore	Disabled
Blob soft delete	Enabled
Blob retainment period in days	7
Container soft delete	Enabled
Container retainment period in days	7
File share soft delete	Enabled
File share retainment period in days	7
Versioning	Disabled
Blob change feed	Disabled

Create   < Previous   Next >   Download a template for automation

Figure 2-30. *Storage accounts review and create*

Step 9: Once deployment is completed, verify that the storage account exists (Figure 2-31).

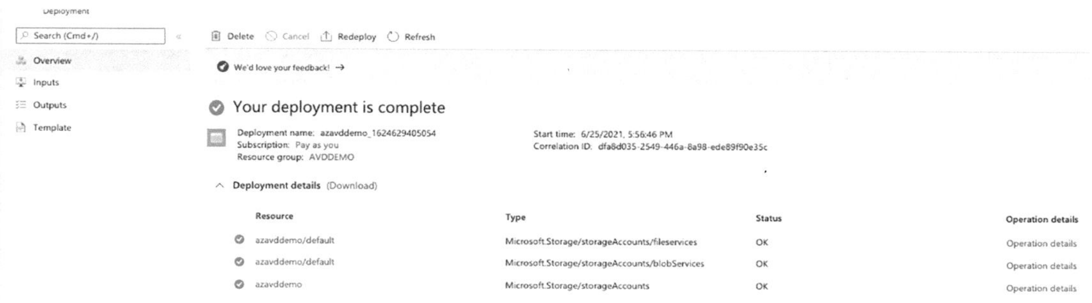

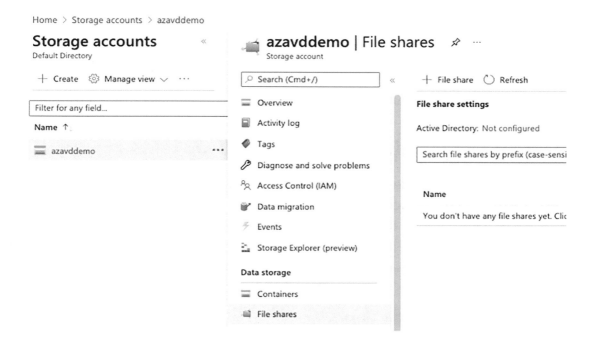

Figure 2-31. *Storage accounts validate the account creation*

Next, the AVD administrator is to create a file share. The following eight-step process demonstrates how to perform an Azure file setup for AVD.

Step 1: Log in to personal or business account into Azure portal. The following is the link: `https://portal.azure.com/`.

Step 2: Choose the storage account that was created and click on file shares (Figure 2-32).

Figure 2-32. *Storage accounts file shares creation*

Step 3: Choose to create a new file share, set name and select a size for share.

Azure file share offers four different tiers of storage, premium, transaction optimized, hot, and cool, to allow cloud consumers to tailor file shares to their performance and price requirements. For AVD, a premium is a preferred choice for users to store documents (Figure 2-33).

Figure 2-33. Storage accounts offering types

The next step integrates with AD authentication on the storage account and configures share folder permissions.

Azure Observability

Azure monitor offers end-to-end observability into cloud consumer applications, infrastructure, and networks.

Observability is critical for managing and improving the complex virtual desktop environment. Through this methodology, any AVD administrator and engineering team can understand system utilization and performance, so the AVD administrator can perform ongoing maintenance and forecast the features needed for the end users. As well as monitoring and logging, the AVD components offer visibility into service-level indicators. Specifically, indicators can lead to actionable tasks, be they automated or manual, to achieve the service-level objective (SLO).

Observability includes monitoring, dynamic service topology, anomaly detection, proactive issues avoidance, alert grouping, incident similarity, ChatOps, advice on next best action, story service, logging, tracing, and messaging critical role for virtual desktop administrators.

Azure Monitor for AVD is a dashboard intensified on Azure Monitor workbooks that supports AVD administrators in understanding cloud consumers' AVD environments. AVD helps to perform gathering and investigative tasks and do telemetry data from AVD Azure and on-premises environments. Azure Monitor benefits cloud consumers to maximize the performance and availability of the AVD environment and proactively identify problems in seconds.

With Azure Monitor for Windows virtual desktop, AVD administrators can detect and troubleshoot predicaments in the environment, view the status and well-being of host pools, diagnose end-user feedback, and follow resource utilization.

Finally, it is the monitoring and logging that gives AVD administrators the end-to-end visibility to drive tasks to maintain SLO with provided context.

To access Azure Monitor for AVD in the Azure portal, follow these steps:

> **Method 1:** Go to `https://portal.azure.com/`.
>
> **Method 2:** AVD from the Azure portal, then choose Insights.
>
> **Method 3:** Azure Monitor from the Azure portal. Choose Insights Hub under Insights, then choose AVD from other tabs (Figure 2-34).

Figure 2-34. *Storage Monitoring view*

Getting started with Azure Monitor for AVD requires an AVD administrator minimum of one log analytics workspace. Use an assigned log analytics workspace for cloud consumers' AVD session hosts to ensure that performance KPIs and events are only received from session hosts in cloud consumer AVD deployment.

Next, the AVD administrator must create a Log Analytics workspace if it does not exist. The following process demonstrates how to perform a log analytics workspace for AVD.

Step 1: Log in to personal or business account into Azure portal.

The following is the link: `https://portal.azure.com/`.

Step 2: In the search pane, type "log analytics" and choose Log Analytics workspaces (Figure 2-35).

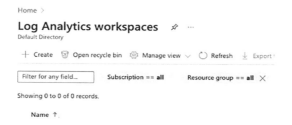

Figure 2-35. *Log Analytics view*

Step 3: Choose a subscription to link to by selecting from the drop-down list if the default chosen is not appropriate.

Step 4: For **Resource Group**, select a current resource group that previously created a new one.

Step 4: Type a name for the new log analytics workspace.

Step 5: Choose a cloud consumer **Region** (Figure 2-36).

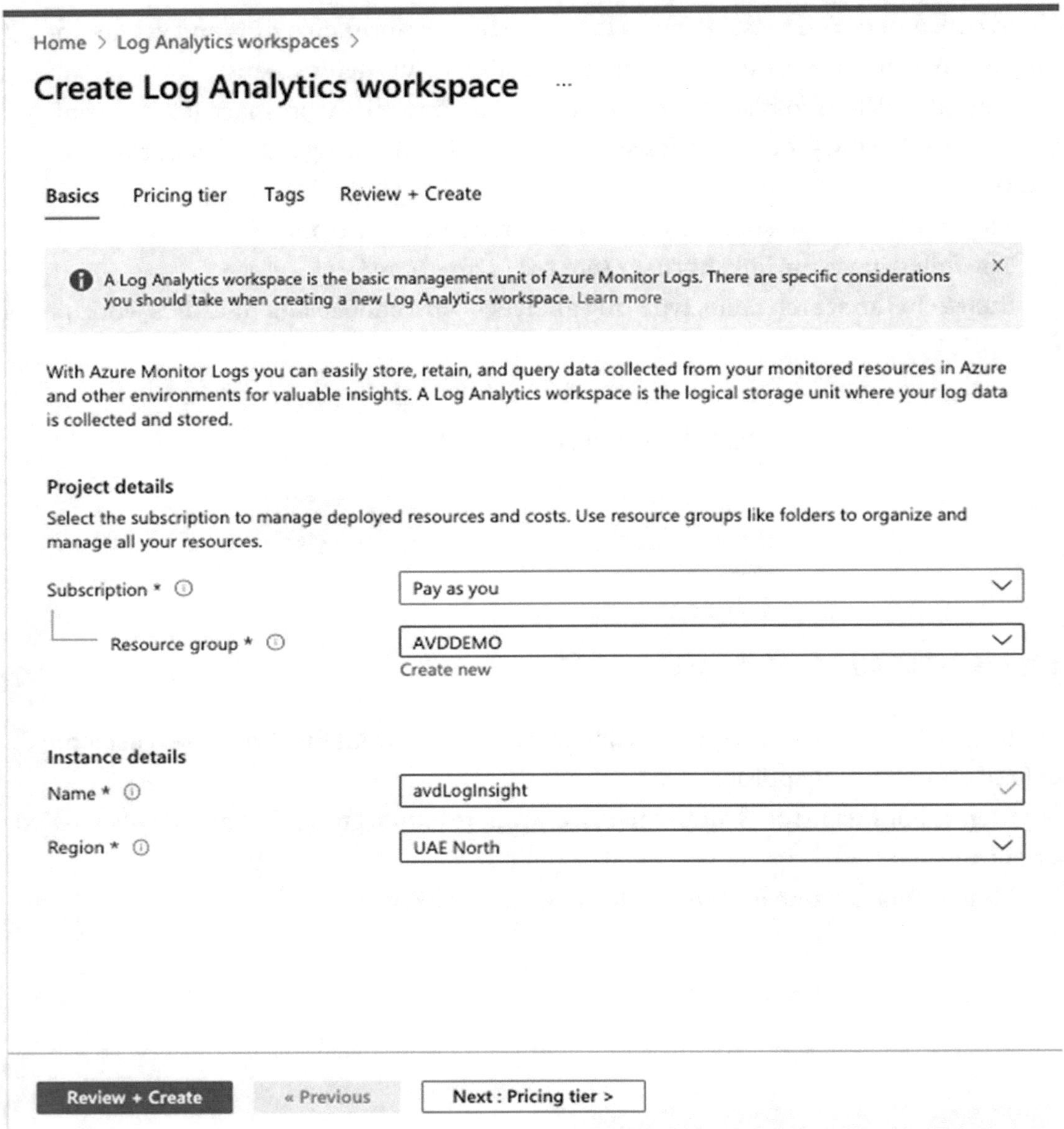

Home > Log Analytics workspaces >

Create Log Analytics workspace   ⋯

Basics   Pricing tier   Tags   Review + Create

> ℹ A Log Analytics workspace is the basic management unit of Azure Monitor Logs. There are specific considerations you should take when creating a new Log Analytics workspace. Learn more   ✕

With Azure Monitor Logs you can easily store, retain, and query data collected from your monitored resources in Azure and other environments for valuable insights. A Log Analytics workspace is the logical storage unit where your log data is collected and stored.

Project details

Select the subscription to manage deployed resources and costs. Use resource groups like folders to organize and manage all your resources.

Subscription * ⓘ | Pay as you   ⌄ |

    └─ Resource group * ⓘ | AVDDEMO   ⌄ |
                              Create new

Instance details

Name * ⓘ | avdLogInsight   ✓ |

Region * ⓘ | UAE North   ⌄ |

[Review + Create]   [« Previous]   [Next : Pricing tier >]

Figure 2-36. Review and create

Finally, Click on Review + **create** to review the settings and then **Create** to deploy the log analytics for AVD environment.

The next step is to configure the workbook, Azure Monitor for AVD; the AVD administrator needs to configure Azure Monitor for the cloud consumer AVD environment. The following process demonstrates how to perform a workbook Azure monitor for AVD.

Step 1: Log in to personal or business account into Azure portal .

The following is the link: `https://portal.azure.com/`. Or directly access: aka.ms/azmonwvdi.

Step 2: Choose configuration workbook.

Step 3: Choose AVD cloud consumer environment to configure under Subscription, Resource Group, and Host Pool.

Step 4: Configure AVD core infrastructure and desktop pool alerts.

Azure Security and Compliance

AVD is a managed DaaS desktop that offers many security abilities for keeping cloud consumer organizations safe. Microsoft manages parts of the services on the cloud consumer's behalf in an AVD design and deployment.

Microsoft maintains the security of physical data centers: the physical network, storage, and hosts that Azure runs on. Microsoft is also accountable for security and compliance for ensuring that the AVD control plane is running securely in Azure. Figure 2-37 depicts a high-level overview.

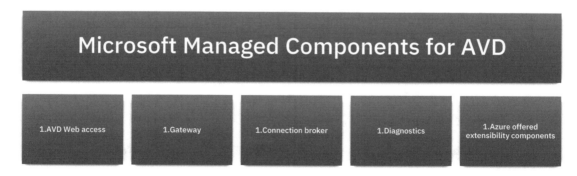

Figure 2-37. *Microsoft managed components for AVD*

It is recommended for all AVD consumers to enable Azure Security Center standard for subscriptions as minimum, AVD core infrastructure VMs, key vaults, and storage accounts. Enablement helps manage vulnerabilities, impose compliance with standard frameworks like PCI, and increase the AVD environment's overall security.

Cloud consumer manages parts of the services for as part of AVD design and deployment. The following depicts a high-level overview.

Network security is a very vital component of AVD. The following critical security baseline is to be applied in the very preparation of AVD design and deployment.

- Perform security for internal traffic

- Connect securely private networks

- Protect client applications from external network attacks

- Plan and prepare network security rules

The business enables end users' access to AVD; thereby, the company also allows end users to store and access data and user profiles. In addition, Azure disk encryption is a security protection mechanism to protect data in rest and transit offered by Microsoft.

Storage security is the next vital component of AVD. following critical security baseline to be applied in the very preparation of AVD design and deployment

- Discover, group, and tag sensitive data

- Preserve sensitive data

- Monitor for unapproved transfer of sensitive data

- Encrypt sensitive data in transit and rest

Backup security is another vital component of AVD. The following is the critical security baseline to be applied in the very preparation of AVD design and deployment.

- Ensure regular automated backups

- Encrypt backup data

- Confirm all backups, including cloud consumer-managed keys

Next, users' identity needs to be protected with multifactor authentication and enabled for conditional access.

Standardize Azure AD as the central identity and authentication system, manage apps' identities securely, and enable single sign on, if possible. Secure administrators' IDs via privilege access management methods.

Users' session host demands security protection with endpoint protection, endpoint detection and response, data loss protection, empower threat and vulnerability management assessments, patch OS and application vulnerabilities, design and deployment of app locker, session active, idle, and disconnected timeout management, and finally a virtualized version of hardware trusted platform module (vTPM) to be enabled wherever it is applicable (Figure 2-38).

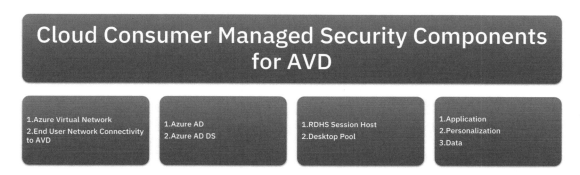

Figure 2-38. *Cloud consumer managed components for AVD*

AVD Licenses

AVD licenses can be considered in two aspects: infrastructure cost and end-user license cost.

An Azure account is needed to deploy and manage core infrastructure components required to host AVD, such as virtual machines for core infra, session, desktop pool, storage for operating system, data disk and user profile, networking, and security.

Microsoft offers free-of-charge license entitlement for users already enabled with Microsoft 365 E3, E5, F1, Microsoft 365 Business, Microsoft A3, A5, used consumer from educational organizations, Microsoft remote desktop services client access license (RDS CAL), and eligible Windows.

The definition of eligible Windows includes any entitled users of Windows 10 Enterprise E3/E5, Windows 10 Education A3/A5, and Windows 10 VDA per user.

Also, Microsoft offers BYOL for Windows Server, Windows 10/Windows 7, per-user access pricing for external users, and pay as you go or reserved instance. it is applicable for both remote application streaming, hosted shared desktop, and dedicated desktops.

When it comes to planning the costing beyond the licenses, the following elements need to be factored as well.

- Region of AVD you have planned to host

- Type of AVD (pooled or personal)

- Type of session (single or multisession)

- Type of workload (light, medium, heavy, and power)

- Total named users

- Total usage hours per month

- Peak concurrency

- Off-peak concurrency

- Size of VM along with storage

- File storage

- Data at rest

- Snapshots

- Bandwidth

  - Inter-region transfer type if DR/HA is part of your solution

  - Internet egress

- Azure support cost

  - Developer

  - Standard

  - Professional direct

- On-premises end user device cost

- On-premises device management cost

- On-premises to Azure network connectivity cost

- On-premises end-user field support management cost

- On-premises help desk support management cost

Design Methodology for AVD

AVD introduces a distinct way of maintaining end-user environments. AVD allows IT administrators to host and administer user desktops on virtual desktop infrastructure in the Azure cloud. At the same time, AVD offers many new and compelling benefits for increasing manageability, performance, and security. Thus, AVD is a solution rather than a product and allows end users to access their AVD apps or desktop pool using a remote desktop protocol; end users can access these AVD apps and pool via endpoints such as PCs, laptops, smartphones, thin client terminals, and tablets, among other devices. In this section, let us explore what benefits AVD can offer by industry.

DaaS (AVD) solutions and services are becoming quite popular among various industries such as IT & telecom, government, healthcare, BFSI, education, and retail, among others, for increasingly mobile and remote teams. Mobile end users, field technicians, contractors, part-time workers, healthcare professionals, and teachers are some of the users who commonly use virtual desktop infrastructure for productive work and high performance while working from remote locations, even during the pandemic.

DaaS (AVD) enhances user mobility and remote access by permitting users to obtain a wide array of virtual apps and data on the move. With the increasing trend of digitalization, automation, and creative workplaces, AVD solutions are anticipated to rise at an extraordinary pace in the upcoming years. The COVID-19 pandemic is considerably accelerating market growth with work-from-home guidelines getting deployed across the world. Primary IT and other companies are expected to invest massively in DaaS solutions such as AVD over the forecast period to reduce physical infrastructure and additional capital expenditure costs.

As banks and financial institutions intend to improve their market significance and growth with new products and Omnichannel bank's end-user's engagement models, digital workplace programs are persuading a top priority for any BFSI institution.

The banking sector can be one of the early adopters of AVD technology. Some of the critical advantages offered by AVDs in the BFSI division incorporate computational finance, access systems from anywhere, and preconfigured, preintegrated, and pretested systems.

BFSI institutions are likely to be victims of cybercriminals, and the refinement of these attacks is developing day by day. With the use of offline features and complicated access authorization policies offered by AVD, BFSI institutions can provide superimposed layers of security and support mobility.

Government authorities worldwide have supported workers to work from home due to the pandemic. With DaaS (AVD) choice, seamless workflow is attained among the workforce working remotely to follow social distancing measures as prescribed by the government bodies.

One of the significant priorities of retail businesses is to extend enhanced buyer experiences and expand their market connection. With increasing online engagement and transformation of the business environment, retail organizations accommodate these changes. To fight efficiently in this highly ambitious business environment, retailers significantly invest in new digital technologies and IT infrastructure. Thus, the modern AVD will help the retail business adapt to a changeable future.

Smart retail, via offline and online, is data-driven, handling everything from online advertisements to in-store price comparisons. And although mobile devices have expanded the range and influence of retail systems, the desktop still plays a crucial part, particularly in point-of-sale units, digital signage, kiosks, and so on.

Telco operators are investing heavily in advanced telecommunication technologies such as 5G. Moreover, the operators are planning to invest more. Considerable investments in seasoned Internet technology would promote DaaS (AVD) platforms to have uniform business operations worldwide.

The modern healthcare sector is highly regulated and complex, making it challenging to change developments and innovate when uncertain results. However, the drive for enhanced cost, quality, and delivery of patients is becoming imperative with the swiftly growing population.

Digital transformation in healthcare focuses on becoming necessary on patients, although there is regularly an accelerator involved. The current technology-driven healthcare foundation contains several mobile devices and apps used by healthcare professionals, establishing a demand for the AVD to handle diverse tasks remotely. The key stakeholders in the DaaS (AVD) are hardware component providers, solution/service providers, cloud infrastructure providers, and end users.

Cloud-based solutions offer businesses smooth scalability and operational adaptability while diminishing costs and risks compared with on-prem's daily operations. Thus, the expanding adoption of cloud-based solutions will complement the request for AVD solutions among enterprises.

This section will introduce Agile approach aids to iteratively generate, qualify, and implement solutions for AVD consumers, along with hurdles and impediments encountered by on-prem virtual desktop infrastructure due to poor design and AVD architecture.

An Agile Approach Design and Deploy Solutions for AVD

Designing a DaaS solution is a solely multidomain subject to a well-defined design framework and regulated technical decisions with business and end-user requirements. Without Agile methodology, architects tend to frequently skip from domain to domain, driving distraction and error. Agile methodology is an iterative, time-bounded, people-oriented, and output-focused approach to delivering AVD design and build.

The architecture method, which must incorporate the TOGAF and Microsoft Azure design guidelines, is a linear sequential method with an iterative approach of prototyping following IT infrastructure architecture, planning, design, and deployment. The Agile methodology follows an iterative process for each major initiative of the AVD project. In doing so, the cloud consumer organization is enabled with a tangible improvement to the workplace environment (Figure 2-39).

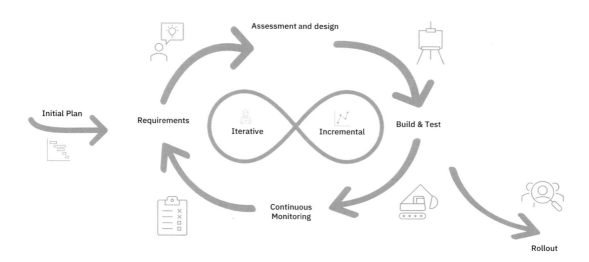

Figure 2-39. *Agile design methodology for AVD*

Initial planning aims to draft a plan, deliver an AVD business strategy, and adopt end-user feedback into the design, deployment, or improvement lifecycle. Kanban boards are famous tools used for continuous planning to continuously address the end-user business needs and prioritize them as per product owner needs and take a considerable amount of end-user feedback aligning with business strategy. It provides the tools and practices to help the IT function to develop accurate ideas or features.

Requirements gathering is an essential part of the design process. Requirements will steer AVD design in a specific direction. Requirements gathering is the manner of discovering what AVD projects need to perform.

AVD requirements commonly split into two categories, usually business requirements and technical requirements.

In the assessment phase, the cloud consumer may be new to the AVD and need to assess what they have, where they are in terms of industry and technology trends, and what they are looking for in a plan to modernize, upgrade, and probably identify fixes for the workplace. Business direction and requirements may affect the plan and the design.

The design phase should define AVD architecture needed to meet critical business drivers, requirements, and success criteria recognized during the assessment phase. The design characteristics for AVD such as reliability, availability, flexibility, recoverability, security, performance, operational excellence, and granular control over the cost need to be enabled for the AVD cloud consumer part of each design.

Elegant AVD solution building blocks are primarily classified into the following:

- Cloud Consumer End-User Layer

- AVD Access Layer

- AVD Resource Layer

- Microsoft AVD Control Layer

- Microsoft Azure Hosting Layer

- Microsoft and End-User Security Layer

Continuous testing reduces the expense of testing while boosting the deployment team's balance of quality and agility. It reduces testing bottlenecks by virtualized dependent services and interprets the totality of virtualized test conditions that can be effortlessly deployed and refreshed as AVD changes. These abilities decrease the cost of provisioning and managing test systems and decrease test cycle times by facilitating integration testing beforehand in the lifecycle.

Continuous automated rollout offers a continuous delivery pipeline that automates AVD deployments from dev, test, and UAT to production environments. It reduces standard time and efforts, resource wait-time, and rewrite by using push-button deployments that facilitate a higher recurrence of releases, reduced mistakes, and fully integrated compliance. Continuous delivery is a range of methods intended to secure that code can be immediately and carefully deployed to production by delivering each update to production and ensuring that business applications and services function as demanded via rigorous automated testing.

Continuous monitoring extends industry-standard monitoring and reporting, helping administrators, developers, and testers achieve their application's performance and availability, even before it is implemented into production. The advanced feedback presented by continuous monitoring is vital to decreasing the cost of errors, updates, and steering projects toward successful closure.

Hurdles and Impediments Encountered by On-Prem Virtual Desktop Infrastructure

More organizations have instituted virtualized desktops in the last two decades. However, what is driving DaaS growth? Business worldwide is embracing digitalization. It offers an extensive opportunity for firms to utilize digital technologies and automation to convert their business models and current processes to improve operational efficiency and raise revenue. In the last few years, the proliferation of intelligent devices, the Internet of Things (IoT), cloud computing, and artificial intelligence (AI) have led to intelligent workplaces.

In general, digital transformation refers to the integration of digital technologies in business processes and organizational activities/models. The rising demand for end-to-end business process optimization, high operational efficiency, and reduced human errors are the key drivers for digital transformation in various industries. For the past few years, VDI has gained popularity among enterprises to virtualize entire workgroups for higher efficiency and reduce end-user footprint, as well as expanded lifespans and lower power footprint of zero clients compared to PCs. The potential is there for simpler desktop management and heavy operational cost savings.

Though VDI offered numerous benefits, it failed many times due to the following Top Five reasons. So the following should be taken into consideration during design and deployment of AVD.

1. The physical desktop is how work gets done in practically every organization. Sorrowful users moaning already about their desktops will undoubtedly sound as harried as c-level executives. And get a VDI project to add to the no-go list.

    Idea to overcome Obstacle 1: Engage them in the DaaS pilot program and arm them with new device work from anywhere, solving the primary production application rollout with VDI.

2. Whether large or tiny IT organizations, it will perpetually be challenging to deliver VDI as one person. Businesses that designed and deployed VDI were successful only when getting everyone aligned.

    Idea to overcome Obstacle 2: Engage everyone in the DaaS pilot program. Adequate resources must be provisioned during peak hours. Use an effective autoscale feature wherever required from cloud, and network managers must govern network changes concerning end users' connectivity.

3. Inadequate storage IOPS (input/output operations per second) is a prescription for VDI failure. On-prem system may have enough storage capacity to host virtual desktops. But when the rotating disks in the old SAN array are all being accessed by many remote shared server-hosted desktops simultaneously, I/O performance will undergo a hurdle. Desktops will act sluggish. And end users will begin requesting the return of their traditional physical desktops.

    Idea to overcome Obstacle 3: Engage power users in the DaaS pilot program. Azure Files has four various performance levels with added costs and performance KPIs. The two tiers, transaction optimized and premium, are estimated and supported for storing user profile data.

    The highest IOPS supported for a transaction file share with large file shares moved with 10,000 IOPS, applicable from a 10-TB to a 100-TB share and with a maximum throughput of 300 MiB/sec along with a wide variety of options combining locally redundant, zone redundant, and geo-redundant with read-only and hot or cold tiering available from Azure. Premium performance extends up to 100 TiB of storage for one file share with 100,000 IOPS, and throughput depends on the deployed size of the file share. An alternate architect can evaluate Azure NetApp files or storage space directly. However, additional cost is involved.

4. Difficulty in packaging all of the end-user client applications: packaging skills are also required for on-prem VDI, and app virtualization tools are remarkable for quarantining apps that conflict with each other. However, it takes time for the packaging administrator to finish setting up his packaging desktop setup, pre-scans, post-scans, scripting workarounds, Windows registry changes, virtualizing service, and including and excluding process and deployment to Dev, TEST, UAT, and Prod Pilot. Virtualizing a single app consumed months, and engaging with a professional service provider cost a lot.

Idea to overcome Obstacle 4: MSIX is a Windows app package format that provides modern packaging knowledge to all Windows apps. The MSIX package format conserves the functionality of living app packages and install files and enables new, innovative packaging and deployment features to Win32, WPF, and Windows form apps. MSIX enables businesses to stay modern and ensure their applications are always up to date. It allows AVD administrators to deliver a user-centric solution while still overwhelming the cost of the application by defeating the need to repackage.

To avoid additional packaging costs, integrate with a solution like chocolatey, which has a known good package 6000 + when writing this book.

5. Single golden image management sprawl. The organization concluded VDI would eliminate the need to patch multiple copies of Windows with the single golden image.

Idea to overcome Obstacle 5: Golden image management combines various elements; each demands multiple solutions, such as operating systems and patches managed in base build. The application demands that native installation must be MSIX;

that isolation needs to be Microsoft App-V; that personalization and context awareness need integration with a third-party solution like Ivanti product but with additional licensing; and that redirection, office, caching, masking, and other drives use FSLogix.

Architecture of AVD

In this section, let us explore the reference use case, success criteria, and reference architecture most widely used by enterprises. Microsoft AVD is a turnkey Microsoft Azure offering a solution to deliver virtual desktops and apps. The AVD administrator can deliver Windows client OS multisession desktops and client OS single-session desktops. Also, Windows server OS sessions or apps run on any server OS using a GUI interface in just a few clicks. Microsoft provides a single bill for the service and the Azure resource consumption if the organization chooses to use managed Azure for the workloads. Microsoft is now enabling customers and partners with the capability to use their own Azure subscription along with Microsoft AVD and apps standard for Azure.

Just as construction AVD blueprints include organizations' structures and internal workings, enterprise AVD solutions also need blueprints that define technical components and interactions. AVD reference architectures are extensive models that assist businesses in planning their AVD workspace implementations. This section lets us explore the reference use case, reference success criteria, and reference architecture most widely adopted by the enterprise before tailoring their own AVD solution.

Reference AVD Use Case

AVD architects must define a use case for virtual apps and desktop solutions, following the example of use cases.

- Security and regulation applications from BFSI, healthcare, government, and other industries demand virtualized desktops and apps.

- Flexible workforce needs like remote work, mergers and acquisition, short-term employees, contractors, and partner access demand remote desktops and apps.

- Provide end users with the capability to operate with business apps and data from any device on demand.

- Employees like bring your own device (BYOD), road warriors, mobile users, call centers, and remote branch workers.

- Operational workloads such as engineering, legacy apps, and development environments demand personalized desktops.

Reference AVD Success Criteria

AVD architects must define a list of completion criteria that established the overarching design and deployment groundwork. The following table illustrates key success criteria.

AVD Key Success Criteria	Description
Minimize CAPEX costs	A large portion of cloud consumer end users work in the office on PCs. The solution empowers cloud consumer end users to work remotely from anywhere via any network.
Flexible digital workplace	Although many users have a primary work environment, the AVD solution supports digital workplace flexibility allowing cloud consumer end users.
Secure digital resources	Must secure critical business applications and data accessing by end users' untrusted endpoints or from unsecured locations.
Reduce data center footprint	Decrease data center footprint to have the versatility and quickness to scale as demanded and minimize physical hardware and appliances that need to be managed.
Enhance user experience reporting	As IT cannot fully establish the links among remote users and the virtual desktops, AVD administrators need to monitor the end-to-end experience and distinguish the areas for reform.
Optimize OPEX costs	Lessen cloud payments by automatically scaling AVD usage patterns based on peak and off-peak working hours.
Secure with multifactor authentication	CIO's top priority is security; MFA is required to ensure an added layer of authentication and cloud consumer resources.
Business continuity	Prospects for resiliency in the event of is an outage with the cloud services provider region.

Reference AVD Logical Architecture

Figure 2-40 depicts an AVD. High-level architecture is classified into six main building blocks. The building blocks are necessary to provide a secure, reliable, multitenant AVD hosting solution based on Microsoft Azure services and the purpose of each building block and how all fit together collectively are show.

Elegant AVD solution building blocks are primarily classified into the following building blocks as depicted in Figure 2-40.

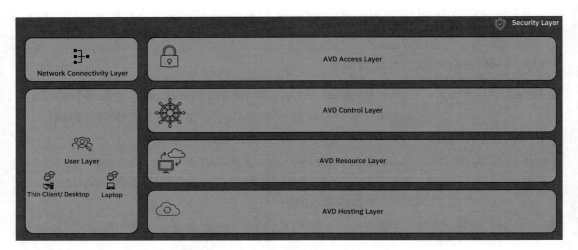

Figure 2-40. *Logical architecture of Microsoft AVD*

User layer building block: The user layer defines the user topology, end-point devices, and AVD clients.

- External users: Access AVD via remote desktop client to access AVD hosted in Azure cloud via the public network.

- Internal users: Access AVD via remote desktop client to access AVD hosted in Azure cloud via the internal or corporate network.

Access layer building block: The access layer defines how users access the resources via an internal network with AD integration and external users connect via multifactor authentication.

- Gateway: The Microsoft AVD remote connection gateway service joins remote users to AVD apps, data, and desktops from any device running an AVD client. The client connects to a gateway, then composes a remote desktop service host (RDSH) or client OS VM back to the same gateway.

- Web access: The web access service within AVD lets users access apps, desktops, and data via an HTML5-compatible web browser built into it as part of the client OS from anywhere on any device. AVD administrators can secure web access using MFA in Azure AD.

Control layer building block: The control layer defines the Azure virtual architectural foundation, Azure infrastructure perquisites, management, and monitoring for AVD solution.

- Connection broker: The connection broker service manages end-user sessions to virtual desktops and apps. The connection broker presents load balancing and session reconnect.

- Diagnostics: AVD diagnostics is an event-based aggregator that checks each end-user action on the AVD deployment as a success or failure. AVD administrators can ask the event aggregation to classify failing elements.

- Monitoring: For the end-user level, monitoring solutions such as control up, login vsi, lakeside, and so on can be integrated with AVD.

Resource layer building block: The resource layer defines deployment models to consume AVDs and applications.

- AVD session pool: A pool can run the following operating systems when writing the book.

  - Windows 7 Enterprise

  - Windows 10 Enterprise

  - Windows 10 Enterprise Multisession

  - Windows Server 2012 R2,

- Windows Server 2016,

- Windows Server 2019 and above

- Your own image preloaded apps, local group policies, or along with golden image customization.

- Third-party integration: For end-user personalization and profile management solutions such as Ivanti, liquit, cloud house, and so on can be integrated with AVD.

Hosting layer building block: The hosting layer defines the underlying cloud infrastructure with resilience and HA.

- Azure provides a wide range of VM sizes and images, enabling AVD administrators to choose the best deployment options for their AVD environments. Azure compute, Azure infrastructure-as-a-service category of services creates and manages VMs, containers, and batch jobs and supports remote application access.

- Azure delivers long-lasting, highly available, and massively scalable storage choices such as blob, queue, file, and disk, which can keep pace with explosive data extension. Azure storage, along with the Azure infrastructure-as-a-service category of services, provides scalable cloud storage for structured and unstructured data.

- Azure offers various networking services to build advanced network topologies and extend data centers to the cloud. Azure networking, along with the Azure infrastructure-as-a-service category of services, provides vNETs, dedicated connections, gateways, and services for traffic management and diagnostics, load balancing, DNS hosting, and network protection against distributed denial-of-service (DDoS) attacks.

Security layer building block: The security layer defines the zero-trust architecture, defense-in-depth, identity, user devices (mobile and PC), app security, session host, deployment configuration, and network controls managed by cloud consumers or managed service providers. Governance takes place on Azure virtualization control plane, physical compute, network, storage, and Azure cloud physical datacenters.

- Azure security center: Azure cloud workload protection solution that presents security management and high-level threat protection across AVD cloud workloads.

- Azure key vault: Azure secure secrets store for the passwords, agent strings, and other knowledge AVD administrators need to keep desktop and apps working.

- Azure monitor logs: Azure monitoring service receives telemetry and different data and renders a query language and analytics engine to deliver operational insights for desktops, data, and apps.

Summary

In this chapter, you read about planning DaaS, a list of components to be prepared for AVD, Agile design methodology for AVD, and Microsoft landscape logical architecture of AVD.

In the next chapter, you will read about the AVD performing requirements for gathering Microsoft AVD, performing due diligence and assessing for AVD, and designing AVD core solutions.

CHAPTER 3

Defining AVD Requirements and Assessment

Requirements organize a foundation for Azure Virtual Desktop (AVD) project vision, scope, cost, and schedule, and they eventually must meet the target state with quality and performance.

Proper assessment evaluation and due diligence are required. AVD architects who neglect to assess the current landscape often find that they needed to, which later drives them to backtrack, probably hampering project delivery.

Designing a desktop and app virtualization solution is simply a matter of following a certified method and following technical decisions with organizational and user requirements. The high-level design for virtual desktops and application delivery solutions is made comparatively straightforward by following the Agile design methodology.

This chapter provides the requirements gathering for apps, data, infra, security, and compliance for AVD, along with a method to perform assessment and a design thinking (DT) framework for AVD module by module and for the conceptual architecture.

By the end of this chapter, you should be able to understand the following:

- Defining AVD requirements

  - Business requirements.

  - Defining AVD functional requirements.

  - Defining AVD nonfunctional requirements (NFRs).

© Puthiyavan Udayakumar 2022
P. Udayakumar, *Design and Deploy Microsoft Azure Virtual Desktop*,
https://doi.org/10.1007/978-1-4842-7796-6_3

- Performing Assessment

  - Assess AVD user baseline.

  - Assess AVD data baseline.

  - Assess AVD application baseline.

  - Assess AVD cloud IaaS baseline.

  - Assess AVD security and management baseline.

- Designing AVD

  - DT approach for AVD.

  - Conceptual architecture of AVD.

Defining AVD Requirements

In this section, let us get started by defining AVD requirements. Defining requirements helps to detail the quality attributes that the design will satisfy to deliver the business goals, objectives, or capabilities.

Throughout this section, you will learn about the fundamentals of requirements gathering for apps, data, infra, security, and compliance for AVD from both the business and the technical standpoint.

Additionally, the better the set of defined requirements, the easier it is to identify and propose viable solutions to meet the business end goal. Requirements gathering is a vital part of the design process. Requirements will direct design in a specific direction.

Business Requirements

Business requirements are high-level needs, purposes, and aims of the business. They should show what is required to occur. It is important to build one source of truth for the study behind AVD business requirements to make it so that the AVD platform, design, deployment, and AVD operations teams and all stakeholders can regularly follow and stay aligned.

Business requirements define a particular remote working requirement, including its purpose, features, functionality, and behavior. Figure 3-1 shows a well-known method to define an Agile way of defining business requirements.

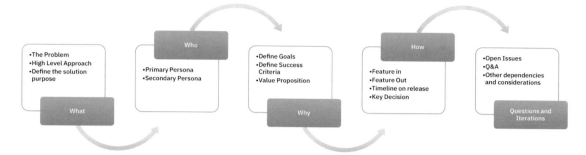

Figure 3-1. *Workflow for defining business requirements*

The method defines what you're going to design and deploy, who it is for, and how it benefits the end user. It also functions as a guide for business and technical teams to help develop, launch, and market the solution.

To help you learn how to apply requirements gathering principles, we're going to look at them in the circumstances of a real-world team from a hypothetical information technology company, Company XYZ, that covered remote work and globally dispersed teams. As we'll see, many of the company's challenges are the same as those that plague small groups today.

What Is the Problem?

Describe the problem that the business is trying to solve (or the business opportunity).

- Why is it important to end users and cloud consumer business?

- What are user experiences issue running with detailed insights? And if relevant,

- What issues are not intended to be solved?

What Is the High-Level Approach?

Describe the approach the business is planning to take to solve the problem. It should be enough for the cloud consumer or client to imagine possible solutions and get a rough sense of this AVD project's scope.

What Is the Solution Purpose?

Creating a business requirement story starts with three simple questions:

- Why do they exist?

- How are you doing it?

- What is the product?

Figure 3-2 shows the sample Agile method to define the ***Business Requirement***

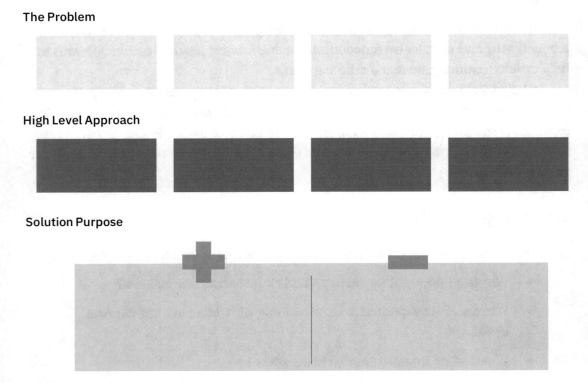

Figure 3-2. *Agile template of agreeing on business requirements*

Who Is the Primary Persona?

Primary personas are target users for AVD solutions. Their needs, pain points, and motivations should inform business requirements. And they should have defined

- Needs/challenges
- Goals/motivation
- Expected outcomes

Who Is the Secondary Persona?

Secondary personas represent profiles of people who might not be ideal users but might also use AVD solution. And they should have defined

- Needs/challenges
- Goals/motivation
- Outline expected outcomes

Figure 3-3 shows the sample Agile method to define key stakeholder needs of the **Business Requirement**

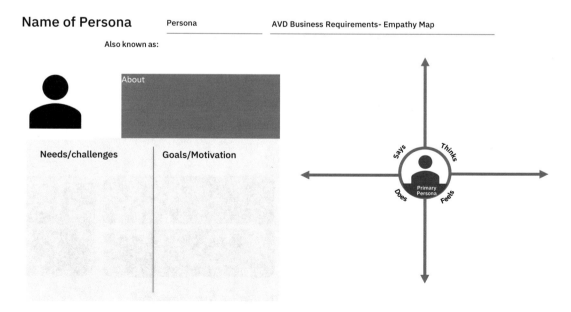

Figure 3-3. *Defining user persona*

Define Goals

If everything runs as per the plan, what will be after six months from now or two years? So define SMART (a.k.a. Specific, Measurable, Achievable, Relevant, and Time-based) goals:

- What are the success criteria? What metrics do DaaS solutions intend to move?

- Explain why these KPIs are vital if they're not visible.

A business goal is something the business aspires to. Goals should be measurable and timebound.

Define Success Criteria

- What critical KPIs will the success of the DaaS solution be measured on?

- How much runway do we have to restrain those metrics?

Define the Fundamental Value Proposition

- What benefits of the DaaS solutions are created for the primary and secondary personas?

- How does your product help the primary and secondary personas achieve their desired outcome or job?

Figure 3-4 shows the sample Agile method to define key stakeholder goals of the **Business Requirement.**

Figure 3-4. *Key business stakeholder inputs gathering template*

Define the Solution Overview

Solution overview provides a summary of the design and deployment model as well as an organized list of features in and out of scope, with priorities if relevant.

Feature in

Defines features that are distinct, prioritized, and provides short explanation of why it is essential.

Feature out

Defines features that are left out, and provides short explanation of why it is out.

Feature 3-5 shows the sample agile method to define key features in and out of the

Business Requirement

Feature in

Feature Out

Figure 3-5. *Feature in scope and out of scope*

Timeline/Release Planning

Recognize any relevant breakthroughs that the end user should know about. Make sure to show the solution phase of the rollout. See Figure 3-6.

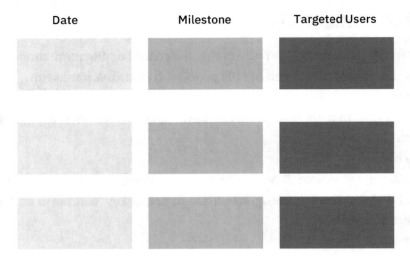

Figure 3-6. *High-level rollout timeline*

Question and Iteration

- Open issues - Factors open to be identified

- List of critical dependencies, assumptions, and considerations.

- Common questions about the DaaS solution, along with the answers to be identified.

Summary of Company XYZ Business Requirements

Remote work has been a component of many organizations' policies for decades, but a comparatively minute proportion of people operated this way till the global pandemic of 2020. A seismic transformation occurred for the numbers of millions of operators worldwide who transferred to a secluded format. End users have almost absolutely come to realize some of the benefits and challenges of remote work.

- Company XYZ has people spread around the globe, and they weren't a small company. The company decided to send everyone home: no more coming into the world's office. The need is the solution, tools, and infrastructure to make everyone productive, to make all cloud-based for all end users' content, and to provide critical apps, data, and information.

- Making all infrastructures in the cloud. Everyone should have a corporate-owned device or bring your device so it automatically became possible for end users to be connected online, and for them to develop a sense of community. If they made it so it's easy for Company XYZ to send everyone home, and they could be productive on day 1.

- Company XYZ loses thousands of dollars a cycle in the form of lost workloads, intellectual resources, and other data due to pinched or lost computers. Company XYZ believes a solution is required in format, in which data is outside the premises and can be quickly restored.

- Company XYZ wants cost savings associated with stolen data and security as a priority. Company XYZ wants to encrypt end-user data and quickly restore it so that end users don't bother about devices being seized and docking in the wrong hands.

- Company XYZ wants the most significant benefits of a solution: the flexibility aspect in letting cloud consumers rent only the infrastructure they need at any given time. Cloud consumers should always be able to add more or remove what isn't necessary later.

- Company XYZ wants to use an easy-to-use solution, flexible and scalable, that provides a secure and robust functionality for end-user workplace resources, that enables automation, that is cost-effective, and that supports specialized instances for workloads, such as floating-point operations, high graphics capability graphical processing units (GPUs), high input/output (I/O), and high-performance computing (HPC).

- Company XYZ's business requirement says that remote work is not new to them. It's been around for decades. But the number of people who are participating in remote or virtual work has grown exponentially and this creates remote work challenges for Company XYZ.

- Company XYZ can feel lost, isolated, out of sync, and out of sight.

- Company XYZ needs to build trust, build connections with limited face-to-face interactions, use tools effectively, and remain productive.

- Company XYZ managers want to know how to lead virtually and how to keep their teams motivated. These are all learned competencies.

Critical business requirements lead to solid performance in remote work. The following are the top five essential business requirements for Company XYZ:

ID	BR-AVD-001	Necessity	Essential
Status (Input)	Reviewed and approved	Status (Output)	Satisfied
Requirement	Method to use digital workplace tools to maximize performance.		
Description	Company XYZ wants remote work to empower digital workplace with tools for communication, connection, collaboration, and, ultimately, productivity. Company XYZ wants to choose the right tools for interpersonal intimacy, immediacy, conveyance, convergency, synchronous, asynchronous, rich media, lean media that employees need to achieve. Company XYZ wants to bypass multiple platforms for the same purpose (e.g., numerous chat solutions). It can be powerful to keep track of chat communications and long-form information on various platforms.		
ID	BR-AVD-002	Necessity	Essential
Status (Input)	Reviewed and approved	Status (Output)	Satisfied
Requirement	Method to foster productivity as a team.		
Description	Company XYZ wants their team to achieve desired outcome with Team Cohesion		
ID	BR-AVD-003	Necessity	Essential
Status (Input)	Reviewed and approved	Status (Output)	Satisfied
Requirement	Method to define trust in a virtual digital workplace.		
Description	Company XYZ wants method to trust in a virtual digital workplace		

(*continued*)

ID	BR-AVD-004		Necessity	Essential
Status (Input)	Reviewed and approved		Status (Output)	Satisfied
Requirement	Method to thrive across national borders.			
Description	Company XYZ wants to leverage skills, talents, and insights of all the remote team members; and many more concrete practices that you can use to set up, maintain, and thrive in remote work.			

ID	BR-AVD-005		Necessity	Essential
Status (Input)	Reviewed and approved		Status (Output)	Satisfied
Requirement	Maximum availability and reliability of digital workplace			
Description	Company XYZ wants to availability of less than an hour of downtime per year to still be compliant to the SLA			

Technical Requirements

When working on an AVD solution, technical requirements describe the technical aspects and issues that the architect needs to address to work and execute successfully.

Technical requirements are needed because they illustrate how the AVD solution should operate and its performance. It helps architect/engineer end users to understand the best way to use the AVD solution.

Requirements are majorly classified into two categories: business and technical. Technical requirements are further classified into functional and nonfunctional requirements.

Defining requirements is essential to develop the vision of the AVD environment, and a result in assessment criteria acts as a critical input factor to design and deployment. See Figure 3-7.

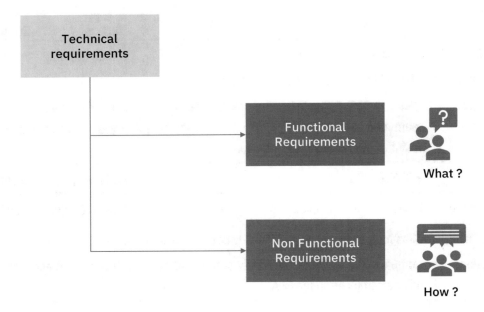

Figure 3-7. *Technical requirements classification*

Functional Requirements

A widely accepted method to define functional requirements defines *what* the solution must do. In contrast, NFRs specify limitations, detentions, or quality attribute values that the solution must comply with or operate while matching its functional requirements. NFRs specify limitations and quality attributes that an AVD solution must meet along with its functional requirements.

Brainstorming to perform requirements gathering is followed industry-wide. Brainstorming is practiced in requirements gathering to arrange as many various ideas as possible from a group of people. It is generally used to classify potential solutions to problems and clarify details of opportunities. Requirements can be captured by brainstorming sessions, by DT workshops, or by distributing questionnaires. A functional requirement defines what the AVD service should do for the end user.

When you capture, ensure that each requirement has an ID; classify the functional requirement between essential or optional, obtain status inputs from the cloud consumer, and confirm status output as satisfied. Define requirements and have a description.

Key benefits of gathering functional requirements:

1. It assists the AVD engineers/architects in checking if the AVD provides all the features mentioned in functional solution requirements.

2. A functional requirement tabulated assists AVD engineers/architects define the functionality of an AVD solution and its subsystems.

3. The functional requirements, together with the requirements analysis, accommodate to recognize the missing needs. They help to establish the expected AVD service and behavior.

4. It is hugely more comfortable to fix defects found during the functional requirements gathering phase.

5. It provides a guide for business goals, AVD architect/engineer tasks, or AVD user actions.

The following are the top ten essential functional requirements for Company XYZ:

ID	FR-AVD-001	Necessity	Essential
Status (Input)	Reviewed and approved	Status (Output)	Satisfied
Requirement	Support for Common Workspace Environment applications		
Description	The solution must support the current Cloud Consumer frequently applications, such as the Microsoft Productivity Suite, Microsoft Edge, Adobe Reader, Java, Media Player and File compressor.		

ID	FR-AVD-002	Necessity	Essential
Status (Input)	Reviewed and approved	Status (Output)	Satisfied
Requirement	H:\ drive mapping (H:\ denotes User Home Drive or One Drive)		
Description	The solution must support the H:\ user personal drive mapping.		

ID	FR-AVD-003	Necessity	Essential
Status (Input)	Reviewed and approved	Status (Output)	Satisfied
Requirement	Support for Personalization		
Description	Cloud consumer end users should be able to save personalized settings.		

(continued)

ID	FR-AVD-004	Necessity	Essential
Status (Input)	Reviewed and approved	Status (Output)	Satisfied
Requirement	Support for Workload		
Description	Solution should support heavy workloads which requires more CPU, RAM, and storage IOPS.		

ID	FR-AVD-005	Necessity	Essential
Status (Input)	Reviewed and approved	Status (Output)	Satisfied
Requirement	Support for persistent settings when roaming across different devices.		
Description	Support the ability to retain user personalization settings between various AVD sessions		

ID	FR-AVD-006	Necessity	Essential
Status (Input)	Reviewed and approved	Status (Output)	Satisfied
Requirement	Support for allocation of desktops		
Description	Support the ability to assign users or groups of users to a specific virtual desktop or types of desktops.		

ID	FR-AVD-007	Necessity	Essential
Status (Input)	Reviewed and approved	Status (Output)	Satisfied
Requirement	Support for multiple web browsers.		
Description	The ability to support multiple web browsers (Internet Explorer, Mozilla Firefox, Google Chrome, Chromium-based Microsoft Edge).		

ID	FR-AVD-008	Necessity	Essential
Status (Input)	Reviewed and approved	Status (Output)	Satisfied
Requirement	Support for caching, application masking, containers.		
Description	The ability to support containers to store user and application profiles, hiding applications from end users for specific groups, and cloud data caching.		

(continued)

ID	FR-AVD-009	Necessity	Essential
Status (Input)	Reviewed and approved	Status (Output)	Satisfied
Requirement	Support for communication and collaboration requirements.		
Description	The solution must support communication and collaboration requirements such as email, instant messaging, and online collaboration.		

ID	FR-AVD-010	Necessity	Essential
Status (Input)	Reviewed and approved	Status (Output)	Satisfied
Requirement	Support for peripherals connected on client devices.		
Description	The solution must support all cloud consumer approved peripherals, such as docking station, webcam, signature pad, barcode scanner, headphones and mics, wireless keyboard and mouse, third-party printer, and scanner.		

Nonfunctional Requirements

NFRs should define *how well* the system must perform in its AVD environment and how it should respond to constraints on its behavior.

NFRs deal with scalability, security, capacity, maintainability, performance, portability, security, reliability, and any other factors impacting an AVD solution's steady state.

NFRs are also called service-level requirements, additional requirements, and quality requirements.

There are many kinds of NFRs. The following are the top ten essential NFRs for Company XYZ:

ID	NFR-AVD-001	Necessity	Essential
Status (Input)	Reviewed and approved	Status (Output)	Satisfied
Requirement	Redundancy for AVD core management components		
Description	There must be no single point of failure within the AVD infrastructure.		

ID	NFR-AVD-002	Necessity	Essential
Status (Input)	Reviewed and approved	Status (Output)	Satisfied
Requirement	Capacity requirements for UAT/Nonproduction		
Description	The solution should maintain a UAT environment outside the production environment to maintain environmental hygiene.		

ID	NFR-AVD-003	Necessity	Essential
Status (Input)	Reviewed and approved	Status (Output)	Satisfied
Requirement	Support for monitoring		
Description	The solution must support the ability for monitoring of alerts and events for AVD user profiles and for AVD infrastructure.		

ID	FR-AVD-004	Necessity	Essential
Status (Input)	Reviewed and approved	Status (Output)	Satisfied
Requirement	Support for application interoperability		
Description	The solution must provide an application which needs to communicate or integrate with other applications.		

ID	NFR-AVD-005	Necessity	Essential
Status (Input)	Reviewed and approved	Status (Output)	Satisfied
Requirement	Support for GPUs		
Description	The solution must support the graphic intensity with a GPU.		

ID	NFR-AVD-006	Necessity	Essential
Status (Input)	Reviewed and approved	Status (Output)	Satisfied
Requirement	Support for single-sign-on (SSO) integration		
Description	The solution must support Enterprise SSO AD for internal access.		

(*continued*)

ID	NFR-AVD-007	Necessity	Essential
Status (Input)	Reviewed and approved	Status (Output)	Satisfied
Requirement	Support for data leak protection		
Description	The solution must support the current mechanisms for data leak protection.		

ID	NFR-AVD-008	Necessity	Essential
Status (Input)	Reviewed and approved	Status (Output)	Satisfied
Requirement	Support for antivirus protection		
Description	The solution must support the mechanisms of antivirus protection.		

ID	NFR-AVD-009	Necessity	Essential
Status (Input)	Reviewed and approved	Status (Output)	Satisfied
Requirement	Support for compliance		
Description	The AVD solution should be secured and compliant with cloud consumer security standards as well as cloud consumer industry and data regulation-specific standards.		

ID	NFR-AVD-010	Necessity	Essential
Status (Input)	Reviewed and approved	Status (Output)	Satisfied
Requirement	Support for audit		
Description	The solution must be auditable by an external entity, in the form of either a formal audit/assessment or an informal compliance check. The solution will need to be included in the security compliance check process. If automated health check cannot be performed, then the cloud consumer may require 90% manual compliance check to be performed.		

This book does not aim to provide all the methodologies or decide which is more reliable. Still, it will stress using a process that helps put a repeatable edifice around providing an AVD solution.

Performing Assessment

Once business and technical requirements are established that affirm a method of delivering a virtual working environment, the next step is to assess.

A proper assessment is required to understand how to scope compute, storage, network, application, data, security, regulatory, and compliance requirements.

An organization that skips the assessment phase and starts with the proof of concept (POC)/pilot phase and goes right into converting the POC environment into production can meet most minor immediate needs. But this will not work for longer-term business outcomes.

An organization fails to assess the current end-user landscape and finds that they required information that does not exist at later stage, forcing them to backtrack, probably hampering the outline and placing it at risk.

The AVD assessment activity works as a focused means of questioning assumptions by a data-driven method. Assessment data will help the team answer a series of significant business and technical viewpoints, verify or revoke their opinions, and polish the scope wanted to support the team's AVD situation. Practicing the two-in-a-box model shown in Figure 3-8, the AVD architect/engineers can expedite the journey of its end-user desktops to AVD.

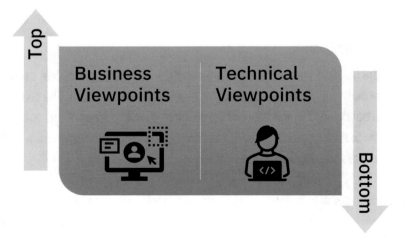

Figure 3-8. *Assessment viewpoints*

The assessment should aim to build a picture of the current landscape from a business, and technical viewpoints.

The first move in an AVD project should commence with a broader understanding and prioritization of strategic imperatives of the business. This task enables the Agile project team to define success criteria KPIs and allows the Agile architectural team to design a simple and optimized architecture.

Business Viewpoints

The following sample discovery questions can be raised to assess the business needs against the AVD solution stack.

- What is the expected total cost of ownership (TCO) reduction?

- What is the anticipated return on investment (ROI) again?

- Is there any expectation of extending desktop hardware lifecycle? Or repurposing them?

- What is the total number of end users who are entitled to connect remotely?

- What is the expected end-user productivity per day?

- Is there any expectation to lock down the end-user devices?

- Is there any expectation of adopting BYOD and company-owned personal enabled (COPE) devices?

- Is there any expectation of reducing administrator overhead?

- Is there any expectation of reducing IT effort to procure, image, and deliver a new PC (hours/PC)?

- Is there any expectation of reducing IT efforts to manage existing PCs (hours/year/physical PC)?

Also, it is good idea to define, SLO, SLA, SLI, MTTR, MTTF, MTBF, MTTD, MTTI, MTRS, and MTBSI with expectations with key business stakeholders. If you are new to these terms, the following provides high-level definitions.

Service-level objectives (SLO) are the user experience success criteria captured as measurable indicators for use as objectives for AVD, engineering, and execution. SLO will be measurable via service-level indicators. SLO gives us the mathematical definition of what end users are happy with in terms of an AVD solution.

Service-level agreements (SLA) is a contractual obligation between cloud service providers and cloud service consumers about measurable metrics like response, uptime, and responsibility.

Service-level indicator (SLI) a carefully defined quantitative measure of some aspect of the service level provided and measures the compliance level with SLO.

Mean time to Repair (MTTR) is an incident management metric that measures the average time needed to troubleshoot and repair AVD solution functions. MTTR is the time taken from the initial time of the incident until the service is restored to the end business user. It uses AVD engineer practices to improve the efficiency of services by baselining the issues. Finally, it is all about measuring how efficiently AVD service can get back to business as usual.

An initial example for calculating MTTR is the following.

Note   Formula to calculate MTTR

Total unplanned maintenance time / Total number of repairs = MTTR

If an AVD engineer has an AVD solution that breaks three times in a workday, and the system engineer spends an hour repairing each of those failed elements, MTTR would be 20 minutes (60 minutes / 3 = 20 minutes).

Mean time to failure (MTTF) is an incident management metric that measures the AVD's unrecoverable system failures. MTTF is the time taken from the initial issue report until the service becomes unrecoverable. It is used in AVD management practices to improve efficiency by baselining the issues. Finally, it is all about measuring how successfully an IT function is managed under the AVD team according to everyday operational workflows.

An initial example for calculating MTTF is the following.

Note   Formula to calculate MTTF

Total hours of operations time / Total number of units = MTTF

Let us consider that you had three identical worker nodes until all of them failed. The first VM crashed after six hours, the second one crashed at eight hours, and the third crashed at ten hours. MTTF would be 8 hours (24 / 3 = 8 hours).

Mean time between failures (MTBF) is an incident management metric that measures the average time between failures. MTBF is the time taken between repairable failures of AVD services. It is used in AVD management practices to measure the availability and reliability of AVD hosted services. Finally, it is all about measuring how successful the AVD team is defending and preventing occurrence or reoccurrences.

An initial example for calculating MTBF is the following.

Note   Formula to calculate MTBF

Total hours of operations time / Total number of failures = MTBF

Let us consider you have one of the AVD functions expected to run for 12 hours, and it worked only for 8 hours. For the remaining 4 hours, it failed to run on three different occasions. MTBF would be 3 hours (12 / 3 = 4 hours).

Mean time to detect (MTTD) is an incident management metric that measures the average time between the start of a problem and when the team notices it. MTTD denotes the period before AVD service management receives an issue ticket and starts the MTTR clock.

An initial example for calculating MTTD is the following.

Note   Formula to calculate MTTD

Single Elapsed Time = Issue detection Start Time - Issue detection End Time

Total Elapsed Time= Sum of Elapsed Time

(Total Elapsed Time) / Number of Incidents = MTTD

Let us consider the following scenario. Five incidents have occurred in IT operations.

Start time	End time	Time elapsed in minutes
00:10 AM	00:30 AM	20
02:30 AM	01:30 AM	60
05:30 PM	06:40 PM	70
00:20 AM	00:50 AM	30
00:10 AM	00:30 AM	20

MTTD would be 40 minutes, which is $(20+60+70+30+20)/5 = 40$.

Mean time to investigate (MTTI) is an incident management metric that measures the average time between detecting an IT incident and when the AVD team works to investigate its cause and solution. The aforementioned denotes the time taken to recognizing issues in IT function.

Mean time to restore service (MTRS) is an incident management metric that measures the average elapsed time from discovering an incident until the concerned system or subsystem is again usable to end users. MTRS differs from MTTR in that MTTR denotes how long it takes to fix an item, while MTRS regards the time taken to restore service after applying the fix.

Mean time between system incidents (MTBSI) is an incident management metric that measures the average elapsed time among detecting two back-to-back incidents. MTBSI can be measured by calculating MTBF and MTRS. It is usually denoted as MTBSI = MTBF + MTRS.

Technical Viewpoints

Businesses that successfully assess, design, and deploy AVD infrastructure services will see a significant reduction in their TCO.

Assessment of organization readiness for AVD solutions impacts many aspects of cloud infrastructure as a service, traditional monolithic apps, cloud native apps, as well as personnel in end-user environments. Assessments should cover compute, storage, network resources requirements, application delivery, software, licensing, personalization, configuration, end-user diagnostics, security, and compliance.

Depending on the end user environment and the desired outcomes, digital workplace assessment can take several forms. Engineers/architects in the AVD field can utilize a variety of methods. It is important to set expectations for DT methods in the early stages of the process. Don't rely only on asset and application inventory. To carry out a technical assessment, we use the framework shown in Figure 3-9.

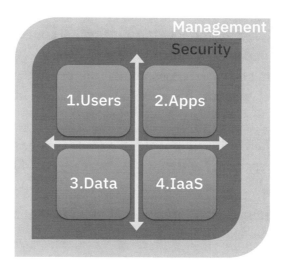

Figure 3-9. *Technical assessment dimension of digital workplace*

AVD Users

User segmentation is a critical essential factor in AVD solutions. Defining personas helps to define the user segmentation. In the past, it was traditionally department-based. As the digital workplace requires accurate results, the traditional method was not always effective.

Each user persona should contain the following key performance indicators.

- Tasks carried out by the persona,

- Apps required to complete the task effectively,

- The volume of data consumed by the user and apps,

- The level of security,

- Workload demand computes or graphical processor,

- The network through which users connect,

- The level of personalization and awareness of context,

- The availability zone which will host the user session.

Creating an exceptional AVD solution requires a deep understanding of your target end user. End-user personas promote a DT team to solve one of their most critical questions: who we are designing the solution for? Engineer/architects can create a solution that will satisfy end users' needs and help them accomplish their goals by gaining insight into target end users' expectations, interests, and impulses. Develop technical insights for each persona. It is essential to assess and identify the answer to the following factors.

- Identify peripherals that potential AVDs could have (e.g., printers, scanners, and specialty) and state whether they are USB or serial/parallel.

- Identify multi-monitor requirements, screen resolution, or color depth requirements.

- Identify endpoint devices (i.e., form factors) that will connect to the AVD solution.

- Identify operating systems the virtual desktop image based on (e.g., Windows 10 Long term Service Release (LTSR) List any disconnected or offline use cases or endpoints that require AVD Solution.

- Identify requirements to allow users to connect to multiple sessions and manage their session (e.g., session resets, change resolution).

- Identify requirements for multimedia (server or client rendered), Voice over Internet Protocol (VoIP), or video. List any local, remote, or direct-attached printing requirements.

- Identify communication and collaboration support requirements.

- Identify location-based services that may require (e.g., location-based printing).

- Identify the number of use cases you anticipate within the AVD solution environment

- Hosted shared model and dedicated model:

- Vendor-managed applications

- Application prerequisites that serve numerous applications

- Determined application compatibility requirements

- Determined application interoperability requirements

- Link users to the application

  - Group the application users' group by commonly used

  - Group the application users' group by business application

  - Group the application users' group by security requirements

  - Group the application users' group by Azure region requirements

  - Group the application users' group by data regulation requirements

  - Group the application users' group by peripheral device access requirements

  - Group the application users' group by extent of resource requirements

  - Group the application users' group by device requirements

- Identify the utilization

  - Application usage by access

  - Application usage by user

  - Application compute usage per user

  - Application frequency of usage

- Application network model

  - Application accessed with a thick client

  - Application accessed with east/west traffic (downstream component hosted inside the private cloud)

  - Application accessed via browsers

- Application accessed with north/south traffic with direct connectivity (downstream component hosted outside a private cloud)

- Application accessed via proxy (downstream component hosted inside the private cloud)

- Application accessed with north/south traffic (downstream component hosted outside a private cloud)

- Possibility for application modernization

  - Corporate-wide accessed application that needs to modernize (i.e., productivity suite like Microsoft Office, browser, etc.)

- Application needs resiliency capability

  - Application that needs out-of-region resiliency defined along with recovery time objective (RTO) and recovery point objective (RPO)

  - Application that needs in region resiliency defined along with RTO and RPO

AVD solution development requires a thorough understanding of the applications that will be hosted in the Azure AVD stack. An application baseline promotes a DT approach to answer one of their most challenging questions: what will they use AVD for? By gaining confidence in target end users' expectations, interests, and impulses, AVD engineers/architects can produce a solution that will satisfy their needs and help them accomplish their goals. Develop technical insights for each application. It is essential to assess and identify the answer to the following factors of applications.

- Identify supported operating system

- Identify minimum system requirements

- Identify CPU minimum required per system/per user

- Identify RAM minimum required per system/per user

- Identify storage minimum required per system/per user

- Identify application architecture (client/server, Web, terminal emulation, etc.)

- Identify whether the vendor supports the application on DaaS deployment

- Identify whether the vendor supports application being virtualized via Microsoft App-V or MSIX

- Identify whether the application requires specific file permissions (i.e., read/write permissions on some applications/any other files or folders)

- Identify software/application license type (Single/Multiuser)

- Identify whether the application has a Dongle for the license

- Identify whether the application requires activation of licensing key

- Identify whether the application installations are packaged, and whether they can be silently installed (i.e., manual or automated)

- Identify whether there is any known specific procedure for installing the application on terminal server or through multisession deployment

- Identify whether the application requires open database connectivity (ODBC) or Oracle TNSNAMES.ORA entries

- Identify where the application writes its log file

- Identify whether there is any post-installation configuration required for DaaS environment

- Identify any admin privileges needed to run the application (i.e., does it require the user to be a member of the power users or administrators local group?)

- Identify whether there is a limit to the number of licenses, hence users who can use app

- Identify Dev/UAT backend server port(s)

- Identify Dev/UAT application database name

- Identify Dev/UAT Application Database Credentials

- Identify Dev/UAT credentials (for testing and verifying application)

- Identify production backend server NAME or IP address

- Identify production backend server port(s)

- Identify production application database name

- Identify production application database credentials

- Identify prod application credentials (for testing and verifying application)

- Identify any special environment-specific configuration

- Identify any other application configuration

- Identify where the application back-end is physically located (on-prem or cloud)

- Identify the application back-end type (SQL, Oracle, database version, application version, or cloud-native)

- Identify whether the application has a middle tier (such as web servers or app servers). If so, where is the middle tier physically located (on-prem or cloud)?

- Identify what type of server does the middle tier reside on (server, OS, application version, database version, etc.)

- Identify whether the application requires network drive mappings or access to file shares (UNC path, etc.)

- If file shares are used, identify what file server they are on (i.e., name of a file server)

- Identify what drive letters are mapped and required by the application (e.g., the application needs an X: or Y: drive). Where is the file server physically located (on-prem or cloud)?

- Identify each application's NFRs

- Identify each application's security requirements

There is a solution that supports application assessment by Lakeside. SysTrack from Lakeside Software is a cloud-hosted data analytics solution that provides information about end-user environments, including metrics and data about those environments.

This assessment tool is free and powered by Lakeside's Digital Experience Cloud platform. This technology uses agent-based deployment and is deployed quickly without affecting the end-user experience. Dashboards and customized reports allow you to see IT performance and usage data on your environment within 24 hours, such as OS types, the most used applications, and more.

Without investing any time, effort, or capital, you will obtain accurate recommendations on whether your environment is ready for AVD. The AVD assessment aims to help you determine your readiness for AVDs and collect data on your system performance and usage. During the 60-day assessment, the AVD architect/engineer will access dashboards that display the data collected and analyzed on the business environment and will provide a customized report on the resources that the AVD architect/engineer needs to consider when migrating to or adopting AVD.

AVD Data

The application assessment is now complete; the next step is to perform a data assessment. User data assessment requires careful capacity planning. The following are user behaviors that need to be taken into consideration.

- Users tend to store a lot of non-corporate-related data (e.g., pictures)

- Users tend to store duplicate files in multiple locations (e.g., , one file on desktop and the same file in the downloads folder)

- Users tend to have partially downloaded incomplete large files

- Users tend to have temporary unknown files

- Multiple users tend to have the same file on everyone's devices

The total volume of data consumed by every end user in the current landscape should be reported, and this report should include the following at a minimum. The data assessment report should have the following key performance indicators.

- The volume of data consumed by users

- The volume of data consumed by the folder and subfolder

- The volume of data consumed by file type

- The volume of data consumed per user by last access

- The volume of data consumed per user by last modified

- The volume of data needed to be backed up per user

The development of an AD solution requires a deep knowledge of the data stored in Azure files or another Azure cloud-native file storage solution. A data baseline promotes an approach that encourages creating a DT process to answer the following most challenging question: where and how much will be stored in AVD? AVD engineers/ architects utilize end-user expectations, interests, and desires to develop a solution that will satisfy their needs and help them achieve their goals. Analyze all data from a usage perspective. A file system cloud-native storage architecture must consider the following factors.

- Identify each end user's data storage requirements

  - Home drive storage

  - Additional application drive storage

  - Cloud cache storage requirements

- Identify each end user's data storage regulation requirements per user/department

- Identify each end user's data classification requirements per user/department

- Identify organization-wide data backup requirements per user

  - Active user data backup requirements per user

  - Offboarded user data backup requirements per user

  - Identify restore SLA per user

  - Identify restore SLA organization-wide

- Identify organization-wide data retention requirements per user

  - Active user data retention requirements per user

  - Offboarded user data retention requirements per user

  - Identify restore SLA per user

  - Identify restore SLA organization-wide

AVD IaaS

After completing the data assessment, the next step will be to assess the infrastructure. Planning and sizing the compute, memory, storage, and network require an infrastructure assessment. One of the most challenging aspects of the design phase is sizing.

Nowadays, sizing is tricky due to resource demand such as graphical enhanced operating systems and applications.

Infrastructure assessment should contain the following key performance indicators.

- CPU and memory requirements per pooled AVD

- CPU and memory requirements per dedicated AVD

- Storage requirements per pooled AVD

- Storage requirements per dedicated AVD

- Network requirements for total session per site

- GPU requirements per users based on user persona

As business requirements become increasingly sophisticated, technology is changing, and end-user expectations rise. Cloud technologies from Azure enable simplified remote working and data protection, easy desktop management, and cost savings. The success of this product will ultimately be determined mainly by its ability to provide a good user experience.

For total consumption of infrastructure consumed by every end user in the current landscape, a report should include at minimum the following. The infrastructure assessment report must consider the following factors.

- Identify total users for each pool

    - Number of users per hosted shared desktop pool

    - Number of users per dedicated desktop pool

    - Number of users per application pool

- Identify density for shared desktop pool

- Identify IOPS and throughput requirement for each pool

- Identify network latency, bandwidth, redundancy, congestion, and scalability requirement for each site

- Identify current landscape network usage

- Identify existing network problem

- Identify external connectivity requirements

AVD Security

After completing the infrastructure assessment, the next step will be to assess the security. Security and compliance should focus on the desktop, apps, and data assessment. The design phase is challenging in terms of security.

Security assessment should contain the following key performance indicators.

- Way to protect all end-user identities

- Way to protect all end-user devices

- Way to protect all the applications that are running in AVD

- Secure the AVD session host OS

- Secure the AVD deployment configuration

- Apply AVD and endpoint network controls

- Way to meet all auditing, retention, eDiscovery, or compliance requirements (such as GDPR, HIPAA, PCID SS, and so forth) that need to be met or accounted

The security assessment report must consider the following factors.

- Identify any access requirements for the AVD

- Identify whether there is any security requirement around the configuration or status of the endpoint connecting to AVD

- Identify whether there are any requirements in supporting a segmented network

- Identify whether there are any requirements for multifactor authentication (MFA), SSO, Web application firewall, CDN cache for external user access

- Identify whether there are any requirements for endpoint threat detection and response

- Identify whether there are any requirements for data loss protection

AVD Management

After completing the security assessment, the next step will be to assess the monitoring. AVD monitoring should take place in conjunction with end-user management and AVD solutions. Managing AVD solutions during the design phase is challenging.

Management assessment should contain the following key performance indicators.

- Way to manage all the end-user devices,

- Way to manage all the end-user identities,

- Way to manage all the application access,

- Way to manage all the users onboarding onto AVD,

- Way to manage all the users offboarding from AVD,

- Way to monitor all the users' devices

- Way to monitor all the users' logon sequences

- Way to monitor all the users' logoff sequences

- Way to monitor all the application usage

- Way to monitor all the network connections

- Way to monitor end users' golden signals

- Way to monitor all the network site connectivity

- Way to monitor all the security incidents associated with AVD stack

The management assessment report must consider the following factors.

- Identify performance monitoring metrics

- Identify AVD service monitoring metrics

- Identify events monitoring metrics

- Identify logs monitoring metrics

- Identify workload management metrics

- Identify end-user management metrics

- Identify network management metrics

The technical viewpoint section in this chapter aims to provide you with methods and KPIs to consider in your assessment.

Azure Migrate is an alternate that provides a centralized hub for assessing and migrating to Azure on-premises virtual desktop solution along with applications and data.

Workloads on-premises are assessed for migration to Azure using the Azure Migrate service. On-premises machines are analyzed for migration suitability sized according to performance and cost estimates. Azure Migrate service is reserved for those envisioning lift-and-shift migrations or currently estimating migration choices.

If you're planning on migrating your private cloud-based VDI based on hyper or VMware or public cloud-based AWS or GCP to Azure's virtual desktop, follow these steps.

Step 1: Log in to personal or business account into Azure portal

The following is the link: `https://portal.azure.com/`.

Step 2: Search Azure Migrate (Figure 3-10).

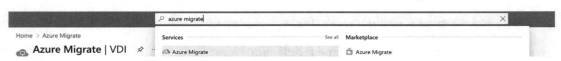

Figure 3-10. *Azure Migrate*

Step 3: Under Azure Migrate, choose VDI (Figure 3-11).

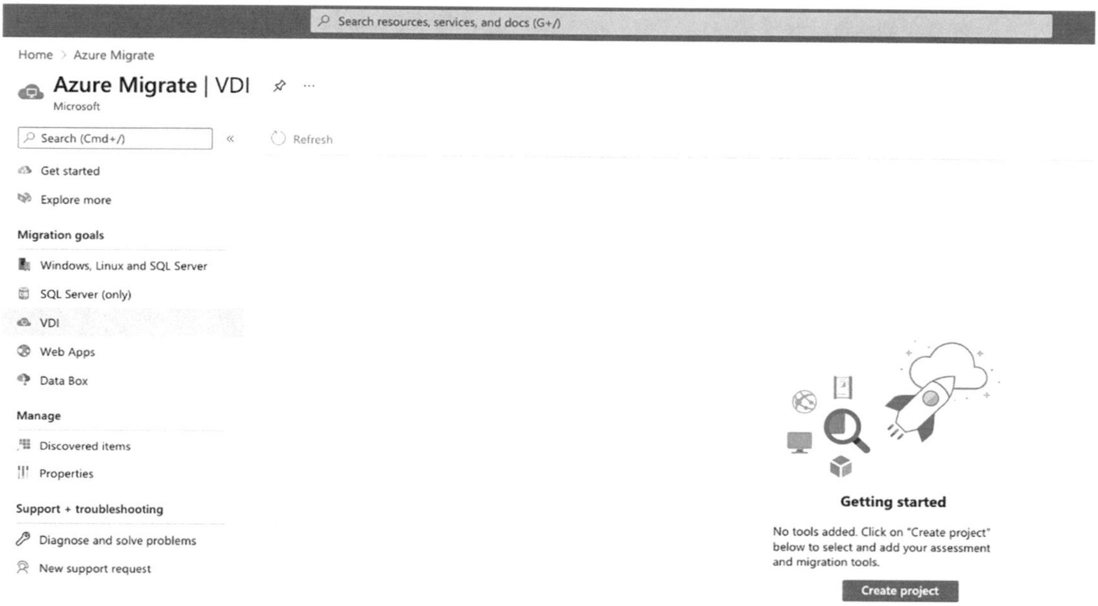

Figure 3-11. *Azure Migrate VDI*

Step 4: Create a project with your subscription and resource group; set the project name and location (Figure 3-12).

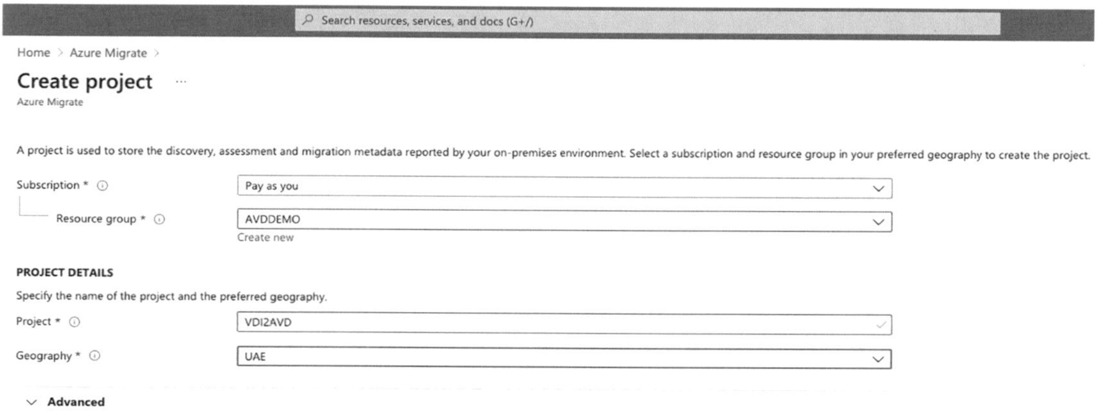

Figure 3-12. *Azure Migrate VDI – create project*

Step 5: Choose Azure Migrate (Figure 3-13).

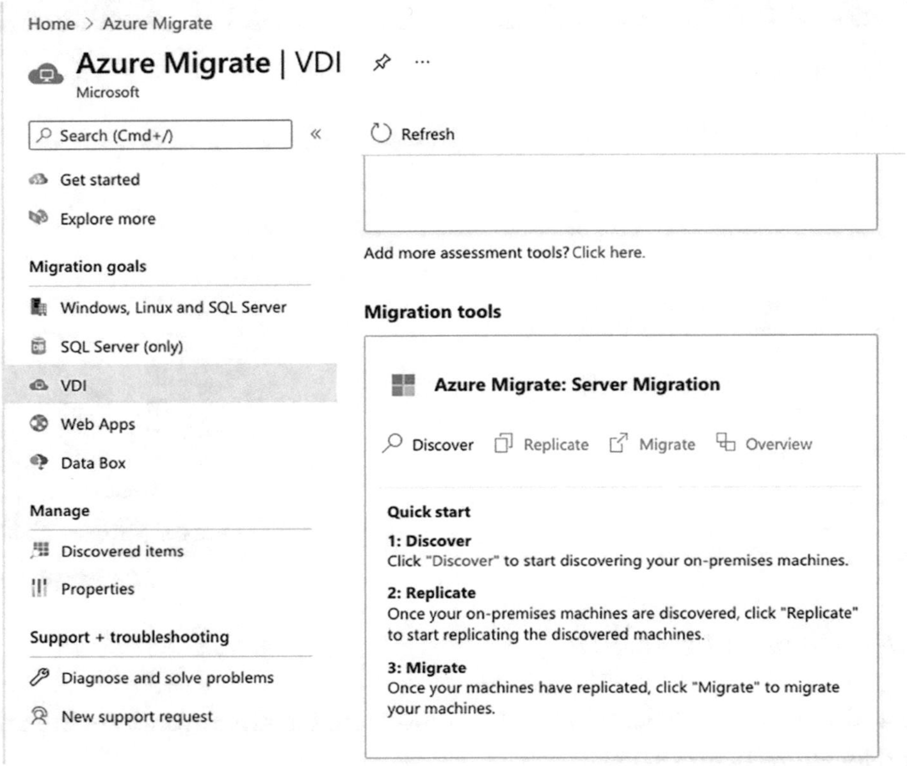

Figure 3-13. Azure Migrate VDI – server migration

Follow the wizard to complete your discovery planning and migration.

Designing AVD

The assessment data, the requirements, and the validated assumptions contribute significantly to designing something (Figure 3-14).

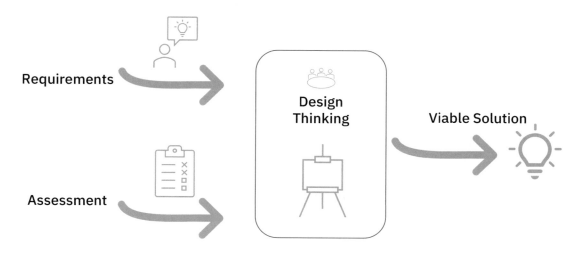

Figure 3-14. *Process of designing solution*

AVD architects and engineers can implement DT methods to design digital workplace using AVD solution. The process of DT helps to transition from the current state to the target state. As an AVD architect/engineer, you will always be asked to solve a digital workplace problem that will be unique, and sometimes very complex and time-consuming.

In the DT process, ups and downs are part of the journey. You must be disciplined and engage, but it is well worth it. To overcome hurdles and secure opportunities, AVD architects/engineers require the right tools and insights.

As an AVD architect/engineer, you should consider user experience as the top priority, and the end user does not necessarily care about your AVD design and deployment methods. They look for cloud-based desktops and apps that are functioning, performing, and with features that are working as expected.

AVD architects/engineers are guided by the principles of DT in their everyday lives. As an AVD architect/engineer, you must ensure that your solution prioritizes end-user critical functional requirements, that you work with a diverse group, and that your solution is continually enhanced.

DT principles guide the AVD architect/engineer team to immerse themselves in real-world design practices. Interact with end users, stay with them when performing AVD desktop function usage, and perform pilot testing activities with key executives who make the final decision and understand the overall benefits and implications.

Let us examine the DT process briefly. We will look at the six-stage DT method followed by the IT industry as depicted in Figure 3-15.

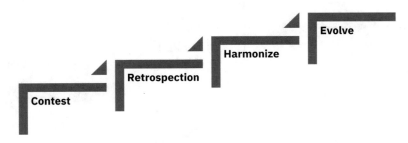

Figure 3-15. *Agile DT approach for AVD*

Note   Every IT service provider/function has its DT methodology and pattern. You can follow either your company-provided process or apply the following approach since it is also in line with industry standards.

First and foremost, DT seeks a **Contest**. To produce a design/solution, an AVD engineer/architect needs to gain a comprehensive insight into the problem. In this process, the AVD architect/engineer engages, observes, understands, and empathizes with the end user to learn more about the area of concern. By conducting the contest, AVD engineers can better understand end-user current experiences and levels of understanding.

The next phase of the DT process is **Retrospection**; AVD architect/engineers put together the information assessed, and requirements gathered during the assessment stage. With available data and facts, AVD architect/engineers need to analyze end users' observations. AVD architect/engineers need to synthesize them to define the AVD architect/engineer team's core problems up to this point. AVD architect/ engineers should seek to determine the issues as a problem description in an end-user-centered way.

The retrospection stage will ease the AVD architect/engineer team from developing and gathering great ideas to establishing concepts, features, functions, and any other vital components that will allow AVD architect/engineers to build the design for the problems.

The next phase of the DT process is **Harmonize**. An AVD architect/engineer is fully ready to kick start developing a design. The AVD architect/engineer has grown to understand end users and their essential, critical, and complex needs in the contest stage. The AVD architect/engineer has analyzed and synthesized their observations in the Retrospection stage and ended up with an end-user-centered issue statement. With this end-to-end visibility, facts, and data, AVD architect/engineer team members can start to apply their thinking process to identify practical solutions to the problem statement the AVD architect/engineer has created. The AVD architect/engineer can begin to look at alternative ways of resolving the problem. Iteration and Pi planning sessions can be scheduled and conducted. Sessions help stimulate free thinking and deep dive into the problem arena of transforming into a digital workplace. It is essential to get as many thoughts, ideas, and solutions as possible at the beginning of the Harmonize phase. It is important that the AVD architect/engineer prioritizes the development of the solution and ensures that the critical dependencies are identified before moving forward.

DT's next phase is **Evolve**. A product or feature should be strategically and pragmatically developed and launched at this stage. The goal of an AVD architect/engineer is to build an AVD solution that will solve a given problem of transforming into the digital workplace. The AVD architect/engineer is obligated to develop a fix for a trial. You can build several solutions based on priority. AVD architect/engineers should focus on a logical approach for each answer, by which we mean a spot should demonstrate tangible benefits in the shortest amount of time and effort.

You can apply this DT approach across each layer of the AVD solution and in continuous improvement while introducing new features from AVD to end users.

Conceptual Architecture of AVD

The conceptual architecture defines the overarching strategies for the entire AVD solution based on the business objectives, technical viewpoint, and assessment. It is worthwhile to start the design phase by defining the long-term objectives around preliminary building blocks, even if AVD conceptual architecture evolves.

AVD allows IT departments to run remote desktops and applications remotely in Azure as a managed service. Administrators can improve efficiency, security, and productivity by centrally managing desktops, apps, and data.

Figure 3-16 depicts conceptual architecture, which is classified into three main building blocks. The building blocks are necessary to provide an efficient, robust, highly available, reliable, secure AVD solution based on Microsoft Azure services.

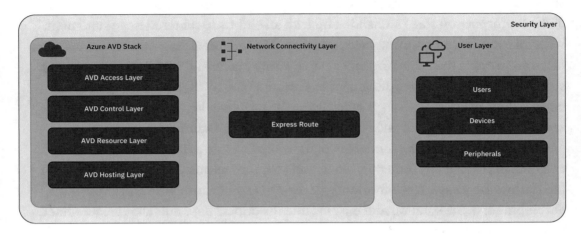

Figure 3-16. *Logical architecture of E2E AVD solution*

During the last two decades, technological advances have given rise to hyperscale public clouds, current cloud services, microservice architectures, DevOps/Agile delivery frameworks, subscription licensing models, and "evergreen" software and systems. Technology has been revolutionized across nearly every industry in the world by these advancements in procurement, selection, delivery, and support. AVD level 0 consists of three mainstream building blocks.

Azure AVD Stack

Today, many of the components or layers that comprise an AVD are available "as a service." Cloud consumers "subscribe" to various services. The service provider takes on the responsibility for delivering and managing these services.

AVD solution offers:

- End users to run applications and desktops independently of the device's operating system and interface.

- Administrators to manage the user and control their access from selected devices or restrict from all devices.

Access layer building block: The access layer defines how users access the resources via an internal network with AD integration and external users connect via MFA.

- Gateway: AVD remote connection gateway connects remote users to access AVD apps, data, and desktops from any device running an AVD client. Once a client connects to a gateway, it composes an RDSH or client OS VM and sends it back to that gateway.

- Web Access: Using the web access service within AVD, users can access apps, desktops, and data remotely from anywhere on any device using an HTML5-compatible web browser built into the client OS. Administrators of Azure AD can secure web access using MFA.

Control layer building block: The control layer defines the Azure virtual architectural foundation, Azure infrastructure perquisites, management, and monitoring for AVD solution.

- Connection Broker: This service manages virtual desktops and applications virtualized by Connection Broker. Using the Connection Broker, you can perform load balancing and reconnect sessions.

- Diagnostics: AVD diagnostics is an event-based aggregator that evaluates the success or failure of each user action. Event aggregation can be asked to classify failing elements by AVD administrators.

- Monitoring: End-user-level monitoring solutions such as control up, login vsi, lakeside, and so on can be integrated with AVD.

Resource layer building block: The resource layer defines deployment models to consume AVDs and applications.

- AVD session pool: A pool can run the following operating systems when writing the book.

  - Windows 7 Enterprise

  - Windows 10 Enterprise

  - Windows 10 Enterprise Multi-session

  - Windows Server 2012 R2,

  - Windows Server 2016,

- Windows Server 2019 above

- Your own image preloaded apps, local group policies, or along with golden image customization.

- Third-party integration: End-user personalization and profile management solutions such as Ivanti, liquit, cloud house, and so on can be integrated with AVD.

Hosting layer building block: The hosting layer defines the underlying cloud infrastructure with resilience and high availability.

- Azure provides a wide range of VM sizes and images, enabling AVD administrators to choose the best deployment options for their AVD environments. Azure compute, Azure infrastructure as a service category creates and manages VMs, containers, and batch jobs and supports remote application access.

- Azure delivers long-lasting, highly available, and massively scalable storage choices such as blob, queue, file, and disk, which keep velocity with explosive data extension. Azure storage, Azure infrastructure as a service category provides scalable cloud storage for structured and unstructured data.

- Azure offers various networking services to build advanced network topologies and extend data centers to the cloud. Azure networking, Azure infrastructure as a service category provides virtual networks, dedicated connections, gateways, and services for traffic management and diagnostics, load balancing, DNS hosting, and network protection against distributed denial-of-service (DDoS) attacks.

AVD resources with greater agility and elasticity are becoming available, adjusting usage as requirements change. Microsoft Azure provides all the necessary control and workload components for end users. Integrating Microsoft Azure's control plane for global operations establishes identity, governance, and security. Please conclude your decision and document it as follows.

ID	Decision
LOD01	Microsoft will provide a DaaS solution
Decision Description	Centralized platform to administer, deploy, and connect to virtual desktops and published applications

Network Connectivity

Accessing AVD resources requires building blocks of network and security. The goal is to allow only legitimate traffic to pass through via the managed network when it is internal. Azure includes a robust networking infrastructure that supports the connectivity requirements of business applications and services. You can connect Azure AVD resources to on-premises resources, Azure resources to the Internet, and Azure resources to resources on-premises. Connecting Azure virtual networks with AVD cloud consumers' local/cloud networks is called hybrid networking.

The following are options for network connectivity and network service routing. AVD cloud consumers can connect their on-premises computers and networks to a virtual network using any combination of the following options:

- Azure ExpressRoute: A connection between the customer's network and Azure through an ExpressRoute partner. This connection is private. Traffic does not go over the Internet.

- Virtual private network (VPN): Connects two virtual networks or multiple virtual networks to a single computer at a site in a customer's network. To establish connectivity with a virtual network, you must configure each end-user device. Over the Internet, the communication between your device and the virtual network circulates through an encrypted tunnel.

    - Site-to-site VPN- Establishes a VPN connection between on-premises VPN devices and Azure virtual network gateways. Any on-premises resource can access a virtual network that the AVD cloud consumer authorizes. Through an encrypted tunnel over the Internet, an on-premises VPN device communicates with an Azure VPN gateway.

- Point-to-site VPN- An individual client computer can connect
  to a virtual network via a point-to-site (P2S) VPN gateway
  connection. AVD cloud consumer end devices initiate a P2S
  contact. Telecommuters can use this solution to connect to Azure
  virtual networks (vNETs) from a remote location, such as from
  home or a conference. When you only have a few clients who
  must connect to the same vNET as you, P2S VPN is a practical
  alternative to S2S VPN.

As the next step, let us do deep dive into network connectivity with a use case.

Use Case

Consider Company XYZ, which wants two-mode connectivity toward AVD: it wants
to deploy a design that allows internal users to gain direct access to the session host
and external users to connect via public Internet with a highly secure connection. See
Figure 3-17.

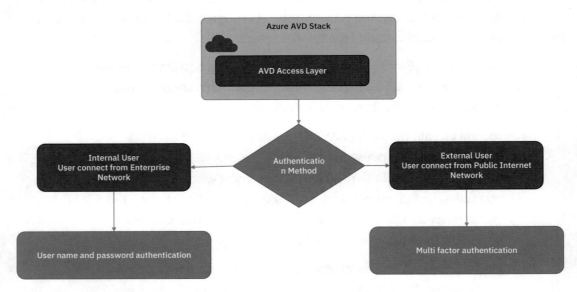

Figure 3-17. *End user access method*

Internal Users Access

AVD published desktops, published applications, and remote access to the system should be available to end users via the enterprise internal network. The enterprise internal network needs to have direct connectivity via the following methods supported by Microsoft:

- ExpressRoute private peering

- IPsec based either on site-to-site or on point-to-site VPN

An ExpressRoute circuit is a logical connection between AVD cloud consumer on-premises infrastructure and Microsoft cloud services through a connectivity provider. An enterprise can order a single ExpressRoute circuit. Circuits can be in the same or different regions and connected to cloud consumer premises via various connectivity providers.

No physical entity maps to an ExpressRoute circuit. The service key (s-key) identifies a circuit by its standard GUID. Only the service key is shared between the enterprise, Microsoft, and the connectivity provider. Security reasons do not require a secret s-key. The mapping between an ExpressRoute circuit and an S-key is 1:1.

Two independent peerings can be included in a new ExpressRoute circuit: a Microsoft peering and a private peering. Peerings may be configured on existing ExpressRoute circuits as follows:

- Azure public

- Azure private

- Microsoft

The peering is accomplished by configuring each border gateway protocol (BGP) session redundantly to ensure high availability. There are eight different bandwidth options for each circuit (50 Mbps, 100 Mbps, 200 Mbps, 500 Mbps, 1 Gbps, 2 Gbps, 5 Gbps and 10 Gbps).

Microsoft, Azure, and Azure public are all routing domains/peerings associated with ExpressRoute circuits. High availability is achieved by configuring each peering identically on a pair of routers (active-active or load sharing). There are two types of Azure services for representing the IP address schemes.

AVD deployed in a virtual network can be accessed through the private peering domain of Azure compute services. The private peering domain is treated as a trusted extension of the AVD cloud consumer core network into Microsoft Azure. AVD cloud consumers can set up bidirectional connectivity between enterprise core and Azure vNETs. This peering lets AVD cloud consumers connect to the published desktops, apps, and dedicated desktops directly on their private IP addresses. See Figure 3-18.

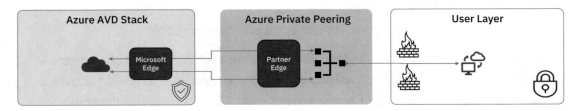

Figure 3-18. *Internal end users access method*

The Network Performance Monitor (NPM) is a tool that facilitates the monitoring of ExpressRoute circuit availability, connectivity to virtual networks, and bandwidth utilization.

During a complete end-to-end network, it's essential to maintain the reliability, high availability, and redundancy of ExpressRoute circuits. Additionally, it would be best not to compromise the redundancy in your service provider's network while maintaining redundancy in the AVD cloud consumer network. A central point of failure is to be avoided whenever possible to keep redundancy at a minimum in your AVD solution design. See Figure 3-19.

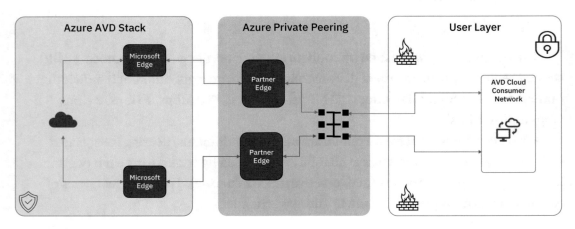

Figure 3-19. *Azure private peering*

Microsoft AVD solution recommends operating both the connections of an ExpressRoute circuit in active-active mode. If you let the links work in an active-active design pattern, the Microsoft network will load the traffic across the connections on a per-flow basis.

Designing the primary and secondary connections of an ExpressRoute circuit in active-passive mode faces the risk of both the links failing following a failure in the active path. Lack of operational management and stale routes advertised by passive connections are the two most common causes of switching.

If an ExpressRoute connection is lost, running the primary and secondary links in active-active mode results in about half the flows failing and rerouting. Therefore, active-active is expected to reduce the MTTR.

ExpressRoute supports peering over bidirectional forwarding detection (BFD). Using BFD, Microsoft Enterprise Edge's Layer 2 network can identify failure in less than a second over BGP neighbors on-premises. ExpressRoute circuits terminated on a single customer premises equipment (CPE) are not highly available on AVD cloud consumer on-premises network. Consider, too, configuring both the primary and secondary connections on the same port of a CPE (either by terminating the two links on different sub interfaces or by merging the two links within the partner network). By making the partner compromise high availability on their network segment, you compromise your partnership.

You may compromise connectivity performance if you terminate primary and secondary ExpressRoute circuits in different geographic locations. Suppose traffic is actively load-balanced across the primary and secondary connections but is terminated on other office locations or on-premises located in a different geo. Due to the significant difference in network latency between these two paths, performance will be suboptimal.

Peering between Microsoft systems is designed for public-to-public communication. On-premises private endpoints are network address translated (NATed) before communicating over Microsoft peering with public IP addresses in the AVD cloud. This is based on the assumption that both primary and secondary connections are active-active.

Your design can use a familiar NAT pool by splitting the traffic between the primary and secondary ExpressRoute connections before you divide it. Before breaking the traffic, it is imperative to realize that introducing a single point of failure does not present a shared NAT pool.

Consider avoiding a single point of failure at each connection termination point.

So, as a result, use ExpressRoute private peering with high availability. A vast user base is located, so consider using site-to-site VPN for disaster recovery and branch office with fewer users. Please conclude your decision and document it as follows.

ID	Decision
LOD02	End users can consume AVD solutions via an internal network from the HQ/main office.
Decision Description	Users consuming internal enterprise networks can access the AVD solution via Azure ExpressRoute private peering.

ID	Decision
LOD03	End users consuming AVD solution via internal network from remote office.
Decision Description	Users consuming internal enterprise networks can access AVD solutions via site-to-site VPN (IPSec).

External Users Access

AVD published desktops, published applications, and remote access to the system should be available to the end users via the Internet.

The authorization rules specify what functions a particular user is allowed to perform on a system. The process of establishing specific system privileges or access rights to resources is known as authorization. AVD provides access control. Assignment within AVD occurs on multiple levels.

AVD's Windows client provides an excellent way to integrate AVD with local machines. Nevertheless, when AVD administrators configure the AVD account to work with the Windows client, the AVD architect must consider some safety precautions in the AVD design. When AVD end users first log in, the AVD client prompts for username, password, and Azure MFA.

After that, the next time the end users log in, the client will remember the token from Azure AD. When the end user chooses "Remember me" on the prompt for credentials for the session host, the end user can log in after restarting the client without needing to provide credentials. Though remembering credentials is comfortable, it can also make a design on enterprise solution less secure. It is a great decision to integrate the AVD solution with Azure MFA to enhance security.

To ensure additional security, we support MFA. When users access the system, they need to provide at least two authentication factors - something they know, their password, and something they have, a token. One-time passwords, proprietary devices, smartphone apps, emails, voice calls, and texts can serve as authentication tokens. See Figure 3-20.

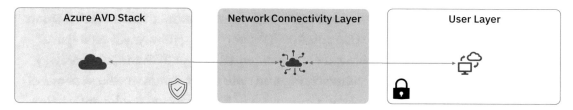

Figure 3-20. *External access method*

There are three prerequisites for setting up MFA in AVD. It's essential to understand the prerequisites as they impact the architecture and configuration of AVD design.

- End users should be given a license for Azure AD P1 or P2.

- The group will have your users assigned to it.

- Set up conditional access and enable all users with Azure MFA.

Please conclude your decision and document it as follows.

ID	Decision
LOD04	End users consuming AVD solution via Internet
Decision Description	Users consuming external networks can access AVD solutions via Internet

ID	Decision
LOD05	End users consuming AVD solution via Internet should be enabled with MFA
Decision Description	Users consuming external networks that can access AVD solutions via the Internet authenticates with MFA

Network Workflow

How clients connect to resources is one of the main differences between traditional remote desktop services (RDS) and AVD. Reverse connect is a feature built into AVD by Microsoft.

In the legacy world, RD gateways typically provide external access to RDS resources. The RD client connects via TCP 443 to the RD gateway and authenticates via AD. Upon selecting/choosing the resource (RemoteApp/Desktop), the gateway will establish a secure inbound session. For improved connection quality over TCP, the RDS gateway can also use the UDP port 3391 (when configured) when using more recent versions of Windows. Despite its high latency and randomness, UDP performs significantly better than conventional protocols.

The following model involves external users connecting to a WVD gateway service accessible over the Internet. WVD can be accessed externally using this method. Access to the appropriate desktops and applications is controlled by Azure AD. Broker connections are proactively established on desktops of backend pools before users connect. Microsoft's managed PaaS services include the broker and gateway services that orchestrate the desktop/application sessions for users. Because of this, there is no direct access to the backend desktop/applications via the Internet.

The key advantage of accessing via the Internet is the ease of configuration, Reverse connect also provides new benefits like setting policies, including conditional access policies. There is no requirement to configure or open any inbound ports on a VM to connect to AVD via RDP. The feature is essentially a reverse proxy security feature straight from Azure. Microsoft AVD makes use of reverse connect technology to establish remote sessions and carry RDP traffic. It does not allow incoming RDP connections to be received via a TCP listener, unlike the on-premises deployments. The AVD infrastructure is directly accessed via HTTPS over the outbound connection instead.

Virtual desktops run on Azure's session hosts and can host client sessions. The software giant manages portions of the services on behalf of the customer and manages the secure endpoints and connections between clients. Figure 3-21 provides a high-level overview of how AVD uses network connections.

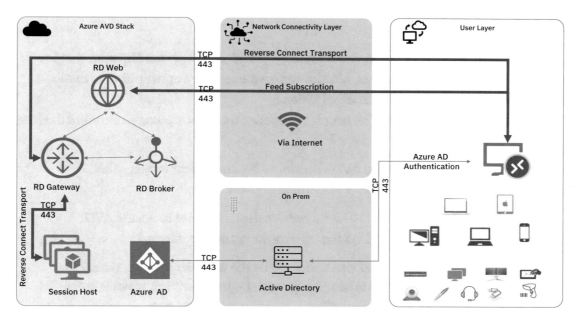

Figure 3-21. *Network flow of AVD*

1. A user subscribes to the AVD workspace by using supported AVD clients.

2. By successful authentication of a user with Azure AD, resources get enumerated to the end-user workspace.

3. A token is sent from the AVD client for the feed subscription service, and in turn, the service validates the token.

4. This service passes back to the client a digitally signed configuration containing a list of available published desktops and published applications.

5. Connection configuration is stored in .rdp files for each resource available to the client. And once the client is connected to an AVD resource, it uses its associated .rdp file, establishes the secure TLS 1.2 connection, and transmits connection information.

AVD End Users

Each user's primary endpoint device should align with the business objectives and their role and associated requirements. Multiple endpoints may be appropriate in many situations, each offering different capabilities.

User layer building block: The user layer defines the user topology, endpoint devices, and AVD clients.

- External Users: Access AVD via remote desktop client to access AVD hosted in Azure cloud via the public network.

- Internal Users: Access AVD via remote desktop client to access AVD hosted in Azure cloud via the internal or corporate network.

Endpoints are usually owned and managed by the organization. The bring-your-own-device (BYOD) trend is becoming more popular as it improves employee satisfaction, reduces costs, and simplifies device management. It does not follow that every individual should be allowed to use their own device within the corporate environment, even if BYOD is a business priority.

Given their application needs, their expected use of the AVD desktop/applications and their location, a desktop/thin client is likely to be the primary device assigned to an end-user persona A. Additionally, an end user may receive a smartphone as a secondary device if their role requires flexibility, service, and application needs. An end-user persona B is likely to use a laptop/thin client for their primary device, depending on their application requirements, their expectation of using these AVD desktops/applications, and their preference for mobility. The use of a secondary device by persona B is likely to provide additional flexibility for their usage pattern. Maybe it's a tablet or smartphone. Please conclude your decision and document it as follows.

ID	Decision
LOD06	Endpoint device standards supported such as desktops, laptops, thin clients, smartphones, and tablets.
Decision Description	Endpoint device standards should be aligned with digital workplace strategy.

Security layer building block: As part of the security layer, there are zero-trust architectures, defense-in-depth programs, identity, user devices (mobile and PC), app security, session hosts, deployment configurations, and network controls managed by cloud consumers or managed service providers. These include the Azure virtualization control plane, the Azure cloud physical datacenters, and the Azure cloud network and storage.

- Azure security center: Azure cloud workload protection solution that presents security management and high-level threat protection across AVD cloud workloads.

- Azure key vault: Azure secure secrets store for the passwords, agent strings, and other knowledge AVD administrators need to keep desktop and apps working.

- Azure monitor logs: Azure monitoring service receives telemetry and different data and renders a query language and analytics engine to deliver operational insights for desktops, data, and apps.

Summary

In this chapter, you read about requirements gathering for apps, data, infra, security, and compliance for AVD, a method to perform assessment, and a DT framework for AVD module by module and conceptual architecture.

In the next chapter, you will read about the designing each layer of AVD solution such as access, control, resource, hosting layer, and end-user layer.

CHAPTER 4

Designing and Deploying AVD Solution

The Microsoft Azure Virtual Desktop (AVD) service provides a corporate-class virtual desktop experience available from anywhere globally, allowing organizations to boost business resilience with remote access to desktops and applications. Besides simplified management, Windows multisession, and optimizations for Microsoft 365 apps for business, it supports migration of remote desktop services (RDS) environments. A virtual desktop deployed on Azure can be deployed and scaled in minutes, and it has built-in security and compliance features to help keep your apps and data secure.

AVD is a Platform-as-a-Service (PaaS); many infrastructure-related parts are managed for cloud consumers by Microsoft. Other factors, mainly relating to the desktop and application workloads, are controlled by cloud consumers. This does not mean that whenever something is managed by Microsoft, you do not need to worry about your design. Still, in architecture practices, it is recommended to apply design thinking concerning operational excellence, performance, cost efficiency, reliability, high availability, resilience, security, and compliance.

Cloud consumers should understand that Microsoft has already contributed to some services' security when they use AVD. Azure is running on physical hosts, data centers, and networks that Microsoft maintains. Additionally, Microsoft is responsible for ensuring that the virtualization of its AVD services are secure. However, as an architect, you must also adjust other security measures to meet the needs of the cloud consumer organization.

© Puthiyavan Udayakumar 2022
P. Udayakumar, *Design and Deploy Microsoft Azure Virtual Desktop*,
https://doi.org/10.1007/978-1-4842-7796-6_4

This chapter provides the way of designing each building block of the AVD solution. By the end of this chapter, you should be able to understand the following:

- Design of AVD layer

  - Design Access Layer

  - Design Control Layer

  - Design Resource Layer

  - Design Hosting Layer

  - Design User Layer

Design and Deploy AVD Solution

You must be in some way interested in designing and deploying AVDs based on the Microsoft Azure platform if you are reading this book. Thanks to this common interest, we now have something in common!

With Microsoft Azure, you can spin up new virtual desktops and remote applications resources quickly and flexibly, so they fit your changing needs. Microsoft Azure supports all the necessary control and workload functions for a virtual apps and desktop service deployment.

The cloud provider Azure has the most functionality, largest enterprise customers, unsurpassed experience, and the highest maturity of all cloud providers, causing end users, applications, and data to move to its clouds. Here, we discuss the common patterns and designs in the apps and desktops domain and recommend deploying apps and desktops to Azure. This chapter focus on designing an architecture and deployment model of AVD services, as well as highlighting the design decisions and deployment considerations across the following three critical architectural principles: operational excellence, governance, and security. In turn, these align to three layers of building block: AVD layer, network layer, and user layer.

Figure 4-1 depicts building blocks around AVD.

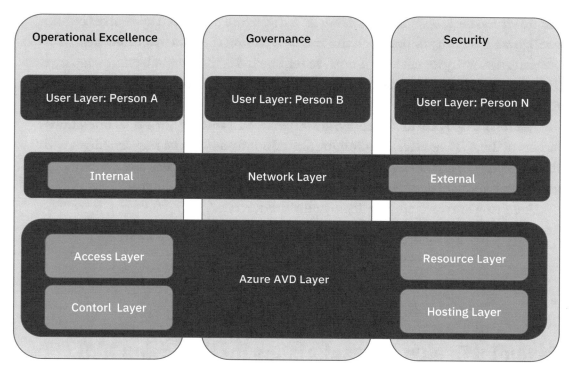

Figure 4-1. *Building blocks around AVD*

Let us explore each design pillar explanation. End users can securely access their entire digital workspace on any device, anytime, anywhere, thanks to Microsoft AVD. Operational excellence is a crucial element to achieve this in your design. For operational excellence, with the ability to support the AVD end users and run their workloads effectively, AVD administrators must gain insight into their operations and continuously improve supporting processes and procedures to deliver end-user experiences and increase productivity.

Reduce costs and improve business outcomes with hybrid and cloud-native deployments and modernized operations that simplify Day 2 management. Governance is the next crucial element to achieve those mentioned above in your design. AVD governance involves establishing policies, processes, and procedures associated with planning, architecting, acquiring, deploying, and managing the resources.

Microsoft AVD should encompass the ability to protect data, systems, and assets from taking advantage of cloud technologies to improve your end-user identity, apps, and data protection. Security is the last crucial element to achieve those mentioned above in your design. Secured Microsoft AVD delivers high performance, intrinsically secure virtual desktop, and application delivery. Azure provides a wide array of configurable security options and the ability to control them so that customers can customize security to meet the unique requirements of their organization's deployments. This section helps to understand how Azure security capabilities can help you fulfill these requirements.

Microsoft AVD provides identity, governance, and security for global operations as part of the AVD services. Fine-tuning and adopting additional ring-fencing is with the enterprise or architects. This chapter also guides prerequisites, architecture design considerations, and deployment guidance for customer environments.

Following are the common deployment models used.

- Cloud-Native - uses Azure cloud services for all remote working system subsystems, plus Azure public cloud services.

- Hybrid Cloud - uses Azure cloud services for all disaster recovery services and production running on-prem.

Essential Design Characteristics for Deploying AVD Hosting Layer

A well-defined framework for AVD solution to provide services, availability, flexibility, recoverability, and performance is required for AVD cloud consumers. Figure 4-2 shows key design principles that can be followed in your AVD design.

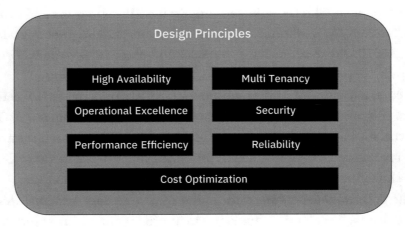

Figure 4-2. *Design principles around AVD*

Multitenancy - AVD design should focuses on isolation of resources and networks to deliver AVD desktop and application with quality. It includes

- AVD create virtual desktop and apps for AVD end user under available high-level compute nodes that offer specific service-level agreements (SLAs).

- The AVD management plane functions reside in the Edge management domain at the AVD.

- Compute Isolation - Allocation of compute and storage resources ensures that there is an optimal footprint available to the AVD end user.

- Network Isolation - The advanced networking model of vNET 97 provides fully isolated and secure traffic paths across AVD end-user Workloads.

High availability - AVD design should focus on avoiding single points of failure across the design.

- AVD system should be highly available when it can withstand the failure of an individual or multiple components (e.g., hard disks, servers, network links). Implement automating recovery and reducing disruption at every layer of AVD architecture by introducing redundancy.

- Introduce redundancy by having multiple resources for the same task. Redundancy is implemented in standby mode (functionality is recovered through failover while the resource remains unavailable) or active mode (requests are distributed to multiple redundant compute resources, and when one of them fails, the rest can simply absorb a larger share of the workload).

- Detection and reaction to failure should both be automated as much as possible via Azure Automation – Runbook Management

- Have a durable data storage to protect data availability and integrity. Redundant copies of data are implemented by synchronous, asynchronous, or Quorum-based replication based on data requirements.

Operational Excellence – AVD design should focuses on running and monitoring systems to deliver AVD end-user business value, and continually improve processes and procedures. The ability to run and monitor systems to deliver business value and to continually improve supporting processes and procedures includes

- managing and automating changes

- responding to events

- defining standards to successfully manage daily operations

- performing operations with code

- aligning operations processes to business objectives

- making regular, small, incremental changes

- testing for responses to unexpected events

- learning from operational events and failures

Security – AVD design focuses on protecting AVD cloud consumer information and systems. Security is the ability to protect information, systems, and assets while delivering business value through risk assessments and mitigation strategies. It includes

- confidentiality and integrity of data

- identifying and managing who can do what with privilege management

- protecting systems

- controls to detect security events

- applying security at all layers of AVD

- enabling traceability

- implementing a principle of least privilege

- focusing on securing your system

- automating security best practices

Reliability – AVD design focuses on the ability to prevent, and quickly recover from failures to meet business and AVD cloud consumer demand. Reliability is the ability of a system to recover from infrastructure or service disruptions, dynamically acquire computing resources to meet demand, and mitigate disruptions such as misconfigurations or transient network issues. It includes

- foundational elements around setup

- cross-project requirements

- recovery planning

- how we handle change

- testing recovery procedures to automatically recover from failure

- scaling horizontally to increase aggregate system availability

- stopping guessing at capacity

- managing change in automation

Performance Efficiency – AVD design should focuses on using computing resources efficiently. Performance efficiency is ability to use computing resources efficiently to meet system requirements, and to maintain that efficiency as demand changes and technologies evolve. It includes

- selecting the right resource types and sizes based on workload requirements

- monitoring performance

- making informed decisions to maintain efficiency as business needs evolve

- Democratizing advanced technologies

- Experimenting more often

- Mechanical sympathy

Cost Optimization – AVD design should focuses on avoiding un-needed costs. Cost optimization is the ability to run systems to deliver business value at the lowest price point. It includes

- understanding and controlling where money is being spent,

- selecting the most appropriate and right number of resource types

- analyzing spend over time

- scaling to meet business needs without overspending

- adopting a consumption model

- benefitting from economies of scale

- analyzing and attributing expenditure

- using managed services to reduce cost of ownership

Design Pattern for Implementing AVD Solution with Reliability

Survive the failure of its AVD session hosting component: A hypervisor's failure or underlying bare metal spreads to all hosted AVD virtual machines (VMs), further causing their hosted AVD functions to abandon. So, the solution is to implement bare metals in a clustered system so that if one hosting component fails, active VMs are transferred to different working hosts within the cluster. This design pattern applies if you use bare metal solution via Azure. See Figure 4-3.

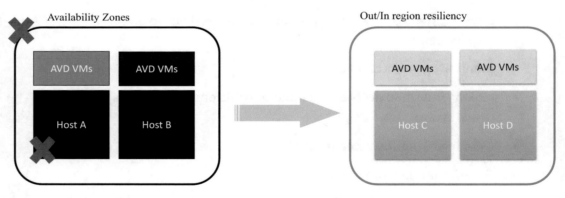

Figure 4-3. *Compute reliability within and out/in region resiliency*

Failure of cloud storage solution: Cloud storage appliances are irregularly subject to breakdown and interruptions created by general hardware failure, network connectivity issues or controller, or security infringements. A jeopardized cloud storage device's reliability can directly impact matters and create problems across all the AVD functions, AVD user sessions, and remote apps; data hosted can also become impacted. So, the solution is to deploy redundant storage. Redundant storage will act as a secondary duplicate data from the primary cloud storage system and secondary storage device. As part of a failover operation, it will sync its data from the primary cloud storage device. A storage service gateway redirects cloud consumer calls to the second device if the primary device fails. See Figure 4-4.

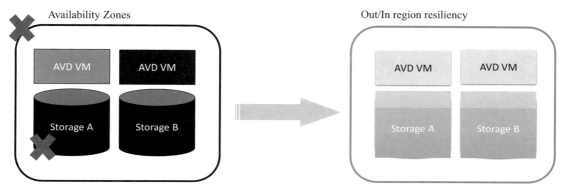

Figure 4-4. *Storage reliability within and out/in region resiliency*

AVD functions need to be reached while its defined route is lost or shifts are unavailable: This can risk an entirely cloud-based solution's stability until the cloud provider can supply the cloud consumer with the missed or refreshed path. So the solution is to implement an alternative route to AVD function presented to cloud consumers to automatically or manually succeeding path failures.

Distributed systems depend on network connectivity to interconnect segments, such as AVD session host. AVD function workloads must work with certitude despite data loss or latency in interconnects. Elements of the distributed system must work in a style that does not negatively crash other segments or the workload. See Figure 4-5.

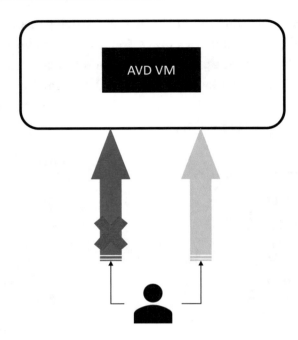

Figure 4-5. *Network reliability with resiliency*

Deploy loosely coupled provinces: Provinces such as queuing, streaming, workflows, and load balancers should be loosely coupled. Loose coupling promotes quarantine of a component's behavior from other cloud components that depend on it, increasing resiliency and readiness. It can be synchronous or asynchronous. Always-tight coupling will add unreliability problems into your solution. See Figure 4-6.

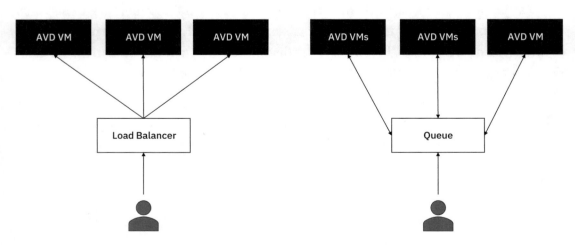

Figure 4-6. *Loosely couple for system reliability*

Failure notification and automate recovery: When cloud-based AVD function fails, the hand-operated interruption may be unacceptably ineffective. So, the solution is to implement a watchdog system to monitor AVD function status and deliver notifications and apply retrospective recovery endeavors during failure circumstances. You can use the artificial intelligence for IT operations (AIOPs) monitoring solution to recovery AVD function. See Figure 4-7.

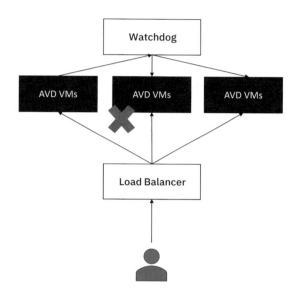

Figure 4-7. *Watchdog to remove failed component and autorecover for system reliability*

Relocating cloud service either temporarily or permanently without generating an interruption: There are situations under which moving cloud service to a functioning site is a good idea. However, moving cloud services or live migrating a cloud service implementation can cause downtime, thereby upsetting the cloud service availability. So the solution is to implement a hot or cold clone of the primary instance that can be created as a second instance in a secondary site after the primary service is deactivated or removed. See Figure 4-8.

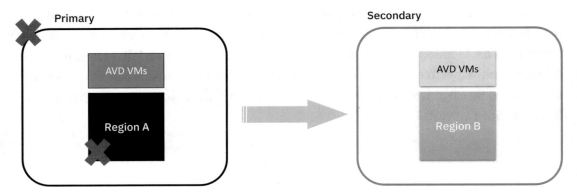

Figure 4-8. *Clone from primary region to secondary region*

AVD core VMs need to be available when high availability and clustering components fail together: A cloud consumer may be restricted from using high availability and clustering technology for its VM or guest operating systems (OS), thereby making them more vulnerable to failure. So, the solution is to composite failover system to not function based on clustering or high-availability characteristics but alternatively to use heartbeat information to synchronize VM, containers of guest OS. See Figure 4-9.

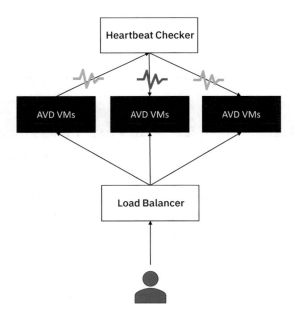

Figure 4-9. *Heartbeat check to synchronize systems*

Handle errors that force taking a time to resume from failure: Detect failures and apply the logic of limiting a loss from regularly recurring sustenance, short outside system failure, or accidental system complications. The solution is to execute a further request that quickly states the AVD function's unavailability and should not wait for the timeout. The method should be used when the crash is temporary. However, if this is not the case, then the run is likely to crash. The circuit breaker method restricts the consumer request from offering a call that is likely to break. When consumer requests are treated as BAU, the circuit breaker is locked, and workflow is as per the original pathway. If one of the active systems rises, returning errors or slowness or a condition defined as per the trigger, the circuit breaker unlocks. Systematically, the trigger endeavors to call the province to discover if it has reached to steady-state. When that happens, the circuit breaker is locked. See Figure 4-10.

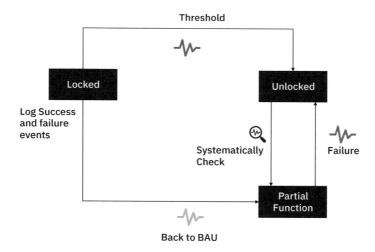

Figure 4-10. *Circuit breaker for system reliability*

Some more methods and patterns exist in real-world usage. For you, we trust this will be an eye-opener in getting started as AVD architect. Whether you are fresh to the topics of availability and reliability, or an established AVD architect seeking insights to increase a mission-critical workload's availability and reliability, we hope this section has triggered your system thinking, offered design principles, or introduced a line of the pattern. We hope this leads to a deeper understanding of the right level of availability and reliability based on your environmental needs and helps you design and deploy the reliability to achieve it. That said, let us move on to software engineering essentials for the AVD architect.

Design of AVD layer

In the last chapter, we have seen conceptual architecture for AVD solutions, including functionality. We describe the logical architecture. It also has essential components, such as Gateway, connection brokers, desktop pools, application delivery components, profile solutions, monitoring solutions, and these are well defined. Now it is the moment to do a deep dive into each element of the AVD stack.

Microsoft PaaS-based AVD solution eliminates the need to design, deploy, and manage web access, gateway, and global load balancing servers' roles. Using this cloud-based service, you can securely access remote applications while managing your identity and access, delivering a unified experience across apps that use PaaS and virtual desktops.

Figure 4-11 depicts cloud-native deployment for the AVD core stack.

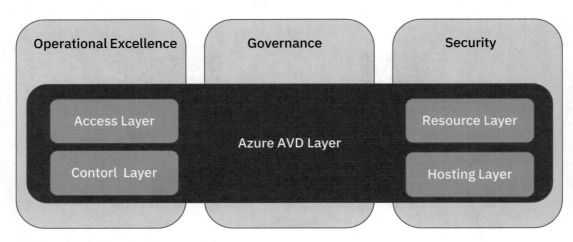

Figure 4-11. *Cloud-native deployment model of AVD core stack*

Building Block 1: Design of Access Layer

Let us get started with the access layer. It is crucial to your design part of the AVD design process.

Access layer building block: The access layer design should make sure users access the AVD resources with secure access via various networks; the design should meet excellent functional requirements, nonfunctional requirements, and operational excellence and governance.

Figure 4-12 depicts design principles around Azure AVD access layer.

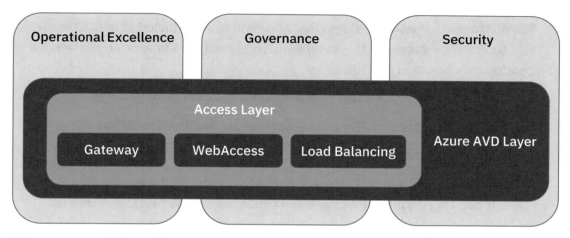

Figure 4-12. *Microsoft managed access layer*

Microsoft manages AVD following services as part of Azure PaaS service itself.

Gateway: AVD Remote Connection Gateway connects remote users to AVD apps, data, and desktops from any device running an AVD client. Once a client connects to a gateway, it composes an RDSH or client OS VM and sends it back to that gateway.

Web Access: Using the Web Access service within AVD, users can access apps, desktops, and data remotely from anywhere on any device using an HTML5-compatible web browser built into the client OS. Administrators of Azure Active Directory (AD) can secure Web Access using multifactor authentication (MFA).

Load Balancing: Availability and scale of web access, gateway, and connection brokers components fully managed by Microsoft.

This layer implements a secure virtual desktop connection by orchestrating access to all the components required by facilitating user authentication. Authentication and authorization are critical elements of the access layer.

This is a complete digital workspace solution that allows an AVD architect/ administrator to deliver secure access to the apps and desktop relevant to a person's role in your cloud consumer world. A connection to an AVD resource is not enough to protect the access to the AVD resources. The appropriate level of access should be granted based on the location of the AVD end user and the organization's security policies via a conditional access policy, MFA, and so on; this is the critical design consideration to be made.

AVD Access layer design decisions are based on security and monitoring requirements. An access layer specifies how users will gain access to an AVD resource.

The AVD access layers are resilient due to several features included in AVD services.

Microsoft fully manages AVD core infrastructure services. The access layer service will continue to operate even if there's an

- Microsoft Azure local corruption of data, metadata, and resources

- Outage in the availability zone within the Microsoft Azure region

- Microsoft Azure regional outage.

In the event of an unplanned failure, the access layer will fail over to multiple locations. It will help to ensure that the cloud consumer AVD access layer remains accessible. It is Microsoft's responsibility to restore service within the provided SLA.

So, the preceding gives the architect/organization a check in the box against operational excellence and governance because Microsoft already fulfills high availability and disaster recovery, as built in for AVD access layer components. However, the open item is security and monitoring. Let us do a deep dive in the next section.

Securing and Monitoring the Access Layer

A virtual desktop infrastructure deployment on-premises typically requires the customer to be responsible for all security aspects. With AVD, these responsibilities spilt between the AVD cloud consumer and Microsoft.

Microsoft has helped secure some of its services when you design AVD. Azure is running on physical hosts, data centers, and networks that Microsoft maintains and the control plane of AVD. Now, let us focus on some of the enterprise-essential security needs.

- Securing cloud consumer's end-user identities based on the context they request access to the resource.

- Collecting and examining audit logs for every end-user transaction.

Now, let us see securing cloud consumer's end-user identities based on the context they request access to the AVD resource. This section will discuss user credentials, applying for conditional access, and maintaining audit logs.

You can directly integrate AVD with your local machine using the Windows client for AVD. You will need to take a few design and deployment considerations to ensure AVD cloud consumers and you stay safe when configuring AVD accounts into the Windows client.

A username and a password are required to sign in for the first time. Following that, the client will remember your Azure AD enterprise application token the next time you sign in. Users can sign in after restarting the client without re-entering their credentials if they select the "Remember me" option on the session host credential prompt. The credential manager stores the certificates for these. It is undoubtedly convenient to remember credentials, but it can reduce the security of deployments on corporate-owned devices.

In your design, consider users always sign into their AVD sessions using their Azure AD credentials, so you must protect this identity from meeting the nonfunctional security requirements. Also, keep in mind the devices and other context they will use to access their sessions. See Figure 4-13.

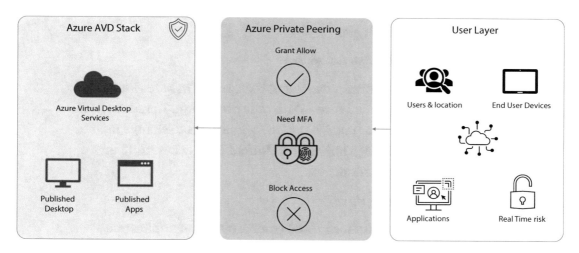

Figure 4-13. *Securing access layer*

Identity checking for users and devices has become an essential part of digital workplace security in the modern age. Enterprises that use the AVD have access control capabilities that can deploy with the help of the following identity signals.

Groups or users

- Administrators can customize policies for specific AVD users and groups, giving them fine-grained control over access.

Information about the IP location

- A policy decision can assign trusted IP address ranges to an enterprise.

- Admins have the option of blocking or allowing traffic from entire countries/regions.

Devices

- End users whose devices are on specific platforms or are tagged as up to date can enforce conditional access policies.

Application

- Users attempting to access specific applications can trigger different conditional access policies.

Real-time and calculated risk detection

- Conditional access policies can identify risky sign-in behavior using signals integration with Azure AD identity protection. To reduce AVD end-user security risk, policies can now force users to change their passwords or use MFA. They can be blocked from access until an administrator takes action.

Microsoft Cloud App Security

- Provides real-time monitoring and control over user application accesses to your cloud environment, increasing visibility and controlling activity within it.

By combining signals, making decisions, and applying organizational policies, Azure AD's conditional access tool accomplishes these tasks. The control plane is identity-driven, and consistent access is at its core.

- Enable conditional access to apply MFA for the Azure WVD client itself.

Using MFA in Azure AD adds another layer of security to data and applications, helping to safeguard their access. Passwords alone are a relatively weak form of authentication. An MFA system – something you know (a password), something you are (a biometric), something you possess (a key, a token, a device, etc.) – results in stronger authentication. Microsoft recommends two-factor authentication for AVD workflows.

- Enable MFA for AVD cloud consumers in Azure AD.

Now you can protect your users' IDs and control the devices, they can access the AVDs. When configuring conditional access policies for AVD, you can ensure that the client keeps asking for Azure MFA credentials more frequently when designing and deploying a protected digital workplace using AVD. With this design approach, you meet the security requirements and significantly improve overall AVD security.

- By enabling MFA for all users and administrators in AVD, your deployment will be more secure.

- Together with MFA, conditional access allows admins to select which specific users should be granted access based on which devices they are using, where AVD cloud consumers are located, how they log in, and so on.

Consider you have an additional functional requirement in your access layer; AVD end users want to quickly unblock themselves and continue working no matter where they are or the time of day. By allowing the end users to unblock themselves, the enterprise can save considerable amounts of support cost, time, and effort spent on the IT service desk in resolving password reset. Azure self-service password reset (SSPR) brings the following benefits into your design.

- Users who use self-service can reset their passwords without contacting a system administrator or the IT service desk.

- Self-service permits users to modify, update, and troubleshoot their environments independently without needing guidance. Most companies have security policies requiring AVD end users to change their passwords every 45-90 days. AVD end users have various endpoint devices with saved passwords, and it is straightforward for AVD end-user accounts to be locked out.

- Consider having your design with the following capabilities:

  - If the AVD end user's account is locked due to too many aborted login attempts, familiar with multiple devices, they can unhitch their AVD user account if they know the keys to their security questions.

  - If the AVD end user forgot their newly formed password, they can reset their password if they know the keys to their security questions.

- Microsoft Azure provides the capabilities to manage the passwords on-premises and resolve account lockouts through Password Writeback.

- The password management activity report provides administrators with insight into the password resets and registrations within their organization.

Azure conditional access combines signals, makes decisions, and enforces organizational policy via Azure AD. Identity-driven control plans are built around conditional access in Microsoft Azure. If AVD users want access to an AVD desktop/ app resource, they must perform one or more actions, forming Microsoft Azure conditional access policies. When using conditions of access policies for AVD, your AVD administrator can apply the proper access controls when needed to protect the enterprise and eliminate interference with AVD end users securely. Among the challenges is maintaining the right balance between security and usability.

Let us get on to deployment now. Creating a workspace is the most frequently deployed first step in setting up the AVD. Workspaces are logical groups of application groups within AVD. Users must be assigned a workspace before seeing remote apps and desktops published to them by AVD application groups.

Step 1: Log in to personal or business account into Azure portal

- The following is the link: `https://portal.azure.com/`.

Step 2: Search and start the **Azure Virtual Desktop** services; look for **Workspaces** blade and click on **Create** (see Figure 4-14).

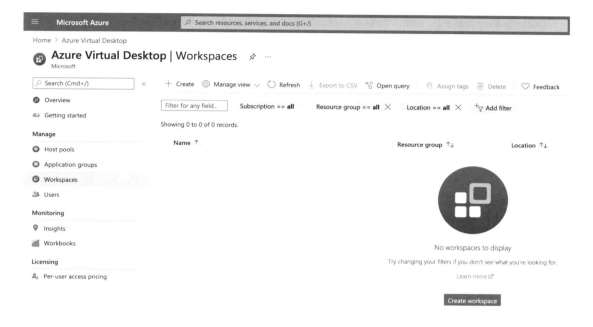

Figure 4-14. *Create workspace for AVD*

Step 3: On the Basics tab, Enter the Subscription and Resource Group

- Type your own (e.g., MYAVD) into the Workspace name box

- Type your own (e.g., Demo Pool) into the Friendly name box

- Type your own description into the Description name box

- Choose the Location

Step 4: Review + Create the workspace (see Figures 4-15 and 4-16).

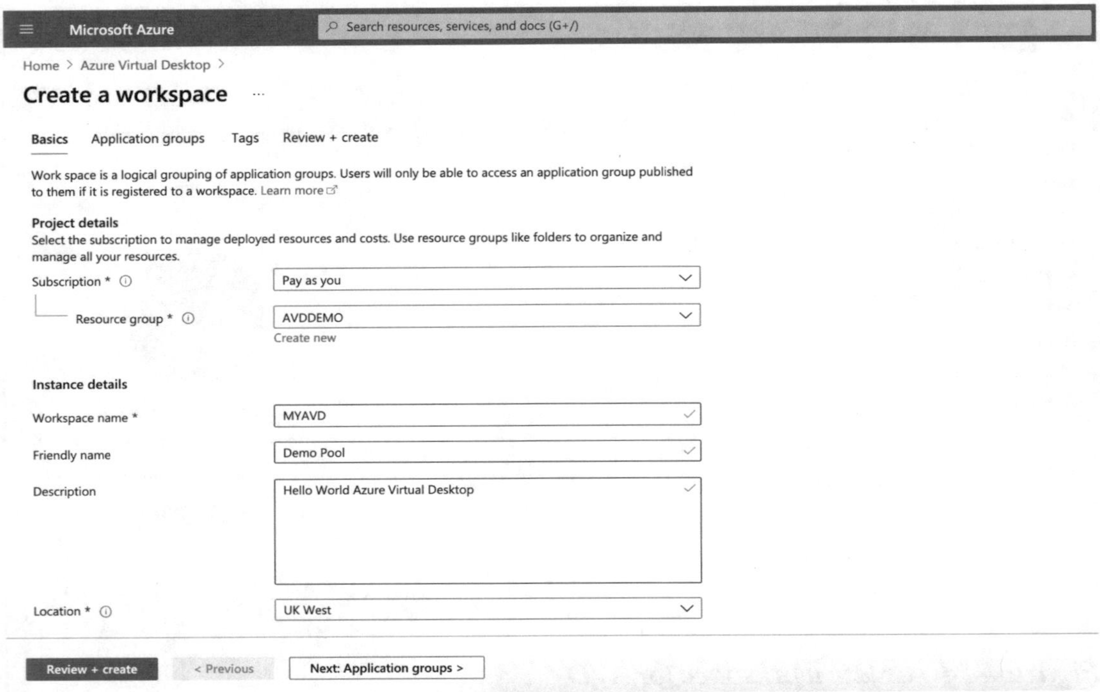

Figure 4-15. Create workspace for AVD

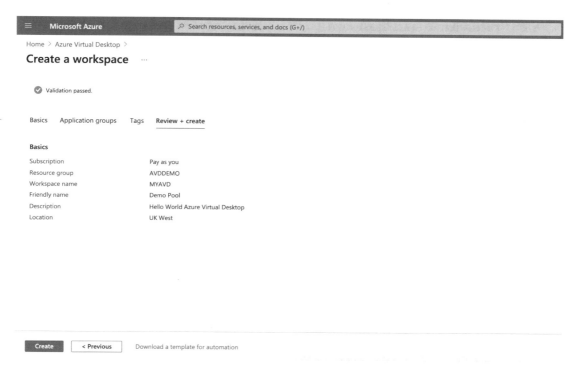

Figure 4-16. *Create workspace for AVD*

For the next step, let us explore how to set up the conditional access policy for AVD, and the following are prerequisites.

- Provide users with a license that includes Azure AD Premium P1 or P2.

- The group has users assigned to it from Azure AD.

- Set up MFA for every user in Azure

Step 1: Log in to personal or business account into Azure portal

- The following is the link: `https://portal.azure.com/`.

Step 2: Search and start the **Azure AD Conditional Access** services. See Figure 4-17.

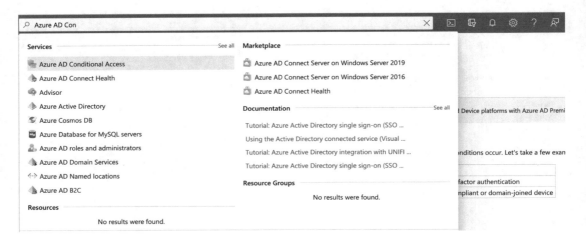

Figure 4-17. *Workflow for creating conditional access*

Step 3: Click the + **New policy** button,

- Give the conditional access policy a name; in this case, I will name it
  AVDDEMOLAB-MFA. See Figure 4-18.

Home > Conditional Access >

New   ...

Conditional Access policy

Control user access based on Conditional Access policy to bring signals together, to make decisions, and enforce organizational policies. Learn more

Control user access based on users and groups assignment for all users, specific groups of users, directory roles, or external guest users Learn more

Name *

AVDDEMOLAB

Include   Exclude

○ None

○ All users

◉ Select users and groups

Assignments

Users and groups ⓘ

Specific users included

☐ All guest and external users ⓘ

☐ Directory roles ⓘ

Cloud apps or actions ⓘ

1 app included

☑ Users and groups

Conditions ⓘ

0 conditions selected

Select

1 user

Figure 4-18. *Workflow for creating conditional access*

- Click under **Assignments** on **Users and groups** and choose the users or groups that you want to apply this policy. See Figure 4-18.

- Click **Done**

Step 4: Click on **Cloud apps or actions,**

- **Choose apps** and search and select the **Windows Virtual Desktop**.

- Click **Select** and **Done**.

  - In case you're using Windows Virtual Desktop (classic), choose these apps (see Figure 4-19):

    - Windows Virtual Desktop (App ID 5a0aa725-4958-4b0c-80a9-34562e23f3b7)

    - Windows Virtual Desktop Client (App ID fa4345a4-a730-4230-84a8-7d9651b86739)

  - In case you're using AVD, choose this app instead:

    - Azure Virtual Desktop (App ID 9cdead84-a844-4324-93f2-b2e6bb768d07)

Figure 4-19. *Workflow for creating conditional access*

Step 5: Click on Conditions **and select Client apps**.

- **In Configure, choose Yes, and then select where to apply the policy**:

    - Choose **Browser** if you want the policy to apply to the web client.

    - Choose **Mobile apps and desktop** clients if you need to use the policy for other clients (see Figure 4-20).

    - Click **Done**.

Figure 4-20. *Workflow for creating conditional access*

Step 6: Click on **Access Control**.

- Choose **Grant** and search and Select the **Requires multi-factor authentication**

- (Optional) **Require the device to be marked as compliant** (if you plan to make exceptions for managed and compliant devices). At the bottom of the page, select **Require one of the selected controls**.

- Click **Select** and **Done**. See Figure 4-21.

Figure 4-21. *Workflow for creating conditional access*

Step 7: Click on **Access Control** and **Session**

Set the sign-in frequency value according to the time between prompts, and then **select**. An hour after the last connection, for example, choosing the by the unit Hours, would require MFA. See Figure 4-22.

Figure 4-22. *Workflow for creating conditional access*

Step 8: Finally, **Enable Policy** setting to **On** and click **Create.** Once created, you confirm the policies exist. See Figure 4-23.

Figure 4-23. *Verification of successful deployment of conditional access*

By using the web client to log in to AVD through your browser, the client app 9cdead84-a844-4324-93f2-b2e6bb768d07 (AVD client) will appear in the log because the client app is linked internally to the server app ID. It is the standard app ID.

Your design widely recommends deploying conditional access to stay secure by applying the proper access controls in the right circumstances. However, one of the challenges with deploying a conditional access policy in deployment is limiting the impact on end users.

AVD administrators may now use the report-only mode for conditional access policies to evaluate the impact in their environment before enabling those policies with the release of report-only mode.

Azure AD log-in reports contain details about the authentication processes used by AVD end users when they request MFA and when conditional access policies are applied. Additionally, users registered for MFA can be reported using PowerShell and MFA Logs can be viewed from **Security blade ➤ MFA ➤ Activity report**. See Figure 4-24.

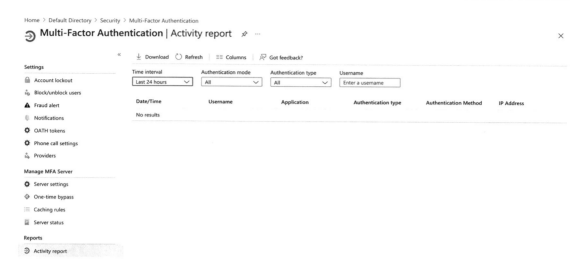

Figure 4-24. *MFA activity report*

Now, let us see collecting and examining audit logs for every end-user transaction. This section will discuss how securing user identities, collecting, and examining audit logs are essential too. With audit log collection enabled, your design and deployment gather and gain insights into AVD end-user and AVD administrator tasks related to AVD.

Log analytics workspaces are unique environments for analyzing Azure Monitor logs. There are specific data repositories, configurations, data sources, and solutions for storing data in a workspace. In your AVD design, you can collect data from any of the following sources

- Azure Activity Log

    - Activity logs provide insight into subscription-level events in Azure. A change in a resource or a login by a user is included in this information.

- Azure AD Activity Log

    - Azure AD activity logs are kept on several endpoints for long-term retention and data insights.

- AVD Session Hosts

    - Log analytics agent deployed on Windows server OS and Windows client OS

- AVD Diagnostic Log

    - In addition to monitoring and alerts, AVD makes use of Azure Monitor. It gives administrators an easy way to identify issues. Activities are logged both by users and by administrators.

- Key Vault Logs (Optional)

    - As soon as you've set up your key vaults, it would be prudent to monitor their access. Azure Key Vault creates a storage account in Azure for the information it saves, so enable the logging feature to do this.

You will need to deploy a log analytics workspace. The following are steps to configure before you see events in Azure conditional access.

Step 1: Log in to personal or business account into Azure portal

- The following is the link: `https://portal.azure.com/`.

Step 2: Search and Start the **Log Analytics Work** services. See Figure 4-25.

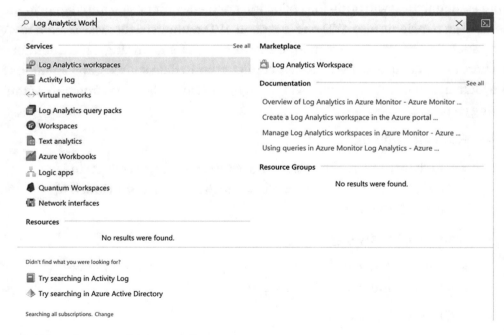

Figure 4-25. *Log analytics work*

Step 3: Search and start the **Log Analytics Work** services.

Select a **Subscription** from the drop-down list. If a **resource group** is already set up, you may choose to use it or **create a new one**. Create a new workspace for log analytics, name **AVDDEMOAL**. Per resource group, this name must be unique. Select an available **Region** and Click Next: **Pricing tier**. See Figure 4-26.

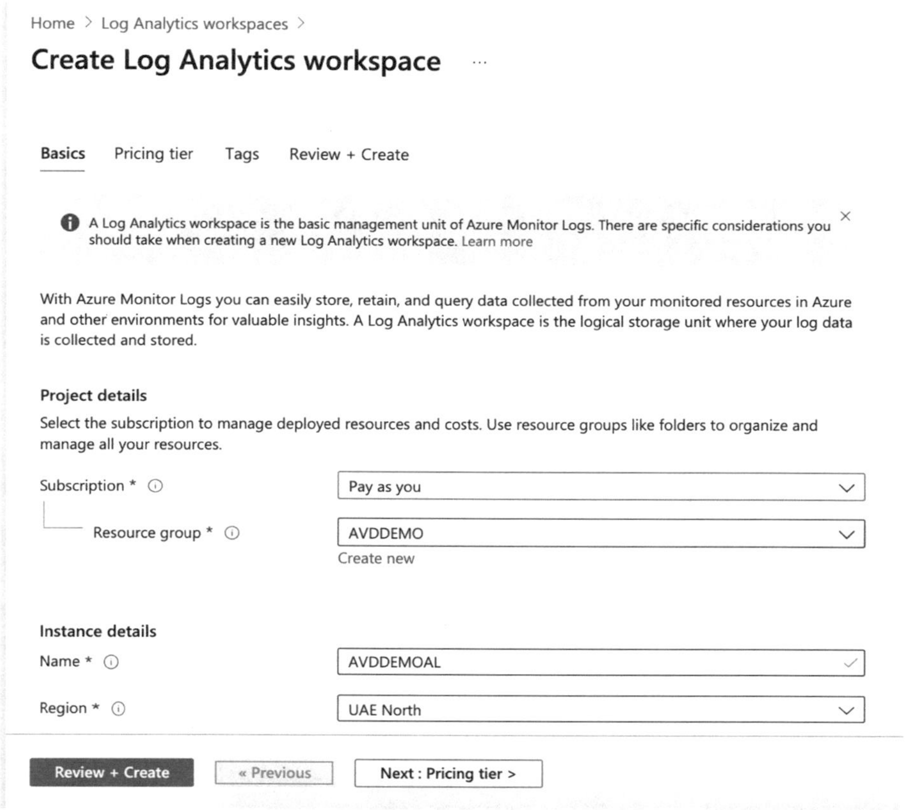

Home > Log Analytics workspaces >

Create Log Analytics workspace ...

Basics   Pricing tier   Tags   Review + Create

ⓘ A Log Analytics workspace is the basic management unit of Azure Monitor Logs. There are specific considerations you   ✕
should take when creating a new Log Analytics workspace. Learn more

With Azure Monitor Logs you can easily store, retain, and query data collected from your monitored resources in Azure and other environments for valuable insights. A Log Analytics workspace is the logical storage unit where your log data is collected and stored.

Project details

Select the subscription to manage deployed resources and costs. Use resource groups like folders to organize and manage all your resources.

Subscription * ⓘ

| Pay as you | ⌄ |

Resource group * ⓘ

| AVDDEMO | ⌄ |
Create new

Instance details

Name * ⓘ

| AVDDEMOAL | ✓ |

Region * ⓘ

| UAE North | ⌄ |

Review + Create   « Previous   Next : Pricing tier >

Figure 4-26. *Workflow for creating log analytics workspace*

Step 4: Click **Review + create** to review the settings and then **Create** to create the Log Analytics workspace. See Figure 4-27.

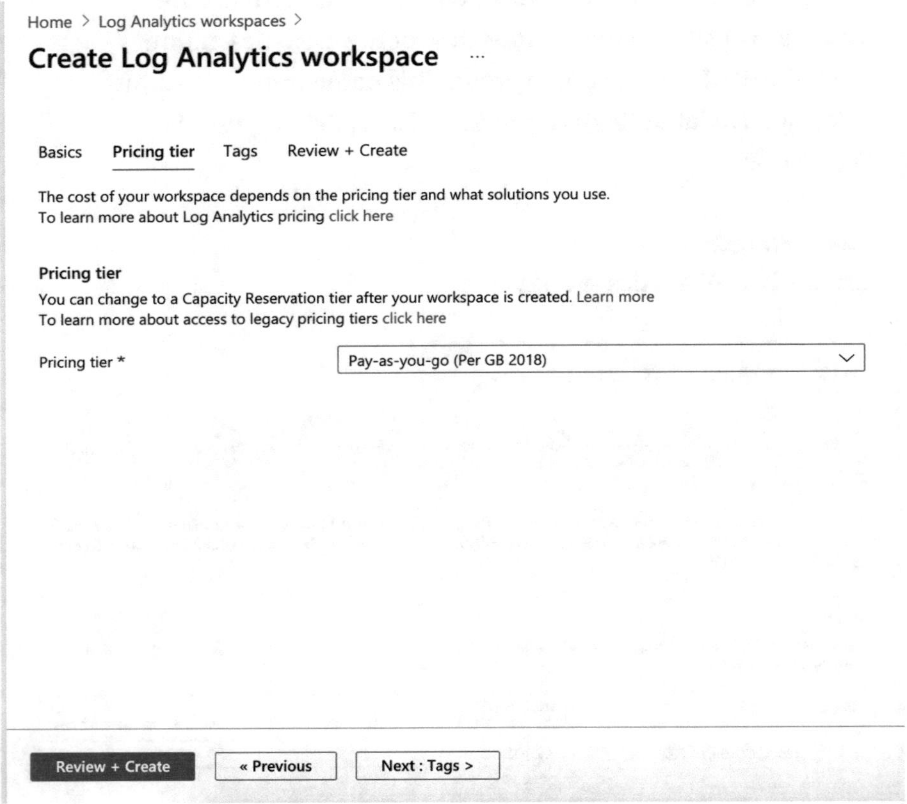

Figure 4-27. *Workflow for creating log analytics workspace*

Step 5: On **Default Directory**, go to **Diagnostic Setting and Enable Audit Logs, Sign in Logs**, and store in log analytics workspace. See Figure 4-28.

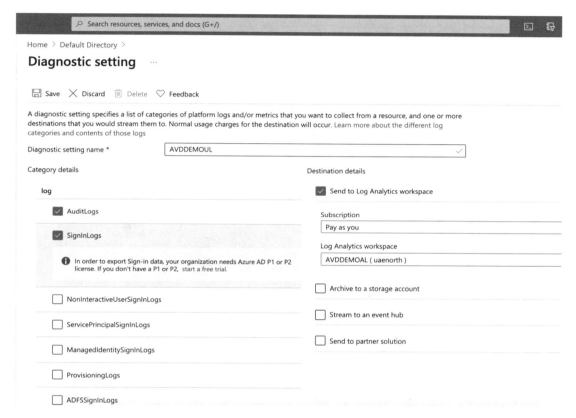

Figure 4-28. *Enable diagnostic settings*

Step 6: On **Conditional Access**, go to **Insights and Reporting**, which provides a dashboard with insight.

> In this downloadable dashboard, you can visualize how conditional access policies impact your AVD over time. Conditional access policies can apply during sign-in, granting access in certain circumstances or blocking access otherwise. See Figure 4-29.

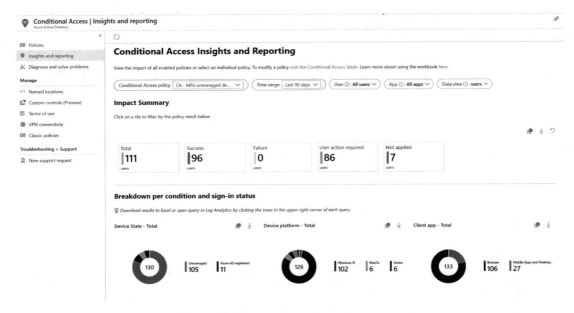

Figure 4-29. *Conditional access insights and reporting*

Additionally, you can search for a specific AVD user's logins located at the bottom of the dashboard. The most popular queries are shown on the left. Filtering the queries to the right happens when you select an AVD end user. See Figure 4-30.

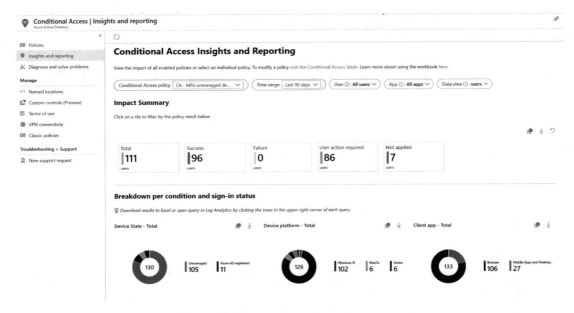

Figure 4-30. *AVD end-user events*

Building Block 2: Design of Control layer

The next building block of the AVD stack is the control layer. It is imperative to your design part of the AVD design process.

Control layer building block: AVD's control layer is the cloud-native system fully managed by Microsoft and helps to maintain the overall solution throughout its lifecycle. Connection broker and diagnostics are critical elements of the control layer. See Figure 4-31.

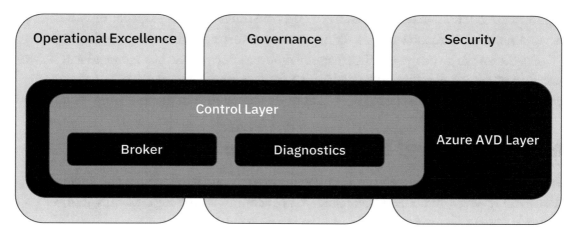

Figure 4-31. *Microsoft AVD control layer*

The control layer defines the Azure virtual architectural foundation, Azure infrastructure perquisites, management, and monitoring for AVD solution.

- **Connection Broker**: Clients can access remote desktops, client-hosted desktops, and server-hosted applications using a remote desktop connection broker. Connection brokers are used in Microsoft AVD environments to connect the desktops in Azure (hosted VMs, shared terminal servers, and blades) to the clients that access the desktops (thin clients, soft clients, and mobile devices, among others).

- **Diagnostics**: An AVD deployment is marked as successful or unsuccessful by remote desktop diagnostics based on the events associated with each action taken by the user or administrator. Administrators can use event aggregation to identify failing components.

The AVD control layers are resilient due to several features included in AVD services.

Microsoft fully manages AVD core infrastructure services. The control layer service will continue to operate even if there is

- Local corruption of data, metadata, and resources

- Outage in the availability zone within the Microsoft Azure region

- Regional outage

In the event of an unplanned failure, the access layer will fail over to multiple locations. It will help to ensure that the cloud consumer AVD access layer remains accessible. It is Microsoft's responsibility to restore service within the provided SLA.

So, the above gives the architect/organization a check in the box against PaaS service because Microsoft already fulfills platform, however management, monitoring, security components around PaaS being open. Let us do a deep dive in the following section.

Management and Monitoring the Control Layer

For end user and Enterprise AVD, more components need to be focused on such as Azure AD services, Azure AVD licensing, Azure Monitor, Azure log analytics, Azure Sentinel, third-party monitoring, and management solution.

Figure 4-32 depicts design components around the Azure AVD control layer.

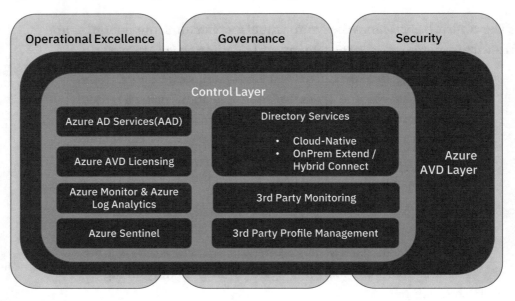

Figure 4-32. *Microsoft AVD control layer design components*

Microsoft Azure AD Services

The Azure AD service, developed by Microsoft, is a cloud-based identity and access management service that allows end users to log in and access AVD resources.

The deployment and management of AVD as an administrator and setting up desktops and applications require an Azure AD tenant. In terms of Microsoft cloud services (Office 365, and Azure hosted services), Azure AD is the highest-level object in the hierarchy. Each entity has a unique domain name associated with Azure AD: for example, myenterprisedomain.onmicrosoft.com.

Having an Azure AD tenant is an advantage if your enterprise is already using Microsoft Office 365. When an O365 administrator signs up for Office 365, an Azure AD tenant is created, and that is the tenant you need to deploy for AVD as well. You will need an Azure AD tenant global administrator account access for deployment and management.

Microsoft Azure AD is offered in four licensing types: Azure AD Free, Azure AD Premium P1, Azure AD Premium P2, and "Pay as you go" feature licenses.

Users and groups can manage their data, sync their directories, run basic reports, change their passwords for cloud users, or log in with just one login across Azure, Microsoft 365, and other popular cloud services.

In addition to Free's features, P1 allows hybrid users to access both on-premises and cloud resources. Additionally, it supports advanced administration features such as dynamic groups, self-service group management, Microsoft Identity Manager (an on-premises identity and access management suite), and cloud write-back capabilities, which allows you to reset your on-premises users' passwords online.

P2 offers many of the same features as Free and P1, plus Azure AD identity protection to provide risk-based conditional access to critical company data and privileged identity management to discover, restrict, and monitor administrators' access to resources, thus enabling just-in-time access.

Azure AD Services offers a variety of features for securing users' identities outside of AD and publishing applications. The following are some of the services to highlight for cloud-native deployment.

- **Application Proxy** makes it possible to publish internal web applications without publishing the website using public IP addresses. An Azure AD reverse connection is then used to access the websites.

- **Universal Print** – Publish and manage printers using the Azure AD service through Universal Print. The new universal print protocol or a Universal Print Connector can connect printers directly to Azure AD, so print servers are not required.

Microsoft Domain Controller

An AVD (RDSH Windows Servers OS and Windows Client OS) needs to be a domain member, so it must be connected, and required GPOs to be applied, especially computer policies, must be applied.

Microsoft offers three choices today, as follows, to achieve the previously specified demand.

- Domain controller (DC) deployed in VM running in Azure cloud a.k.a. Windows Server AD in Azure)

- DC as a service which is Azure AD Domain Services (DS)

- An existing on-premises DC with a site-to-site VPN from on-premises to the Azure VNET

The best design decision will depend on your existing enterprise deployment pattern.

Domain Controller Deployed in VM Running in Azure Cloud

A design and deployment of Microsoft AD will use the well-known AD users and computer, sites and services, domains and trusts, and group policy management tools on a traditional Windows Server machine.

The biggest pro of this approach is that if a VPN or ExpressRoute is used, it syncs with on-premises DCs. You can use any AD group policy you're familiar with. You can pause or stop VMs when necessary to reduce costs.

One of its cons is that VM and AD can be managed more easily in Azure; however, cloud consumer management involves higher costs.

Domain Controller as a Service Which Is Azure AD Domain

Your design can have Azure AD DS for the cloud-native enterprise because it is simple to deploy.

The Azure AD DS provide host-managed DS, including domain join, group policy, lightweight directory access (LDAP), and Kerberos / NTLM authentication. You do not have to deploy, manage, or patch DCs in the cloud.

Microsoft manages, monitors, and updates Azure AD DS in Azure with limited access for administrators. In addition, it is not dependent on a VPN for synchronization with the on-premises domain, and it does not require deployment and management of VMs.

Its biggest pro is that it is ideal for an enterprise that does not require on-premises connections, such as test environments. You will be able to manage your identities with Azure AD.

One of its cons is that there will always be an ongoing charge per month for AD DS.

An Existing On-Premises DC with a Site-to-Site VPN or Express Route from On-Premises to the Azure vNET

Cloud consumers' premises are connected to Azure through Azure VPN gateways. AD DS is commonly used to authenticate identities associated with users, computers, applications, or other resources in a security boundary. Directory and identity services are hosted in enterprise on-premises. Still, if your Enterprise application is hosted on-premises partly and partly in Azure, there may be latency sending authentication requests from Azure back to on-premises. Implementing directory and identity services in Azure can reduce this latency.

Regardless of which option you choose, they need to synchronize with Azure AD. For either of the DC options, your design and deployment should configure Azure AD Connect, whereas Azure AD DS synchronizes directly with Azure AD.

Its biggest pro is that no AD DS or DC runs in Azure.

One of its cons is that latency could be increased by adding delays during user authentication to VMs. This assumes your enterprise has an on-premises DC, not suitable for cloud-native tests.

Design Consideration for Azure AD

- Overall consideration should focus on three main areas: define identity requirements, plan for enterprise-wide data security through robust identity solution, and hybrid identity lifecycle

- If your deployment model is a cloud-native/greenfield deployment model, then you prefer this over Azure AD.

- Suppose your access layer design decision is enabled with a high level of security protection based on conditional access and MFA. In that case, Azure AD is to be licensed with P2.

Key Design Consideration

- Suppose your deployment model is a cloud-native from Azure deployment model; then you prefer this over Azure AD DS.

- Suppose your deployment model is a cloud-native from the Azure deployment model. You prefer this over Azure AD DS or Windows VM running in Azure enabled with DC role, depending on security and compliance requirements.

- Suppose your deployment model is a hybrid-cloud/disaster recovery from Azure deployment model; then you prefer this over Microsoft AD and integrate with AD.

  - The scalability consideration is to configure the VMs running AD DS with the correct size for the cloud consumer enterprise end user's workload requirements, monitor the workload on the VMs, and scale up or down as necessary.

  - The availability consideration is to add the AD DS VMs to an availability set. Depending on your requirements, you may choose to assign the standby operations master role to multiple servers. A standby operations master can replace the primary operations master's server with an active copy of the operations master during failover.

- Manageability considerations are to perform regular AD DS backups. The VHD files of DCs used are backed up via backup software. Never Create a Copy. Because database files on the VHD may not have the same consistency when copied, it is impossible to restart the database.

- Monitor consideration of the resources of the DC VMs and the AD DS Services and develop an action plan to correct any problems quickly.

- **AD forest design**: It includes keeping the AD forest and domain decisions, previously mentioned as multidomain, multiforest, domain and forest trusts, and others, which will define the users of the AVD resources.

- **AD site design**: It includes keeping the number of sites that represent your geographical locations, the number of DCs, the subnets that accommodate the IP addresses, site links for replication, and others.

- **AD organizational unit structure**: Designing the OU structure for easier administration of AVD pool. In multiforest deployment scenarios, having the same OU structure is critical.

- **AD user groups**: Here helps in determining the individual AVD end usernames or groups.

- **Group policy object (GPO) policy control**: Here helps prepare GPOs' ordering and sizing, inheritance, filtering, enforcement, preventing, and loopback processing for defeating the overall processing time on the AVD resource layer.

- **Naming standards**: Designing standard naming conventions for AVD AD objects includes users, security groups, AVD servers, and OUs.

Throughout this book, we will cover initial deployment for cloud-native deployment and hybrid connect deployment.

You can integrate Azure AD DS with an existing or newly created Azure AD tenant of your enterprise. By combining the AVD environment with enterprise credentials, users can sign in to AVD resources with groups and user accounts.

Following are prerequisites for cloud-native deployment.

- An active Azure subscription.

- An Azure AD tenant associated with an enterprise subscription.

- The Azure administrator needs global administrator privileges in enterprise Azure AD tenant to enable Azure AD DS.

- The Azure administrator needs a minimum of contributor privileges in enterprise Azure subscription to deploy the required Azure AD DS resources.

Next step, let us explore how to set up the cloud-native deployment for Azure AD DS. The following are prerequisites.

Step 1: Log in to personal or business account into Azure portal

- The following is the link: `https://portal.azure.com/`.

Step 2: Open Domain Services in the search bar, then pick Azure AD Domain Services from the exploration outlines. And on the Azure AD Domain Services page, select **Create**. See Figure 4-33.

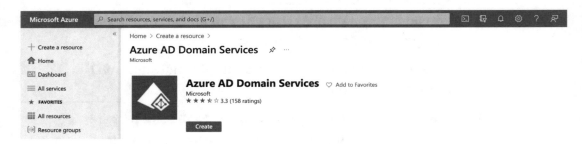

Figure 4-33. *Workflow of creating Microsoft AD DS*

Step 3: Choose the Azure **Subscription** to which you would like to deploy the managed domain and choose the **Resource group** to which the managed domain should belong. Choose to **Create a new** or choose an existing resource group. See Figure 4-34.

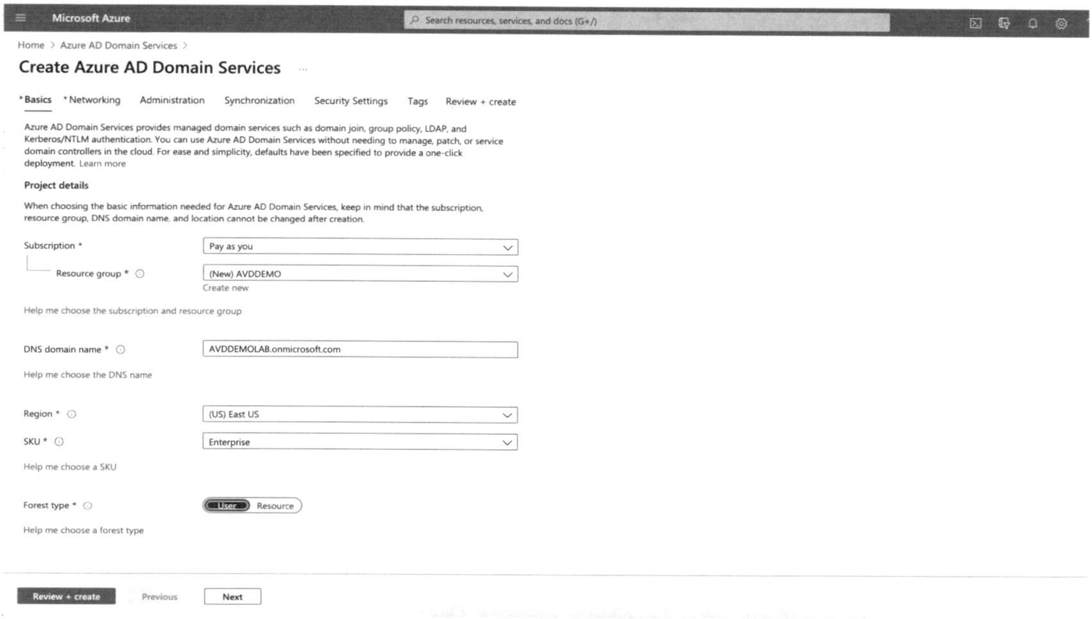

Figure 4-34. *Workflow of creating Microsoft AD DS*

Create a new domain name while keeping existing DNS namespaces in mind. According to Microsoft, all Azure or on-premises DNS namespaces should be separated by a domain name

Step 4: Deploy a virtual network named AVD-vNET that handles the IP address range of 10.0.2.0/24 and deploys a subnet named AVD-subnet using the IP address range of 10.0.2.0/24. See Figure 4-35.

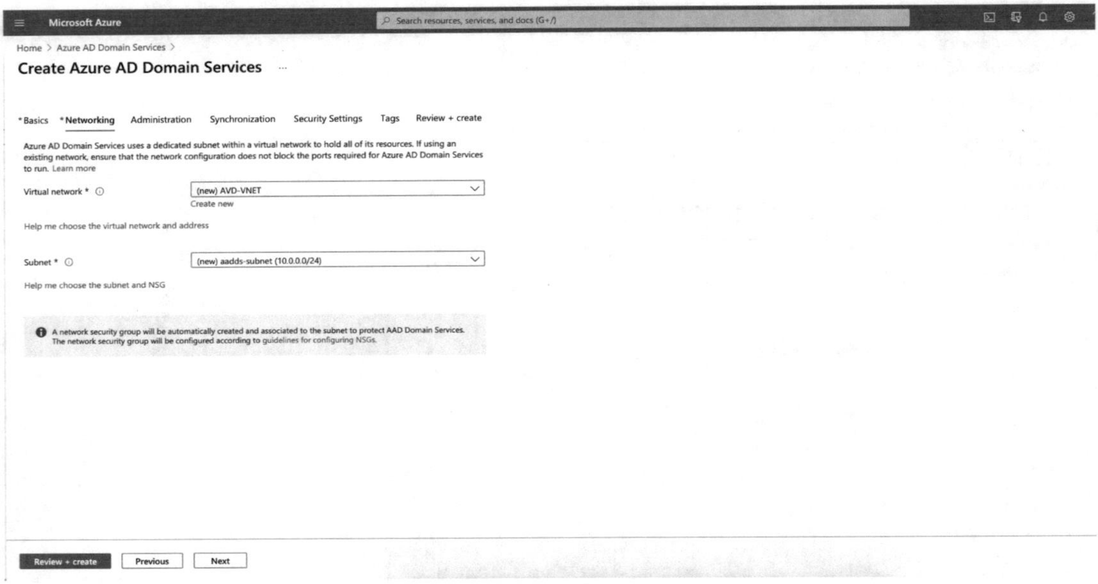

Figure 4-35. *Workflow of creating Microsoft AD DS*

Step 5: On the Administration tab, Choose the Global admin, Member of Azure AD DC, to notify and add additional email recipients if required. See Figure 4-36.

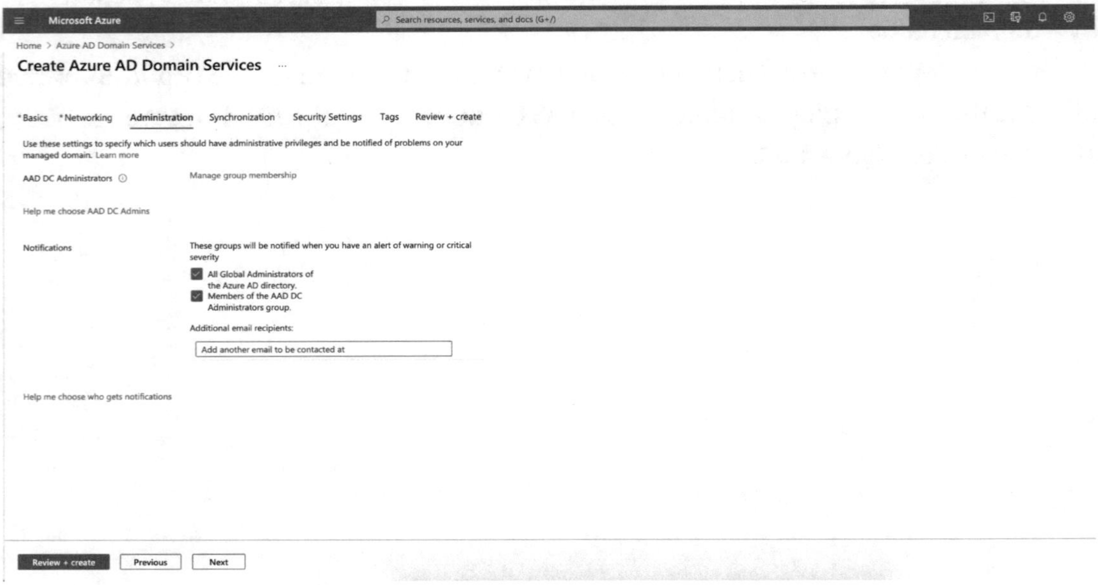

Figure 4-36. *Workflow of creating Microsoft AD DS*

Step 6: Toggle on Synchronizes All Users from Azure AD into the managed domain. See Figure 4-37.

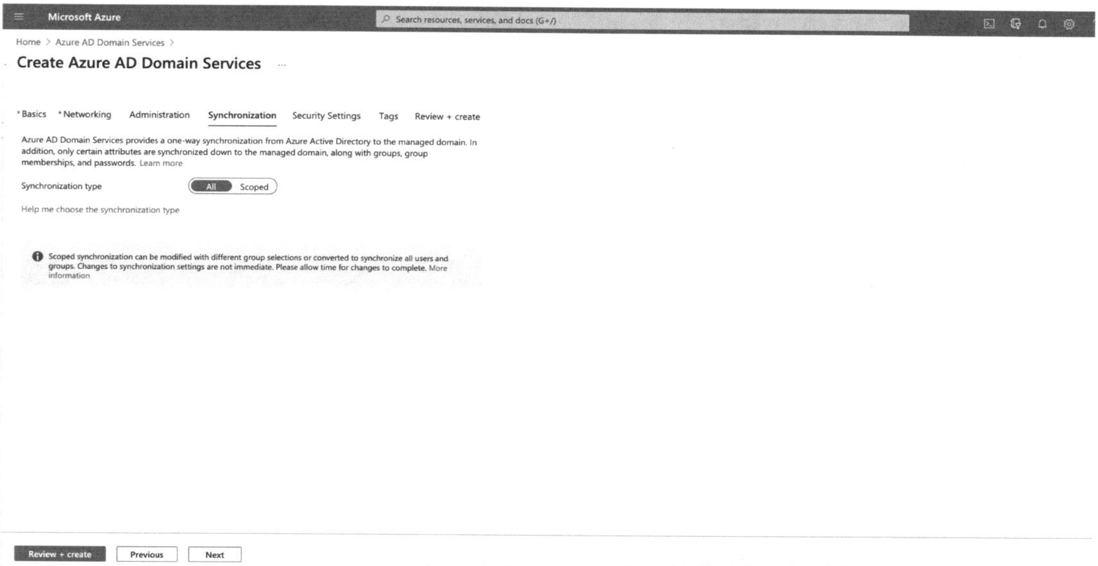

Figure 4-37. *Workflow of creating Microsoft AD DS*

Step 7: NTLM v1 and TLS v1 are the default ciphers available in Azure AD DS. Some legacy applications may require these ciphers, but they are considered weak and can be disabled if they are not needed. You can also disable the synchronization of NTLM password hashes if you use Azure AD Connect for on-premises hybrid connectivity to harden a managed domain by using settings such as:

- Disable NTLM v1 and TLS v1 ciphers

- Disable NTLM password hash synchronization

- Disable the ability to change passwords with RC4 encryption

- Enable Kerberos armoring

Toggle **Enable** or **Disable** for the following settings:

- **TLS 1.2 only mode**

- **NTLM v1 authentication**

- **NTLM Password synchronization from on-premises**

- **Password synchronization from on-premises**

- **Kerberos RC4 encryption**

- **Kerberos armoring**

The Security Audits feature for Azure AD DS stream security events to targeted resources (see Figure 4-38). These resources include Azure storage, Azure log analytics workspaces, or Azure event hub. After enabling security audit events, Azure AD DS sends all the audited events for the selected category to the targeted resource.

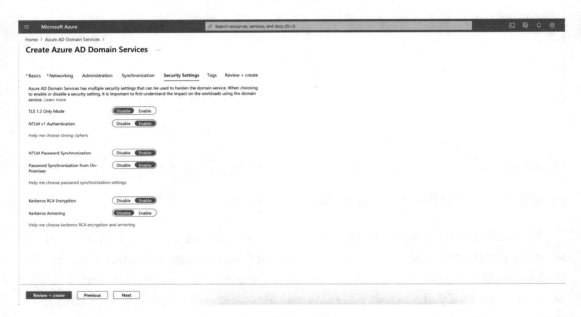

Figure 4-38. *Workflow of creating Microsoft AD DS*

Azure log analytics workspaces from the Azure portal allow users to manage and analyze their log data using Azure storage or your own SIEM software or Azure Sentinel by streaming events into Azure event hubs. You can also archive events into Azure storage and pour them into your own SIEM software or Azure Sentinel from the Azure portal.

Even though disabling NTLM password synchronization will improve security, many applications and services are not designed to function without it. For instance, using an IP address to connect to DNS management or RDP results in an "Access Denied" error. Imagine what happens if you remove NTLM password synchronization and your enterprise application doesn't work.

Step 8: Review and Create is the final setup, and Azure wizard automatically validates your AD DS configuration. See Figure 4-39.

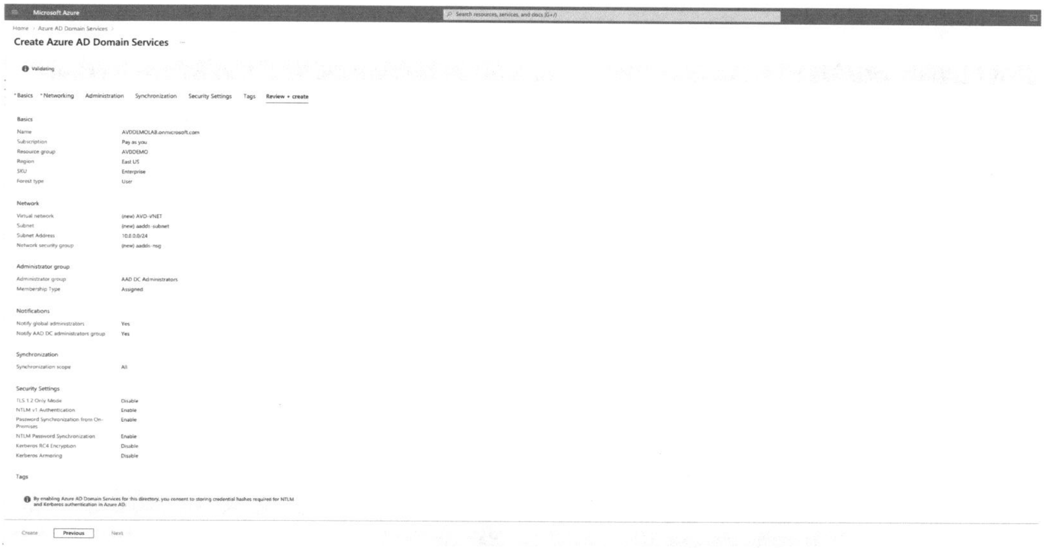

Figure 4-39. *Workflow of creating Microsoft AD DS*

Step 9: Once validation is completed, the Azure wizard automatically lets you review and create your AD DS configuration. See Figure 4-40.

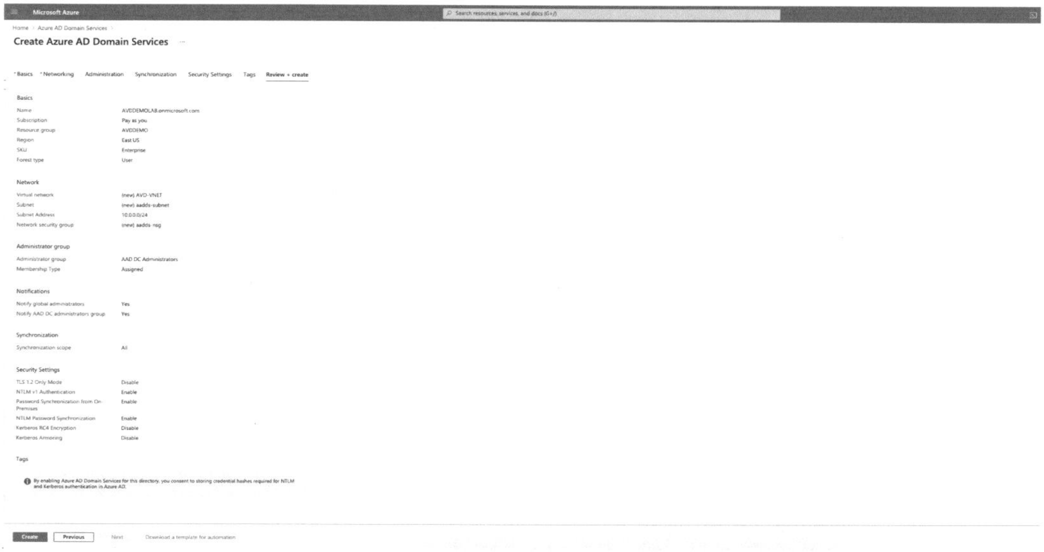

Figure 4-40. *Workflow of creating Microsoft AD DS*

Since cloud-native AD DS is deployed, now let us explore the method to deploy hybrid connect.

AD DS replicates into the Azure cloud for hybrid deployment models. Authentication requests are sent back from the Azure cloud to AD DS running on-premises. This deployment model is used to connect on-premises networks, and the Azure virtual network is connected via VPN or ExpressRoute connection. It supports bidirectional replication between on-premises and the Azure cloud, and both sources will be kept consistent.

- On-premises AD. Cloud consumers' local AD servers perform authentication and authorization for components located on-premises.

- AD servers. These are DCs implementing directory services (AD DS) running as VMs in the Azure cloud. These servers can provide authentication of components running in your Azure virtual network.

- AD subnet. The AD DS servers are deployed in an individual subnet. Network security group (NSG) rules provide a firewall to prevent traffic from unapproved sources on AD DS servers.

- Azure gateway and AD synchronization. The Azure gateway provides a connection between the on-premises network and the Azure vNET. It can be a VPN connection or Azure ExpressRoute. Synchronizing AD between on-premises and cloud servers is done through the gateway. On-premises traffic routing to Azure is handled by user-defined routes (UDRs).

Figure 4-41 depicts the deployment model of AD DS in an Azure virtual network.

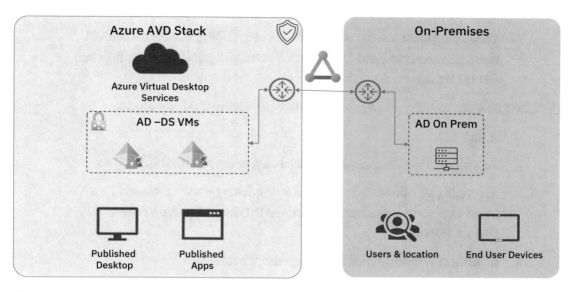

Figure 4-41. *Deployment model for Microsoft AD DS*

Key Design Consideration

Following are the Microsoft recommendations for deploying the DC role in the Microsoft Windows server VM running in your enterprise Azure environment.

- A minimum of two VMs running AD DS as DCs should be installed and configured.

- Do not assign operations masters roles to the DCs deployed in Azure.

- Create AD DS site, including the subnets defined for AVD or Enterprise application in Azure. Then, configure a site link between cloud consumer on-premises AD DS sites, and AD DS will automatically perform the most efficient database replication possible.

- Encryption of the AD DS database disk using BitLocker or Azure disk encryption should be considered when deploying security features.

- A good practice recommendation from Microsoft is to keep the database, logs, and sysvol folders separate from AD DS.

- To fully support the domain name service (DNS), configure the VM network interface Card (NIC) with a static private IP address for each AD DS server.

The following are the prerequisites for hybrid-connect deployment.

- Azure AD.

- Security-related technologies (firewalls, encryption, MFA).

- Managing Windows Server OS and Windows Server workloads in on-premises scenarios, including AD DS and Domain Name System (DNS).

- Common Windows Server management tools.

- Azure Core Microsoft compute, storage, networking, and virtualization technologies.

- On-premises resiliency Windows Server-based compute and storage technologies.

- Deploying and managing IaaS services in Microsoft Azure.

- Windows PowerShell scripting, third-party automation and monitoring.

An Azure VM can be configured as an AD DC in the same way as an on-premises DC. To avoid potential database corruption when deploying an Azure DC, you must place the AD database on the data disk of the VM. In Azure, there are several options for implementing AD DS using the AD DS directory and identity. Corruption of a database might occur due to the read and write cache settings of the OS disk. The following tasks complete deployment of the Azure AD role.

- Deploy an Azure vNET with cross-premises connectivity

- Deploy a storage account

- Deploy a VM and assign an IP address

- Secure VM compute, storage, user, privilege identities, and objects

- Monitor VM compute, storage, user, privilege identities, and objects

- Install and configure the AD DS and DNS roles on an Azure VM.

  - Ensure your on-premises network resources are accessible via the site-to-site VPN connection or the ExpressRoute connection when you are logged into a VM.

  - You can add the AD DS role with Add Roles and Features, or you can use Windows PowerShell cmdlet.

  - Promote new DCs

- Deploy domain-joined AD Federation Services (ADFS) servers on the virtual network for SSO requirements.

- Update DNS to create the Fully Qualified Domain Name (FQDN) to point to the internal load balanced set's private (dynamic) IP address.

The following topics are not covered part of this book, since they are extensive topics.

- Setting up a site-to-site VPN connection from an on-premises location

- Setting up an Express route,

- Securing network traffic in Azure

- Designing the site topology

- Planning operations master role placement

Azure AD Connect can be utilized for sync purposes between on-premises AD and Azure AD to meet the needs of hybrid enterprise organizations. AVD requires Azure AD. Also needed is the synchronization of Windows Server AD with Azure AD. You can deploy Azure AD Connector on-premises to synchronize on-premises AD with Azure AD in a mixed environment. If you are using Azure AD DS (for hybrid or cloud enterprise), Azure AD DS and Azure AD will be synchronized by default.

Microsoft Azure AVD Licenses: Microsoft AVD pricing is calculated by three central building blocks

- AVD resources licensing

- Azure infrastructure

Figure 4-42 depicts the AVD license building blocks.

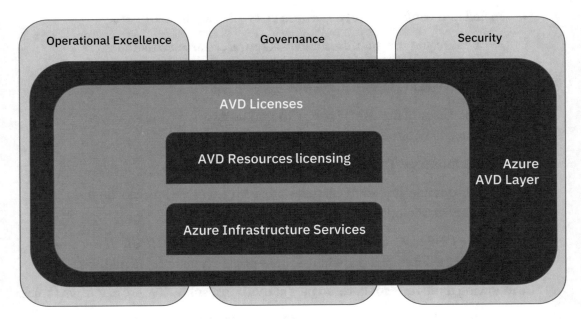

Figure 4-42. *AVD licensing and pricing elements*

Microsoft AVD Resources Licensing

In general, desktop OS have a much shorter lifecycle than server OS, so licenses are issued differently. It means that the license for each desktop might need to be activated every day if one user uses a different desktop every day. AVD resources licensing are available for the following two client OS deployment models.

- Pooled Stateless Desktops / Pooled Random Desktops: Virtual desktops dynamically assigned to users. When AVD end users log off, the desktop becomes free for another user to consume. When rebooted, any changes made to the desktop's personalization and profiles are discarded.

- Private Persistent Desktops / Dedicated Desktops: Virtual desktops statically assigned to respective users. When an AVD user logs off, only the given user can access the desktop, regardless of the desktop is rebooted. During reboots, any changes made will persist across subsequent restarts.

Enterprises will need qualifying licenses or subscriptions per end user to connect to Azure Windows virtual desktop. A valid license allows you to install Windows 7 as well as Windows 10 and 11.

This access is available if you have one of the following per-user licenses for Windows 10/11 and Windows 7. You are eligible to use Windows 7 with AVD if your enterprise has one of these licenses.

- Microsoft 365 E3/E5

- Microsoft 365 A3/A5/Student Use Benefits

- Microsoft 365 F3

- Microsoft 365 Business Premium

- Windows 10 Enterprise E3/E5

- Windows 10 Education A3/A5

- Windows 10 VDA per user

Depending on the license cloud consumers hold today, your design can also use any eligible products the license covers on your design and deployment of AVDs.

AVD resources licensing is available for the following shared services deployment models.

Microsoft Windows 10 Enterprise multisession, formerly known as Windows 10 Enterprise for Virtual Desktops (EVD), allows you to host multiple concurrent interactive remote desktop sessions. Windows Server was the only server that could do this previously. The new feature will enable users to experience a familiar Windows 10 experience. At the same time, IT can take advantage of multisession licensing and use existing per-user Windows licensing instead of RDS Client Access Licenses (CALs).

Single sessions (personal desktops) are typically chosen for users who require administrative rights to modify the OS and want those changes to be retained if the VM is restarted and other users who run applications that are not compatible with multisession.

In addition to being able to connect to Windows client OS desktops hosted in Azure, the subscription license includes usage rights for AVD control plane.

Published Applications Only: Choose applications are delivered without full desktop accessibility. It is typically used when users only need limited access, such as with kiosks. These are individual published applications hosted in the AVD environment, where the users connect to the published application from their endpoint device.

For RDSH deployment model, you need consider in your design a named user/ device or concurrent user along with RDS CALs for each named user and Windows Server CALs for each named user. The critical difference between RDS CAL and Windows Server CAL is that RDS CAL lets users connect to RDSH, whereas Windows Server CAL lets users connect to any Windows Server.

Another option is to access RDSH AVD based on Windows Server rather than Windows client OS such as windows 7/10/11. If this is the Windows Server OS considered in your design, you need a license for Windows Server.

With a CAL for RDS, Microsoft RDS clients can access free desktops powered by Windows Server RDS.

Enterprises are eligible to access Windows Server 2012 R2 and Windows 8 desktops if they have a per-user or per-device RDS CAL license with a current Software Assurance (SA) subscription. Depending on the license you have, you can also use any eligible products the license covers on your virtual desktops. Any Microsoft 365 license grants access to the entire Office365 suite. However, Windows licenses do not and require additional licensing.

Microsoft AVD Infrastructure Pricing

An Azure account must manage AVD virtualization environments in addition to end-user access to AVD resources. Azure VM and storage costs account for the most significant portion of AVD costs. AVDs typically require the following Azure components.

- VM with CPU

- VM with GPU

    - Key performance indicators (KPIs) to factor are the following:

        - Clock speed at peak level

        - Clock speed at average level

        - RAM usage at peak level

        - RAM usage at average level

- Storage – OS Disk

- Storage – Data Disk

- Storage – Profile Disk

- Storage KPIs to factor are the following

  - Aggregated read IOPS

- Networking – Internal

- Networking – External

  - Network KPIs to factor are the following.

    - Networks receive rate at peak level

    - Networks receive rate at average peak level

    - Networks send rate at peak level

    - Networks send rate at average peak level

- Azure AD

- Azure Monitoring

- Azure Sentinel

- Microsoft O365 Enterprise apps

- Third-party monitoring

- Third-party profile management

- Cloud consumer end-user device cost

- Cloud consumer end-user device management cost

AVM infrastructure pricing is determined based on actual consumption. Costs include:

- The price of OS disks.

- The use of Azure files.

- The cost of running AVD RDSH session host VMs.

No usage, no charge following payment when you go with the cloud paradigm. VMs for session hosts are charged based on the Azure subscription level. Egress bandwidth, NAT gateway, VPNs, and firewalls typically come under these charges. Microsoft O365 Enterprise apps for shared computer activation are required for AVD based out of RDSH. There is shared computer activation for every Microsoft 365 package that includes Office Apps. However, Microsoft offers special pricing through Azure Reserved VM Instances and Azure Hybrid Benefits, where Enterprise can use discounts.

The number of named users, usage hours per month, and reserved discounts factor into AVD pricing as well. However, the AVD pricing calculator requires at least 100 users for the first example of budgetary pricing, regardless of the number of AVD users. The pricing calculator and sample scenarios determine the total usage hours to be conservative by default. Calculate the total usage hours based on the number of users and the type of VM.

The cost of licensing and an estimate are not always helpful in evaluating real-world scenarios. The TCO of AVD licensing can be better understood by exploring the following approach.

The following is the practical approach. Your Azure infrastructure relates directly to AVD solution quality attributes. Imagine you plan to increase personnel by 25%, and you would like to have AVD for 1000 users. Interoperability and scalability were not your priorities as an architect on such a relatively small project. You may face problems integrating the existing AVD systems with those that are newly provisioned as a result. Similarly, the system has difficulty handling pickup loads without compromising its overall performance. You end up spending more money to adjust the design for your rising technical demands.

The following is the conservative approach. The alternative would be to overestimate your AVD end-user growth and spend more on building upfront a too-complicated system.

Nevertheless, there is always a way to reduce risk. Based on our experience with the assessment phase, you prepared some recommendations that can help you reduce TCO, regardless of whether you are just starting or in midflight.

The following are the two portals to do pricing.

- https://azure.microsoft.com/en-us/pricing/details/
  virtual-desktop/

- https://azure.microsoft.com/en-us/pricing/calculator/

Designing a product is difficult, especially when it comes to sizing. What's the reason? It was a lot easier when most on-premises VDI was based on hosts with a lot of CPU power and RAM or non-uniform memory access (NUMA) and a shared storage device. Increasingly graphical OS and applications make sizing more challenging these days.

Consider a retail organization's scenario to host 1000 AVD end users in the Azure UAE-North region with the pooled system. Pooled VMs are those whose load-balancing algorithm is used to assign temporary VMs to users when they sign in. AVD retail end users are designated with a different VM whenever they log in. The use of a personal VM is comparable to having a dedicated physical computer for one user.

Assume that a retail organization wants the most cost-effective solution with multisession capabilities.

Multisession is when AVD retails multiple end users connect to the same RDSH Azure VM concurrently.

Consider an AVD end user working 12 PM to 9 PM, which is 9.00 hours, 20 days per month (i.e., 20 days * 9.00 hours = 180 hours), adding a contingency of 10%. This ends up at approximately 200 hours. During peak times of usage, the maximum percentage of all users will be connected at peak concurrency. During off-peak hours, the most considerable fraction of users will connect.

The next element to consider is VM for AVD. Microsoft Azure offers a variety of VM types that are optimized to satisfy various requirements. Machine types vary by the number of virtual CPUs (vCPUs), disk capacity, and memory size, offering multiple options to match any workload. The following are various categories of instance type.

- General-purpose VM sizes provide a balanced CPU-to-memory ratio. Ideal for testing and UAT.

- Compute-optimized VM sizes have a high CPU-to-memory ratio.

- Memory-optimized VM sizes offer a high memory-to-CPU ratio that is great for extensive workloads.

- VMs with GPUs can be configured with a single GPU, multiple GPUs, or fractional GPUs.

- Field programmable gate array (FPGA)-optimized VM sizes are specialized VMs available with single or multiple FPGAs.

- Storage-optimized VM sizes extend high disk throughput and I/O.

- High-performance series VMs are developed to offer leadership-class performance, scalability, and cost efficiency for various real-world HPC workloads.

A large selection of Azure instances is available, each providing different amounts of CPU, RAM, storage, and GPU. Our AVD end-user workloads cannot be scalably tested on all these Azure instances, resulting in different density numbers for our testing results. As part of your POC or extensive assessment phase, you can plan out the VM instance type to be adopted in your design.

Type	General purpose	Compute optimized	Memory optimized	GPU	Storage optimized	High performance compute
Sizes	B, Dsv3, Dv3, Dasv4, Dav4, DSv2, Dv2, Av2, DC, DCv2, Dv4, Dsv4, Ddv4, Ddsv4	F, Fs, Fsv2, FX	Esv3, Ev3, Easv4, Eav4, Ev4, Esv4, Edv4, Edsv4, Mv2, M, DSv2, Dv2	NC, NCv2, NCv3, NCasT4_v3, ND, NDv2, NV, NVv3, NVv4	Lsv2	HB, HBv2, HBv3, HC, H

Each Azure instance has a cost per hour. We need to divide this cost by the number of users the model supports from our scalability testing. It provides a detailed breakdown of the price per user per hour. D-Series and F-Series instance types are widely used in AVD deployments. There are times when D-Series instances are required for user workloads requiring additional memory and beyond what results in F-Series instances. F-Series instances are the most common in the field because they have faster processors perceived as a better user experience.

- RDSH Scale-up scenario chooses Standard_F16s_v2 VMs with remote apps published which were recognized to have the lowest $/user/hr cost compared to other instances. A standard DS5_v2 VM is also competitively priced compared to other instances.

- RDSH Scale-out scenario chooses Standard_F4_v2 and Standard_F8_v2 instances to support a lower user count; these instances provide greater flexibility in power management services due to smaller user containers. It allows machines to be more effectively deallocated to save costs on Pay-as-You-Go models. Also, scalability leads to smaller failure domains.

- Autoscale can run fewer instances to reduce costs. There are fewer user sessions in smaller samples than in more significant ones. Therefore, in smaller models, Autoscale puts machines into a drained state much faster because it takes less time for the last user session to be logged off.

- Standard_F2_v2 has the lowest dual-core cost and performs well with Windows 10 or Windows client OS.

As an architect, you must decide that your cloud consumer workload should assess the instance types with their workloads in all cases.

The next element is storage: Azure storage solutions are developed to deliver enterprise-grade durability. When creating disks, you have the option of selecting from three performance levels: premium SSD disks, standard SSD disks, and standard HDD disks. The disks can be either managed or unmanaged. As a default, managed disks do not have the same limitations as unmanaged disks. As with any compute, VMs in Azure make use of disk storage for OS, applications, and data. Azure VMs come with at least two disks - a Windows OS disk and a temporary disk. Additional data disks may also be attached to VMs as VHD files. Premium SSD is recommended for VM OS disk due to SLA (99.9%) and performance. The other choices, standard SSD or standard HDD, can be selected for non-mission-critical, low-performance scenarios.

Microsoft Intune is an optional service to manage AVD session hosts. However, golden images were used for most of the deployment types. AVD end users may also require additional services, such as extensive support, network connectivity, bandwidth, or hosting in alternative Azure regions. If an enterprise deploys Microsoft's FSLogix management for user profile storage, it will incur additional costs for housing this data. Naturally, the prices depend on the size of the user profiles. An enterprise that requires different virtual desktop applications should add the costs for databases, file servers, and other resources to the estimates.

Microsoft AVD Monitoring Services

A modern digital workplace solution is more than just traditional monitoring. Let us get started by understanding reliability-centric monitoring and altering: how to design and implement digital distribution in a sophisticated way.

AVD administrator/engineers need to focus on reliability and accelerate incident response to service level objectives (SLOs). AVD administrator/engineers need a more reliable way to monitor and react to end-user issues. With the ever-increasing complexity of AVD solutions, AVD administrator/engineers don't have sufficient time to examine all the telemetry data to find oddities manually.

Missed SLOs can impact the entire business. Adopting advanced monitoring design methodology gives AVD administrator/engineers the comfort they need by proactively discovering oddities in multicloud environments before these problems have time to snowball into more significant issues.

To resolve traditional complicated and scattered monitoring, manual management is done from different consoles. An intelligent mechanism must simplify IT integrations and manual control, and must stimulate and automate predicament resolution in a complex digital workplace era.

The AVD monitoring layer part of your design should prioritize predictability, proactivity, security posture, incident response, and operational efficiency. However, it's crucial to realize how quickly AVD administrators can obtain insights from the affluence of data collected in various manners, what details we can create to imagine, and how to automate tasks to be extra efficient and compassionate.

AVD golden signals determine what is needed for the AVD solution to be "reliable monitoring," containing practically all the erudition AVD administrator/engineers need to recognize what is working or not when you design. Build a design with benchmarks for each KPI showing when the AVD solution is reliable. AVD administrator/engineers monitoring solutions need to assure positive end-user experiences and that reliability has been achieved. While an AVD administrator/engineer team could always monitor more KPIs or logs across the AVD solution, the five golden signals are the fundamental, vital building blocks for efficient monitoring maneuvering. Golden signals are crucial for AVD administrator/engineer teams to monitor their AVD solution and identify predicaments.

Let us get started with understanding golden signals. There is no precise agreement, but golden signals are the peak of five main lists in the digital workplace world today: rate, errors, latency, saturation, and utilization. There are various metrics to observe.

Five signals need to be designed and defined well to produce happy user experiences for AVD administrator/engineers' digital workplace. IT monitoring solutions need to integrate well with observability. See Figure 4-43.

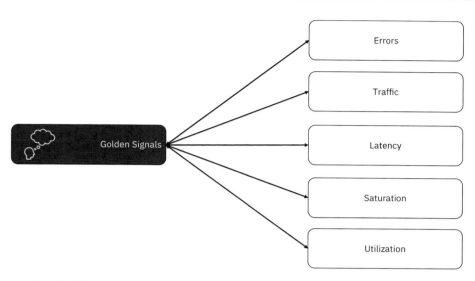

Figure 4-43. *Golden signals*

Errors: The time it takes for the error rate. It's important to distinguish between the priority of error and the reoccurrence of it.

The design thinking question is: How much impact will the end user experience in using the feature of AVD function.

Best metric followed: Type of errors, priority of errors, and end-user issues in milliseconds or custom metrics. AVD administrator/engineer teams need to watch the rate of errors resulting across the AVD solution and at the unique service level. These errors can be either AVD administrator/engineer-defined logic or explicit errors triggered by AVD function. AVD administrator/engineer teams need to monitor these errors constantly. It's also essential to determine which errors are high priority and which ones are low priority. It can help AVD administrator/engineers identify the proper health of service from an end-user perspective and take appropriate action to provide resolution.

Latency: The time it takes to service a request. It's important to distinguish between the latency of successful claims and the latency of failed requests.

The design thinking question is: How much traction can the system withhold at the given time when the end-user performs the transaction.

Best metric followed: Average time for response, queue, and wait time measured in milliseconds or custom metrics. AVD administrator/engineer teams can see precisely how the end-user experience is affected while consuming AVD solution.

Traffic: The network resource utilized fully. It's crucial to measure AVD solution undergoing any network resource constraints.

The design thinking question is: How is the network fulfilled with the request? It is better to define the threshold. Because the network degrades performance prior, it reaches 100% of its capabilities. So the AVD administrator/engineer team needs to define a KPI for a "Network Reliability" percentage of utilization. AVD administrator/engineers need to ensure that the network is reliable in terms of performance and availability for end users.

Saturation: The system resource utilized fully. It's crucial to measure AVD solution undergoing any system resource constraints.

The design thinking question is: How much is the system fulfilled with the request? It is better to define the threshold. Because the system degrades performance prior, it reaches 100% of its capabilities. So the AVD administrator/engineers team needs to define a KPI for a "Reliability" percentage of utilization. The level of saturation ensures that the AVD solution is reliable in terms of performance and availability for end users.

Utilization: The system resource utilized within its threshold. It's crucial to measure AVD solution undergoing any system, network, and storage resource constraints.

The design thinking question is: How much is system used to its capability and available to address the upcoming request? It is better to define the autoscaling capabilities whenever the resource on-demand needs. So the AVD administrator/engineer team needs to define a KPI for a "Capacity" percentage of utilization. The level of usage ensures that the AVD solution is available in terms of performance and availability for end users. AVD administrator/engineers' three essentials of components determine what it intends for the AVD solution to have "reliable observability."

AVD administrator/engineers can use these golden signals for alerting, capacity planning, and advanced troubleshooting.

- Smarter alerts are simplistic alerts originated from smarter metrics-based irregularities.

- More intelligent metrics take problematic behaviors and transform them into benefits.

- The transformation is made viable through operative and Boolean blends of various analytics functions using a powerful, expressive language.

Smart alerts let AVD administrator/engineers derive more significant insight into how AVD solutions are behaving. Signals can give AVD administrator/engineers more advanced notice when something improper arises. By jumping anomalies ahead of an outright failure, AVD administrator/engineers can ensure an excellent experience for their clients.

In extension to alerting, AVD administrator/engineers should visualize golden signals. Well-known solution works has a friendly format, with two graph columns, and the fundamental solution provider has a delightful view. The design should reflect something on the left of the console, a stacked graph of request & error rates, and latency graphs on the console's right. AVD administrator/engineers can also enrich KPIs with tags/events, such as deployments, autoscale events, restarts, and so on. AVD administrator/engineers should be able to add in a third mixed saturation and utilization graph, too. And ideally, all these metrics should be shown on a site architecture map.

The design should consider three essentials such as metrics, traces, and logs. Insightful metrics, traces, and logs are the three essentials of AVD administrator/ engineer observability. AVD administrator/engineers need more in one consolidated platform to enable maximum clarity beyond the AVD solution. See Figure 4-44.

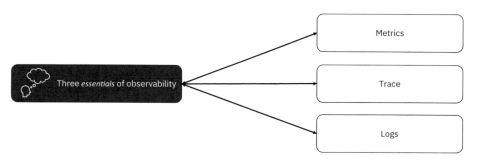

Figure 4-44. *Essentials of observability*

Monitor metrics, traces, and logs into a single glass of management. AVD administrator/engineers should have mechanisms to assemble and visualize KPIs and configure alerts for possible issues for acumen into the performance and reliability of the AVD solution. AVD administrator/engineers should continuously optimize infra and application performance with 360-degree visibility into original requests and code with spread extensive tracing. Finally, AVD administrator/engineers should be cost-efficiently debug, audit, and analyze logs from all AVD solutions such as key services, applications, platforms, and hybrid cloud infrastructure at scale.

Monitor, troubleshoot, and optimize in connection with three essentials of observability. AVD administrator/engineers should be able to pull in KPIs from cross-functional AVD solutions via dynamic and hybrid cloud infrastructures at least with time granularity to consolidate and visualize quintessential data about AVD solution. AVD administrator/ engineers need to use exceptional app analytics and mature evidence search capabilities to connect application performance data seamlessly. AVD administrator/engineers need to analyze, synthesize, parse, and contribute all logs into a readable log console and configure manageable ingestion rules to rank the records from critical AVD solutions.

In a nutshell, monitoring gives AVD administrator/engineers the clarity to manage SLO tasks, and logging provides AVD administrator/engineers with the clarity to support SLO with continued meaning. Microsoft Azure provides a complete monitoring platform and solution to monitor all AVD infrastructure and platform resources. It helps by collecting, analyzing, monitoring, and reporting all logs and telemetry from various resources. It supports being more operationally effective, efficient, secured, and proactive. The first component to consider is to enable out-of-box capabilities from a monitoring solution. It's essential to implement monitoring and observability in the AVD administrator/engineer's way. It will allow AVD administrator/engineers to develop reliable architecture around the monitoring tool rather than retrofit the existing or traditional monitoring solution. Monitoring tools should observe various classes of data feeds, following the breakdown of the most regular types of monitoring deployments.

Compute monitoring: VM monitoring or hybrid cloud infrastructure monitoring operates by gathering data on how VM is working. Resource monitoring tools report on vCPU, vRAM, vCPU load, and remaining disk space. In architecture with bare metal servers, information on hardware health like pCPU temperatures and component uptime can also help AVD administrator/engineers avoid bare metal servers failure.

Network monitoring: Network monitoring looks at the traffic coming in and out of your managed network. The AVD administrator/engineer monitoring tool captures all incoming requests and outgoing responses across all components such as switches, routers, firewalls, servers, load balancers, SDN WAN, and all other networking devices. The information gathered from network monitoring can be as easy as the total traffic coming in and going out.

AVD application performance monitoring: Application monitoring solutions collect data on how an overall application landscape is performing. These tools will send service requests to AVD solution and track metrics such as the response's completeness. The purpose is to accelerate the discovery and investigation of application performance effects to ensure that the AVD solution performs at expected levels.

Other third-party components being monitored: Monitoring third-party components such as security is a component in the overall AVD solution.

The fundamental method of implementing solutions beyond out-of-the-box product capabilities is to use the simulation method. Simulate end-user interaction with the AVD solution. The purpose of simulate is to detect disruptions before end-user impact. It helps AVD administrator/engineers to drive automated or manual rejoinders to decrease the effect. Simulation aids AVD administrator/engineers by providing clarity to disturbances to prevent disruptions or driving AVD administrator/engineers toward quicker recovery.

Simulation is not health assessment run by product on its own. A key difference is that simulation probes the AVD Solution from the end-user perspective. Whereas system health assessments are typically at a lower subsystem that works as expected, AVD administrator/engineers can say that simulation is a way to notify the AVD administrator/engineers' team that there is a predicament, and health assessments help AVD administrator/engineers close the predicament area. It helps to monitor SLO. Implementing data feed in the AVD administrator/engineers' way is critical. AVD administrator/engineers need to have that data presented in the most useful way, following some of the tips that will be useful while you get started.

Key Design Consideration

- Trigger alerts when KPIs surpass determined thresholds.

- Form logs of events, notify based on KPIs.

- Form graphs of KPIs for a specific time as historical time.

- Present a dashboard of crucial health assessment for all components and subcomponents of AVD solution.

- Deploy data warehouse to store and retrieve logs.

- Implement performance KPIs and develop benchmarks to monitor the AVD solution.

- Quickly identify any issues and ensure that a closed-loop support method is in place to resolve issues.

AVD uses Azure Monitor for monitoring and alerts like several other Azure services. It allows AVD administrators/engineers to classify problems through a single console. The service creates activity logs for both AV end-user and AVD system actions. Azure Monitor for AVD will provide a dashboard built on Azure Monitor Workbooks that gives AVD administrator/engineers access to the insides of your cloud consumer AVD environment. The components include connection diagnostics, connection performance, host diagnostics, host performance utilizations, users, clients, and alerts.

In the next step, let us explore how to set up the Azure monitor for AVD: the following are prerequisites.

- An AVD infrastructure and desktop pool are up and running

- Access privilege for deploying and configuring a log analytics workspace in Azure

  - Read access to the Azure subscriptions that hold your cloud consumer AVD resources

  - Read access to the subscription's resource groups that hold your cloud consumer AVD session hosts

  - Read access to the log analytics workspace.

Deploying Azure monitor is a three-phase process:

- Deploy a log analytics workspace

- Enable Windows virtual desktop monitoring

- Adding new VMs to the existing Azure Monitor

Phase 1: Deploy a log analytics workspace

1. Choose the log analytics workspace in the **Log Analytics workspace** parameter

2. Choose **Configure Workspace**

3. Choose **Deploy**. After the deployment is finished, refresh the workbook by choosing the refresh button on the top.

Phase 2: Enable Windows virtual desktop monitoring

1. Choose the log analytics workspace in the **Log Analytics workspace** parameter

2. Choose **Configure Host Pool**

    1. Open the **Insights** tab and

    2. Choose the **Host Pool** which you want to enable monitoring.

    3. Click **Open Configuration Workbook**. The following KPIs are to be enabled by default.

        1. Checkpoint

        2. Error

        3. Management

        4. Connection

        5. HostRegistration

        6. AgentHealthStatus

    4. Against Resources diagnostic settings page, choose the just-created log analytics workspace and click Configure host pool.

3. Choose **Deploy**. After the deployment is finished, refresh the workbook by choosing the Refresh button on the top.

4. After the deployment, open the **Session host data settings** tab and choose the **Log Analytics Workspace** again, which will connect the VMs from the host pool with the log analytics workspace. Click **Add hosts to workspace** and then click Deploy.

5. Configure the workspace performance counter; under **Workspace performance counters** in the configuration workbook, verify **Configured counters** to see the counters the AVD administrators have already been able to send to the log analytics workspace.

6. Configure events logs. Under **Windows Event Logs configuration**, verify **Configured Event Logs** to see the event logs.

7. If the AVD administrator is missing Windows event logs, select Configure Events and choose Deploy.

8. If the AVD administrator is missing the performance counter, select Configure Performance Counter and Apply Config.

9. Refresh the configuration workbook to validate that Windows event logs are visible.

After this deployment, Azure Monitor is deployed for AVD. If the AVD administrator wants to monitor more host pools and workspaces, the AVD administrator needs to repeat the preceding process.

Phase 3: Adding new VMs to the existing Azure Monitor

Also, when the AVD administrator deploys a new session host VMs to AVD host pool after the AVD administrator has enabled the logging, the AVD administrator needs to add them to the log analytics workspace

1. A message will be displayed when the **Insights** tab after the AVD administrator has added new session host VMs. To add the new VMs, click **Configure workbook**.

2. Open the **Session host data settings** tab and click **Add hosts to a workspace** and then click **deploy**.

Microsoft Azure Sentinel for AVD

Security orchestration automated response (SOAR) and security information event management (SIEM) are two functions of Microsoft Azure Sentinel. In addition to providing alert detection, threat visibility, proactive hunting, and threat response, Azure Sentinel offers intelligent security analytics and threat intelligence across the enterprise. As attacks get more sophisticated, alert volumes increase, and resolution times extend, Azure Sentinel's birds-eye view alleviates the stress of the increasing volume of alerts in the enterprise.

At cloud scale, collect, analyze, and visualize data from any source, in any format, with any data format. Using decades of Microsoft security experience, AI lets AVD Security administrators instantly identify, investigate, and respond to real threats.

Azure Sentinel works in three different phases:

- Collect data at cloud scale beyond the enterprise, both on-premises and in multi clouds.

- Generate security alerts, which focus on what's crucial using analytics to build alerts.

- Apply or customize built-in playbooks to automate everyday tasks to reduce toil.

Especially for AVD, Azure Sentinel can ingest Windows event logs from your session hosts, Microsoft Defender for Endpoint alerts, and Windows Virtual Desktop diagnostics. The latter is an AVD service feature that logs information whenever someone is assigned an AVD role and uses the service.

Key Design Considerations

- Firstly, plan out the workspace we will use for log analytics. When setting up Azure Sentinel, you can create a new log analytics workspace or select an existing workspace for the first time.

- Determine the length of time you will want to store the data. It is set to 31 days by default. Although you can extend the workspace setting to two years, you can change this setting.

- Evaluate other security solutions you will be enabling adjacent to Azure Sentinel.

- Plan your security operation requirements such as who needs access and what level of access

- Follow your corporate-wide cloud security guidelines and policies.

- Use Azure policy to apply compliance for deploying and configuring log analytics for AVD VM extension.

- Be selective in deploying Azure monitoring solutions to manage ingestion costs.

In the next step, let us explore how to set up the Azure Sentinel for AVD.

Step 1: Log in to personal or business account into Azure portal

- The following is the link: `https://portal.azure.com/`.

Step 2: Search Azure Sentinel in Azure portal

Step 3: To start ingesting AVD data into Azure Sentinel, connect workplace into Azure Sentinel. See Figure 4-45.

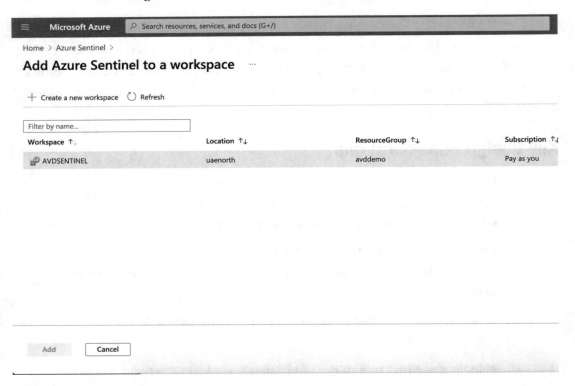

Figure 4-45. *Workflow for creating Azure Sentinel*

Step 4: Once a successful connection is established, run queries in Azure Sentinel against your cloud consumer log analytics data. Figure 4-46 depicts default built-in queries offered by Microsoft Sentinel.

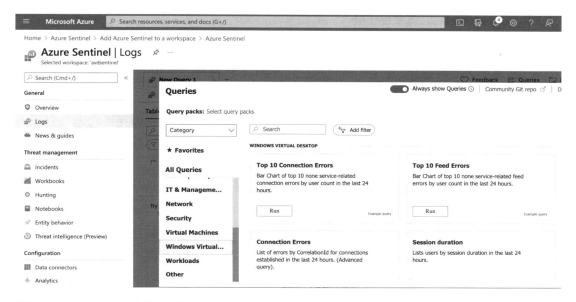

Figure 4-46. *Workflow for creating Azure Sentinel*

Microsoft AVD Monitoring Services via Third-Party Solution

Monitoring, diagnosing, and reporting capabilities are critical to AVD becoming the preferred method for providing digital workspaces. Monitoring can be done with Azure Monitor offered by Microsoft. However, setting up monitoring dashboards is time-consuming and not straightforward. If you have already worked on-prem VDI, then demand SLA, SLO, MTTR, and so on requires a lot more KPIs than offered by Azure Monitor specific to AVD. Operations teams need a simple-to-use, purpose-built monitoring, diagnosis, and analytics solution for AVD. The following are a couple of third-party solutions that exist for AVD on the marketplace today.

- ControlUp – `https://www.controlup.com/`

- uberAgent – `https://uberagent.com/`

- Goliath – `https://goliathtechnologies.com/`

- Ivanti AppSense Insight – `https://www.ivanti.com/products/insight`

- Liquidware Stratusphere UX – `https://www.liquidware.com/products/stratusphere-ux`

- eG Enterprise – `https://www.eginnovations.com/vdi-virtual-desktop-monitoring`

The following critical elements need to be factored into the design if you need extensive monitoring solution capabilities.

- The solution should be able to monitor, troubleshoot, and remediate issues in real time.

- The solution should monitor resource consumption and deliver valuable insights to optimize the AVD end-user experience and efficiently manage Azure VMs.

- The solution should be using synthetic and natural user monitoring, measure the effects of all user experience factors: logon time, application launch time, frame rate, connection bandwidth.

- The solution should provide visibility into the performance of virtual desktops, session hosts, host pools, endpoints, and the Azure cloud infrastructure and network connectivity.

- The solution should work with AIOps technologies, including automatic metrics baselines and intelligent dependency-based correlation rules, so that the AVD administrator can pinpoint the root cause of problems proactively and accurately.

- The solution should aim to increase ROI for the organization, and utilize analytics and insights to optimize the AVD infrastructure.

- The solution should aim to ensure continuous and historical data collection, infrastructure availability, and real-time analytics via multiple devices.

- The solution should aim to determine and resolve any potential issues with end users based on the infrastructure monitoring needs and growth of the network. As infrastructure monitoring needs to grow and develop, scale with them.

A minor change in an AVD image can negatively affect performance, leading to overloaded and unavailable production systems. It is challenging to locate where problems come from and impact end users when they occur with AVD workspaces. AVD is a new technology that can be challenging to adopt without a functional and nonfunctional performance testing toolset. The following critical elements need to be factored into the design if you need extensive functional and nonfunctional testing of your AVD solution capabilities.

- The solution should aim to offer insights into the performance of the application.

- The solution should aim to improve the AVD end-user experience.

- The solution should aim to predict the impact of the AVD solution.

- The solution should aim to provide end-to-end visibility of performance and availability.

- The solution should aim to provide end-to-end visibility of application and infrastructure load testing.

- The solution should aim to provide rich information vital for information security.

- The solution should protect AVD and end-user systems from malware, and detecting sophisticated attacks requires granular application and user activity data.

- The solution should aim to provide application licenses compliance monitoring.

- The solution should aim to provide capacity and sizing planning capabilities.

- The solution should aim to provide SLA compliance monitoring.

Building Block 3: Design of

A good VDI experience starts with a good perception. Users expect an experience like or better than that of a traditional, physical desktop. Codecs, transport protocols, and self-service capabilities affect the overall experience. Users experiencing poor graphics, lagging video, or logging on for 120 seconds can react negatively. Designing a user experience that meets any network challenge is essential.

The resource layer is the third building block of the Azure AVD Stack design methodology. The resource layer defines deployment models to consume AVDs and applications. This layer defines the components and configuration of the VMs assigned to and accessed by users. Sublayers include:

- Azure Virtual Apps and Desktop Delivery

- AVD App Management

- AVD Image Management

- AVD Profile Management

Figure 4-47 depicts the building blocks around the Azure AVD resource layer.

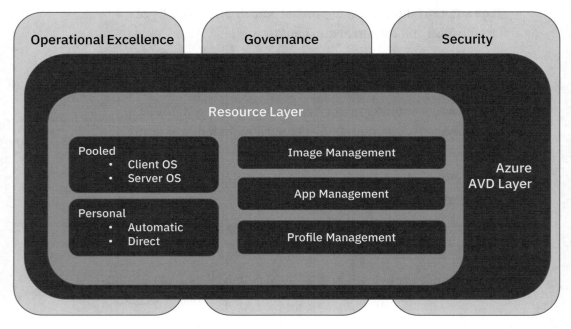

Figure 4-47. *Design elements of resource layer*

Host Pool Type

Remote app and remote desktop delivery methods are available with AVD. A single delivery system will likely not suffice for all your cloud consumer necessities. Determining the appropriate desktop and application delivery system helps increase reliability, scalability, administration, and user experience.

In AVD, session hosts (VMs) are gathered into a host pool. Host pools fall into two types as depicted in Figure 4-48.

238

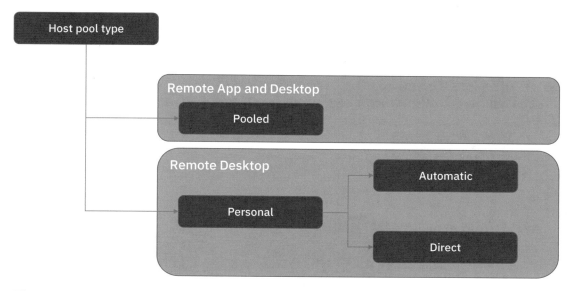

Figure 4-48. *Host pool type*

Type 1: Pooled host pool

Users share a VM on a pooled server. The pool model can run virtualized client Windows server OS in the Azure and offer them to users for multisession access. Pools are a group of more than one identical VM, also known as "session hosts," within AVD environments. Each host pool can contain an application group that AVD end users can interact with on a VM. The AVD agent registers session hosts on behalf of a pool of Azure VMs via the AVD agent. See Figure 4-49.

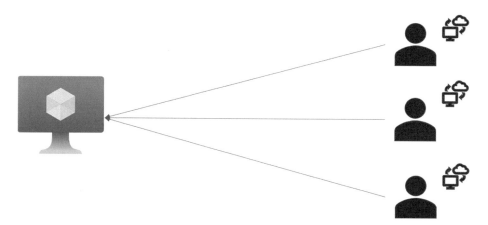

Figure 4-49. *Pooled host pool*

An AVD administrator can set additional properties on the host pool to change its load-balancing behavior. AVD holds two load-balancing schemes. Each process decides which session host will host an AVD end user's session when connecting to an AVD resource in a host pool.

The following load-balancing algorithms (see Figure 4-50) are possible in AVD:

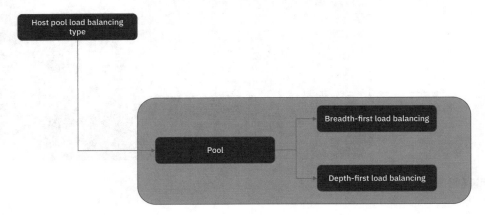

Figure 4-50. *Pool load balancing type*

Breadth-first load balancing assigns AVD end-user sessions against available session hosts in the host pool.

AVD administrators can optimize this scenario by distributing the users' AVD sessions through the breadth-first load-balancing method. This method is ideal for the enterprise that requires providing the most satisfying experience for digital workplace end users connecting to their pooled AVD. See Figure 4-51.

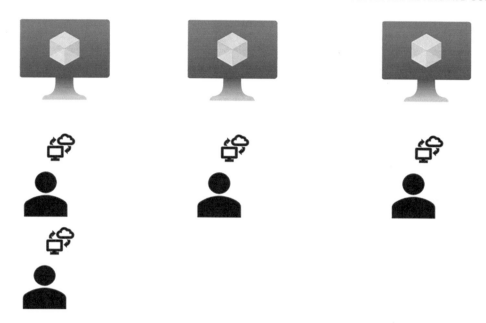

Figure 4-51. *Breadth-first*

Within each session, it looks for hosts that allow new connections. A random session host is selected from the remaining half of the session hosts with the least sessions. A new session won't automatically see the first machine if, for instance, an eight-session host has 15, 17, 19, 21, 23, 25, 27, and 29 sessions. Instead, it can go to any of the first five machines with the lowest number of sessions (15, 17, 19, 21, 23).

Depth-first load balancing assigns AVD end-user sessions to a usable session host with the most connections but which has not attained its most significant session threshold.

To optimize for such scenarios, use the depth-first load-balancing method. This method is ideal for enterprises that want more control over the number of VMs they allocate to a host pool. See Figure 4-52.

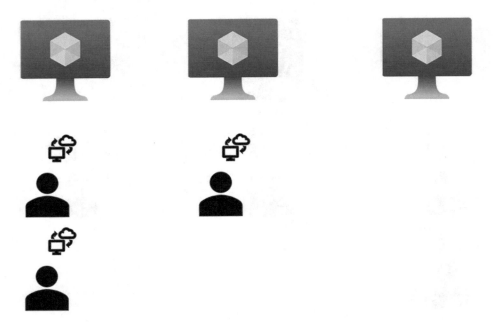

Figure 4-52. Depth-first

It queries hosts that permit new connections and do not exceed their session limit first. Next, the way chooses the session host that has the most sessions. It determines the session host based on the number of ties. For instance, an eight-session host has 17, 15, 21, 19, 23, 27, 25, and 29 sessions. Instead, it can go to directly into of the first machines with the lowest or highest sessions (17) provided 30 is set as the max threshold.

The most significant number of AVD end users have concurrent sessions on a session host. When setting a host pool to have depth-first load balancing, your deployment must decide the applicable max session limit as per your deployment arrangement and the capacity of the AVD. The load-balancing algorithm can be configured for each session host pool only in one way. Regardless of the host pool, both load-balancing methods have the following characteristics:

- Session Reconnect: Consider an AVD end user who already has a session in the session host pool and is reconnecting to that session. In that scenario, the load balancer will favorably redirect them to the session host with their existing session. This protocol implements even if that session host's AllowNewConnections property is configured to False.

- If a user doesn't already have a session in the session host pool, the load balancer won't consider session hosts whose AllowNewConnections property is configured during load balancing.

Applications groups allow AVD administrators to control which resources are made available to the system's end users.

A hosted shared desktop is a Windows desktop running on a remote desktop instead of a local PC. Multiple users can connect to the remote desktop to run the same applications. The Windows server can be accessed from Azure and accessed over the Internet or via the internal network. Because users will share the OS or underlying VM, one user's behavior will not affect the other users' performance. The computing resources of the hosted shared pool model are dedicated to the users. The following are sample use cases.

- Suppose your cloud consumer demands a solution cost-effectively. In that case, you can have inexpensive Windows, a server-based delivery model to minimize the cost of delivering applications to many AVD end users.

- Suppose your cloud consumer performs well-defined tasks and does not require personalization to applications and desktops. Users can include task workers such as call center operators and retail workers or users that share workstations.

This desktop delivery model lends itself to those users who require more flexibility, resource intensity, and compute power than should be offered. The following are key benefits of hosted shared desktop pool.

- Desktop and applications run on client OS in the Azure

- Many-to-one relationship: High volume of users can share one server

- Manageable and scalable model

- Cost benefits for increased user volumes

- Suited to users with predefined set of applications and limited personalization requirements

- Not suited to resource-intense applications

- AVD administrator manages hosted applications. AVD end users cannot add/remove/modify the application deployment type.

There are two subcategories under desktop delivery model:

- Remote Desktop a.k.a. Pooled Stateless Desktops / Pooled Random Desktops: Virtual desktops dynamically assigned to users. When AVD end users log off, the desktop becomes free for another user to consume. When rebooted, any changes made to the desktop's personalization and profiles are discarded.

- RemoteApp a.k.a. Published Application Pool: Enterprise can also deliver a published application to many users by creating application pools. The published applications in application pools run on a Azure host session share pool. An application group is a logical grouping of applications installed on session hosts in the host pool.

In your design, you can use multisession server OS machines to deliver remote apps and desktops via published apps and published desktops.

Type 2: Personal host pool

A personal host pool is where each user has their own dedicated VM. That pool is based on a single master image.

One-to-one mapping of a user to Windows client OS, either Windows 7 or Windows 10. You extend Windows 7 VM on AVD. The method to deploy a Windows 7 VM on AVD somewhat varies from that for VMs running latest versions of Windows. See Figure 4-53.

Figure 4-53. *Dedicated host pool*

The personal host pool further falls into two types: automatic and direct.

Automatic and Direct

He automatic and direct methods are Windows desktops running on remote desktops instead of a local PC. Single users can connect to the remote desktop to run the same applications. The Windows client OS can be accessed from Azure and accessed over the Internet or via the internal network. Because users will not share the OS or underlying VM, one user's behavior will not affect the other users' performance. The computing resources of the automatic and direct desktop are specific to the users.

- Automatic or Shared Stateless Desktops a.k.a. Nonpersistent: Virtual desktops dynamically assigned to users. When AVD end users log off, the desktop becomes free for another user to consume. When rebooted, any changes made to the desktop's personalization and profiles are discarded. In a nutshell, nonpersistent desktops are desktops that revert to a known good state at logoff or shutdown. When these desktops are reverted, any changes that were made are lost.

- Direct or Dedicated Stateful Desktops a.k.a. Persistent: Virtual desktops statically assigned to users. When AVD end users log off, the desktop is powered off. When rebooted, any changes made to the desktop's personalization and profiles are saved. In a nutshell, persistent desktops are desktops that retain their state when the user logs out or the desktop is shut down.

- Graphics Enabled: For the advanced use cases, your requirement may demand to allocate the pass-through GPU for both the cases.

Persistency can be a challenging conversation during the design phase, but it can essentially confidently impact your AVD design and deployment. In the cloud consumer's eyes, nonpersistency means not using a virtual desktop like their personal computer or corporate-owned devices. It includes deploying applications, changing their desktop wallpaper, filling their desktop with shortcuts, and so on.

The persistency requirement needs to be classified into the following categories.

- User personalization layer

  - Advanced user profile management

  - Application management

  - Application, user, device, and so on analysis and reporting

245

- Secure and context aware

- Application licenses compliance

- User application layering

  - User personal disk

  - User profile container

  - System application masking

  - Microsoft Office and O365 container

  - Client application version control (i.e., Java Runtime Environment)

The following are key benefits of shared and dedicated desktop pool.

- Virtual desktops run on servers in the Azure

- One-to-one relationship between users and OS instances

- Dedicated compute power per user

- Scalable model

- Cost benefits for increased user volumes

- Suited to resource-intense applications

- Suited to users who require more flexibility, including the ability to have more applications installed or with persistence requirements beyond the profile.

There are two subcategories under the desktop delivery model:

- Private Persistent Desktops / Dedicated Desktops: Virtual desktops that are statically assigned to respective users. When an AVD user logs off, only the given user can access the desktop, regardless of whether the desktop is rebooted. During reboots, any changes made will persist across subsequent restarts.

- Pooled Stateless Desktops / Pooled Random Desktops: Virtual desktops dynamically assigned to users. When AVD end users log off, the desktop becomes free for another user to consume. When rebooted, any changes made to the desktop's personalization and profiles are discarded.

In the next step, let us explore how to set up the Azure host pool for AVD, and the following are prerequisites.

AVD administrators need to enter the following configuration parameters to deploy a host pool:

- The VM image name (is the image from Azure Gallery or is it a custom image)?

- VM configuration

- Domain, domain joins credential's network properties

- AVD hosts pool properties

Step 1: Log in to personal or business account into Azure portal

- The following is the link: `https://portal.azure.com/`.

Step 2: Access **Azure Virtual Desktop** in the search bar, then locate and choose **Azure Virtual Desktop** under Services and in the **Azure Virtual Desktop** summary page, choose to **Create a host pool**. See Figure 4-54.

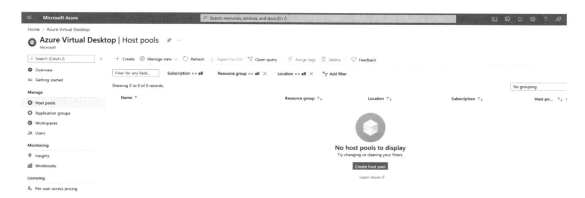

Figure 4-54. *Workflow of create a host pool*

Step 3: In the **Basics** tab, provide the following project details

1. Choose the exact subscription.

2. Register a unique title for your AVD host pool.

3. Choose the Azure region where the AVD objects are to be deployed. The metadata for the object will be in the geography associated with the territory.

4. The validation host pool allows your AVD instance for dev/UAT service changes before production is set up.

5. Choose host pool type, if your AVD administrator chooses the pooled (shared), AVD ends users will still access their personalization and user data using FSLogix.

   Under the host pool type, the AVD administrator chooses whether the host pool will be **Personal** or **Pooled**. If your AVD administrator determines **Personal**, they can select either **Automatic** or **Direct** in the Assignment Type field.

6. Choose load-balancing algorithm.

   • Breadth-first load balancing distributes AVD end-user sessions crosswise all possible session hosts in the host pool.

   • Depth-first load balancing distributes AVD user sessions to a possible session host with the most significant connections but has not relinquished its maximum session limit threshold.

7. Assuming that as an AVD administrator you chose Pooled to meet the requirement for remote host shared application or desktop, then enter the following information:

   Open the maximum number of users you want load-balanced to a single session host during the max session limit. See Figure 4-55.

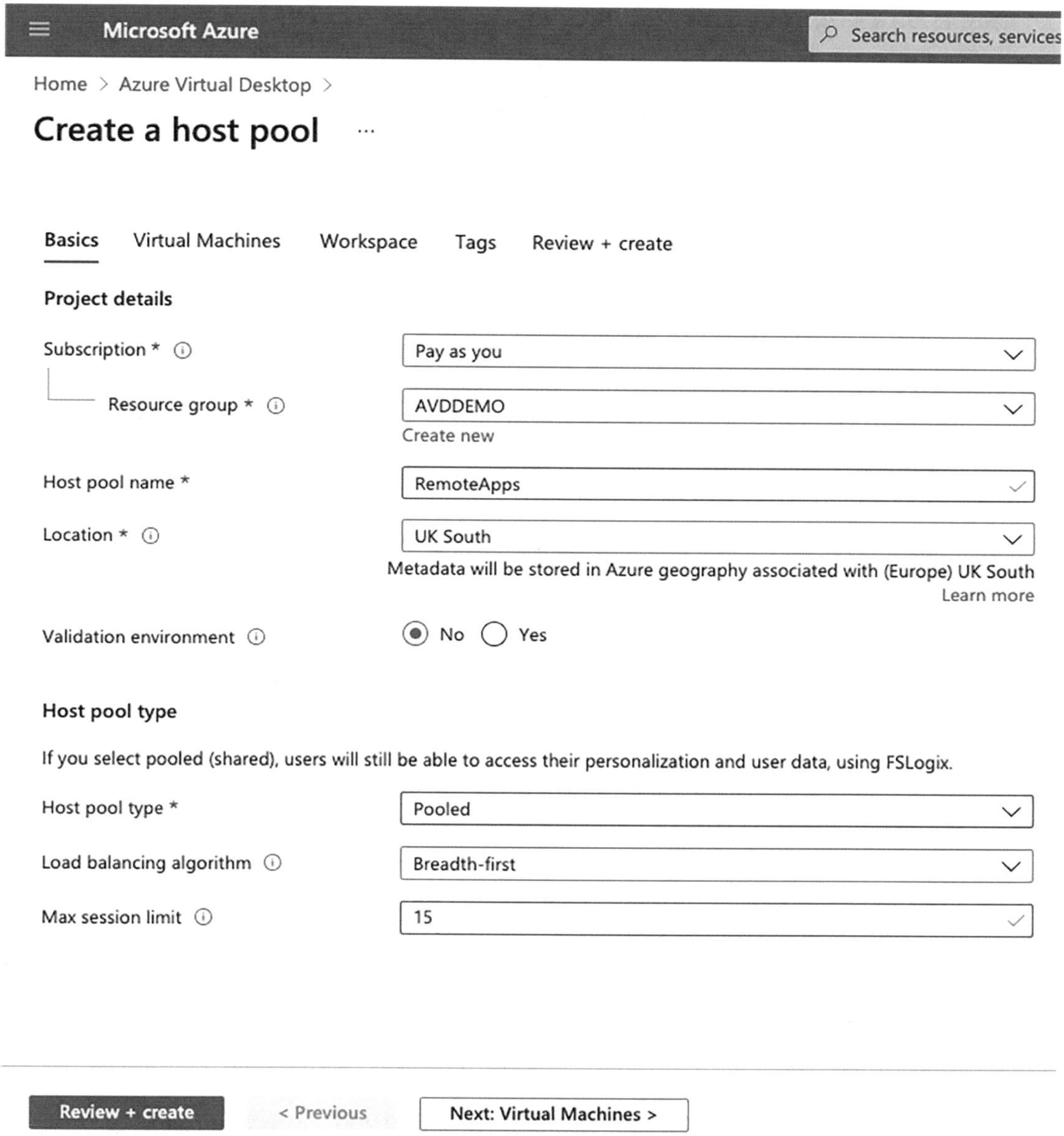

≡   **Microsoft Azure**   🔎 Search resources, services

Home > Azure Virtual Desktop >

Create a host pool   ⋯

Basics   Virtual Machines   Workspace   Tags   Review + create

Project details

Subscription * ⓘ

| Pay as you | ⌄ |

Resource group * ⓘ

| AVDDEMO | ⌄ |
Create new

Host pool name *

| RemoteApps | ✓ |

Location * ⓘ

| UK South | ⌄ |

Metadata will be stored in Azure geography associated with (Europe) UK South
Learn more

Validation environment ⓘ   ⦿ No ◯ Yes

Host pool type

If you select pooled (shared), users will still be able to access their personalization and user data, using FSLogix.

Host pool type *

| Pooled | ⌄ |

Load balancing algorithm ⓘ

| Breadth-first | ⌄ |

Max session limit ⓘ

| 15 | ✓ |

Review + create   < Previous   Next: Virtual Machines >

Figure 4-55. *Workflow of create a host pool*

Step 4: On **Virtual Machines** tab, provide the following VM details

1. Following **Resource group**, prefer the resource group where you want to deploy the AVD VMs. Keynote

2. The session hostname requirement is a unique name within the Azure resource group. Provide a **Name prefix** to name the VM the install process deploys. The suffix will be with numbers starting from 0.

3. Pick the **Virtual machine location** where you need to build the AVD VMs. The site can be the same or different from the Azure region you selected for the host pool. VM costs range by area, and the VM locations should be close to your AVD end user to maximize performance.

4. Next, determine the **Availability** advantage that best suits your requirements.

5. Next, prefer the image that is to be utilized to build the AVD VM. The AVD administrator can choose either **Gallery** or **Storage blob**.

For Pooled host pool: If you use Gallery, pick one of the prescribed golden images from the drop-down menu (the following images were available at the time of writing this book) and it is applicable to pooled:

- Windows 10 Enterprise multisession, Version 1909

- Windows 10 Enterprise multisession, Version 1909 (GEN2)

- Windows 10 Enterprise multisession, Version 1909 + Microsoft 365 Apps

- Windows 10 Enterprise multisession, Version 1909 + Microsoft 365 Apps (GEN2)

- Windows Server 2019 Datacenter

- Windows 10 Enterprise multisession, Version 2004

- Windows 10 Enterprise multisession, Version 2004 (GEN2)

- Windows 10 Enterprise multisession, Version 2004 + Microsoft 365 Apps

- Windows 10 Enterprise multisession, Version 2004 + Microsoft 365 Apps (GEN2)

- Windows 10 Enterprise multisession, Version 20H2

- Windows 10 Enterprise multisession, Version 20H2 (GEN2)

- Windows 10 Enterprise multisession, Version 20H2+ Microsoft 365 Apps

- Windows 10 Enterprise multisession, Version 20H2+ Microsoft 365 Apps (GEN2)

Windows 10 Multisession is a new remote desktop session host that allows multiple concurrent interactive sessions, formerly known as Windows 10 Enterprise for Virtual Desktops (EVD). In the old days, multisession was possible via Windows server. Using this capability, users can experience Windows 10 as if they were using it. Using Windows licensing instead of RDS CALs will allow the AVD administrator to benefit from multisession and save costs.

The virtual edition of Windows 10 Enterprise is known as Windows 10 Enterprise multisession. One of the differences is that Windows Server reports the ProductType value as 3, which is the same for this OS. By maintaining this compatibility, the OS keeps existing RDSH management tooling, low-level RDSH performance optimizations, and multisession-aware applications for RDSH platforms compatible. If they detect that the ProductType is Client, some application installers will prevent Windows 10 multisession installation. To install your application, contact the vendor of your application.

It's not currently feasible to upgrade an existing VM that's working Windows 10 Professional or Enterprise to Windows 10 Enterprise multisession.

As a result, Windows 10 Enterprise multisession cannot run on-premises in production environments since it is optimized for AVDs. There is no way to create Windows 10 Enterprise multisessions outside of Azure, according to Microsoft.

For Personal host pool: In case if you use Gallery, pick one of the prescribed golden images from the drop-down menu (following images were available at the time of writing this book) and it is applicable to personal direct and automatic.

- Windows 10 Enterprise, Version 1909

- Windows 10 Enterprise, Version 1909 (GEN2)

- Windows 10 Enterprise, Version 2004

- Windows 10 Enterprise, Version 2004 (GEN2)

- Windows 10 Enterprise, Version 20H2

- Windows 10 Enterprise, Version 20H2 (GEN2)

If you use **Storage Blob**, can build your golden image via a Hyper-V or Azure VM. It is simply a matter of entering an image's URL location in the storage blob.

1. Next, Select the **Virtual machine** size you want to use. You can either keep the default size as-is or choose Change size to adjust the size. If you choose Change size in the window that appears, pick the size of the Azure VM suitable for your workload.

2. Next, choose the **Number of VMs**, present the number of Azure AVD VMs you require to build for your host pool. (The configuration maximum is that the setup process creates a max of 400 at the time of writing this book.)

3. Choose OS disks you require your VMs to work with, such as standard SSD, premium SSD, or standard HDD.

   Microsoft recommends Azure managed disks for most VM configurations for best performance, reliability, scalability, and access control. Use unmanaged disks if you need to support classic scenarios or manage disk VHDs in your storage account.

   Standard SSD disks offer consistent performance at low IOPS levels and are a cost-effective storage option. With SSD disks, you can run high-throughput, low-latency applications, and production workloads. Standard HDDs are the best choice for TEST/UAT environments and less critical workloads.

You can use the boot diagnostics feature to troubleshoot boot crashes. Using pre-provisioned storage accounts operated by Microsoft to perform boot diagnostics significantly improves the making time of Azure AVD VMs. See Figure 4-56.

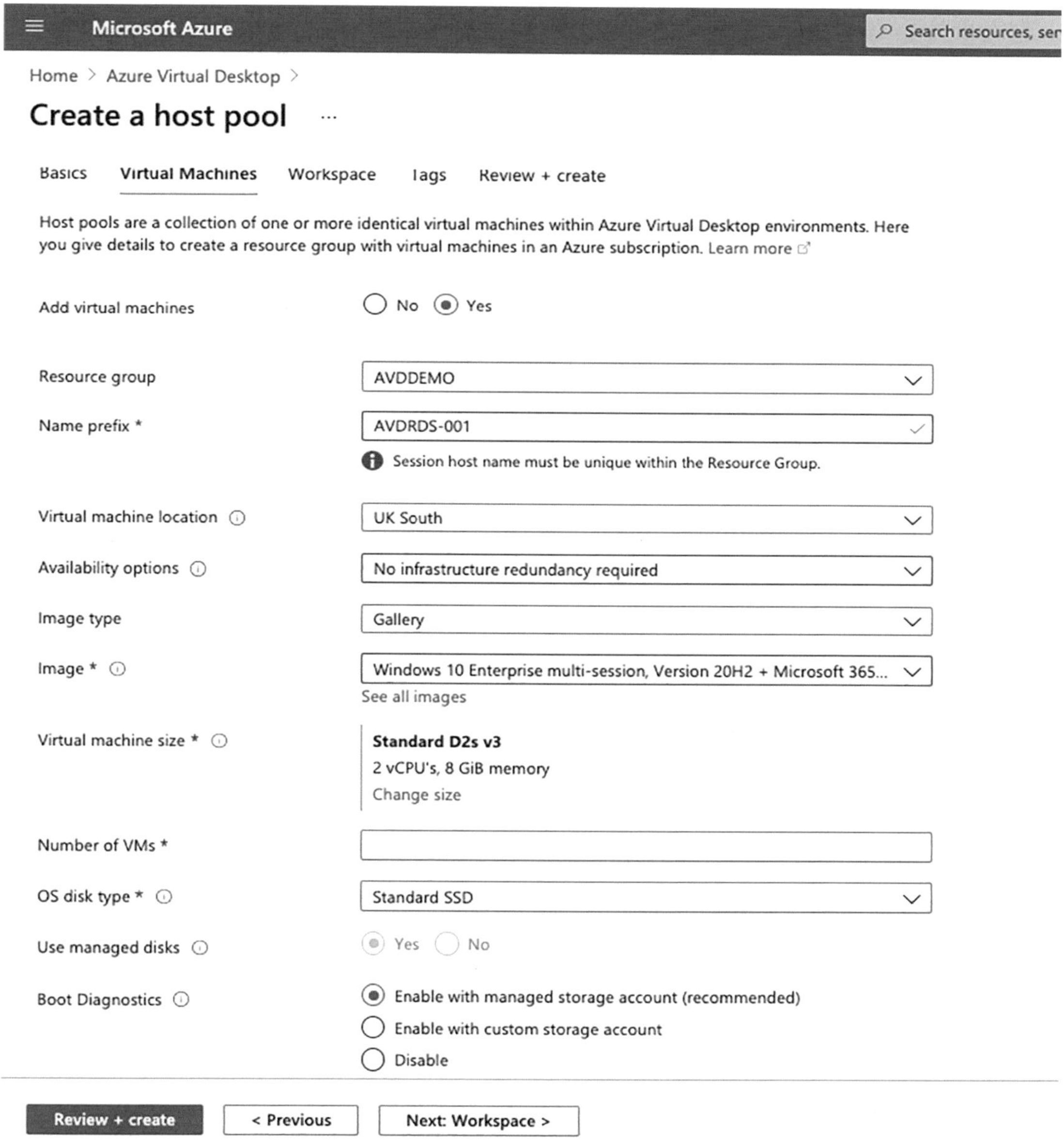

Figure 4-56. Workflow of create a host pool

Step 5: On **Virtual Machines** tab, provide the following networking details

1. Azure logically isolates its virtual networks. Like a traditional network in your data center, you can configure their IP address ranges, subnets, route tables, gateways, and security settings. A VM in a LAN can access other VMs automatically.

2. Choose the virtual network and subnet to place the VMs you create from the network and security section. As part of joining the VMs inside the virtual network, ensure that the virtual network can connect to the DC.

3. The DNS servers of the virtual network you decided on should be set up to use the IP of the DC.

4. Network security groups control which network traffic is allowed or denied from a VM. Microsoft recommends associating network security groups to individual subnets instead of separate network interfaces whenever possible to simplify the management of security rules.

5. Azure load balancing solutions and sources in the same network allow access to the AVD VM by default. The public Internet may use these ports, or you may choose to allow traffic through None.

6. Determine the type of security group you require: **Basic**, **Advanced**, or **None**.

7. Next, choose whether you require the AVD VMs to be joined to **Active Directory** or **Azure Active Directory**.

    If you use AD, present an AD account to join the domain and prefer to join a specific domain and OU.

    - For the AD domain join user principle name (UPN), enter the AD domain administrators of the virtual network you selected.

    - The account you use can't have MFA enabled. When joining an Azure AD DS domain, the account you use necessity be part of the Azure AD DC administrators AD group.

    - The account password must operate in Azure AD DS.

- To designate a domain, choose Yes, then subscribe to the domain's name you want to join.

- You can also attach a specific organizational unit you want the AVD VMs to enter the full path without quotes.

- If you don't want to designate a domain, choose No. The VMs will automatically join the domain that resembles the suffix of the AD domain enter UPN.

  If you use Azure AD, you can choose to Enroll the VM with Intune to make the VM prepared for management automatically. See Figure 4-57.

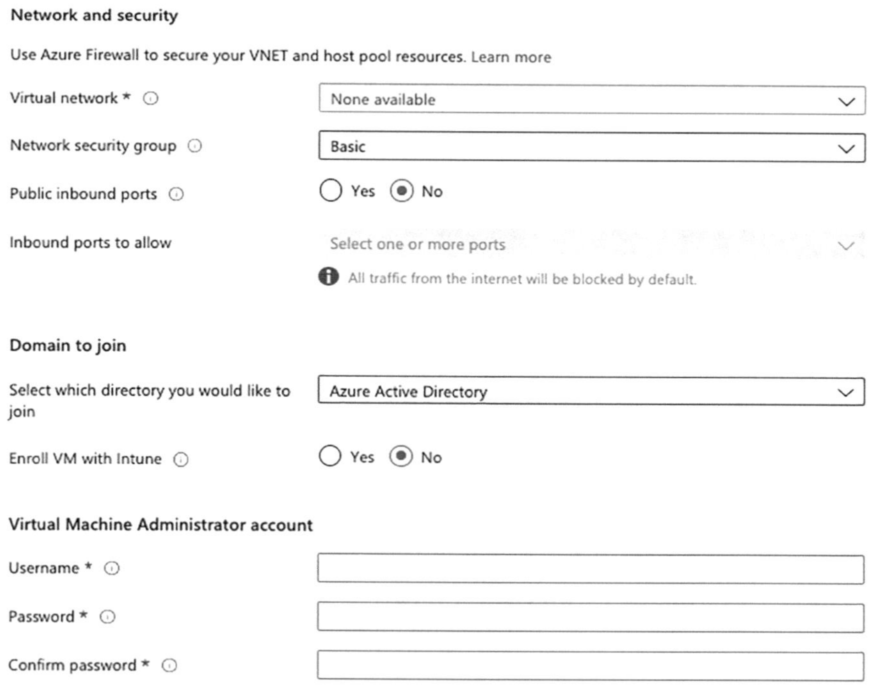

Network and security

Use Azure Firewall to secure your VNET and host pool resources. Learn more

| Virtual network * ⓘ | None available | ⌄ |

| Network security group ⓘ | Basic | ⌄ |

Public inbound ports ⓘ   ◯ Yes ⦿ No

Inbound ports to allow   Select one or more ports   ⌄

ⓘ All traffic from the internet will be blocked by default.

Domain to join

| Select which directory you would like to join | Azure Active Directory | ⌄ |

Enroll VM with Intune ⓘ   ◯ Yes ⦿ No

Virtual Machine Administrator account

Username * ⓘ

Password * ⓘ

Confirm password * ⓘ

Figure 4-57. *Workflow of create a host pool*

Enter the local administrator username for the AVD VM and the local administrator password for the VM.

During the setup process, each VM will have this local administrator. The AVD administrator can delete or disable the local admin, as well reset the password after initial AVD VM setup.

Step 6: On the **Workspace** tab, provide the following registration details to register the desktop app group to a workspace:

1. Choose **Yes**.

   If you select **No**, the AVD administrator can register the app group later. Still, Microsoft recommends that the AVD administrator gets the workspace registration done ASAP, so your host pool works appropriately.

2. Next, choose whether you require to set up a brand-new workspace or choose from already existing workspaces. Only workspaces designed in the exact location as the host pool will register the remote application group. See Figure 4-58.

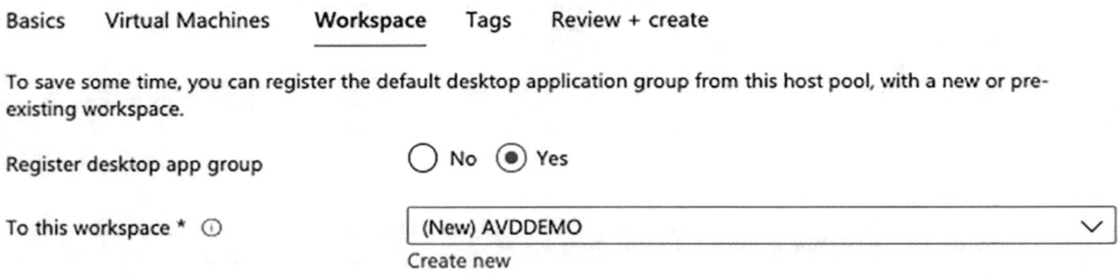

Basics   Virtual Machines   **Workspace**   Tags   Review + create

To save some time, you can register the default desktop application group from this host pool, with a new or pre-existing workspace.

Register desktop app group   ○ No ● Yes

To this workspace * ⓘ   (New) AVDDEMO ⌄
                                Create new

Figure 4-58. *Workflow of create a host pool*

Step 6: On the **Tags** tab, provide the following

- Optionally, the AVD administrator can select **Next: Tags >**.

- Here you can add tags to group the objects with metadata to make things easier for your admins.

Step 7: Finally, select **Review + create.**

Review the information about your install process to make sure all the provided information looks accurate. When finished, choose to **Create**. This kickstarts the deployment process.

Optionally, post deployment, if you want to add GPU, you can add it as VM extension for example.

- Choose your AVD VM size on the first deployment.

- Choose the extensions section within the VM panel and click Add.

- Nvidia GPU driver extension can be performed via azure portal, once the deployment is complete, and you will see the setup worked.

- Log on to AVD VM with the local administrator and verify that the driver is installed in programs & features and device manager. (After driver deployment, a reboot is required.)

- The next step is to Configure GPU-accelerated app rendering.

  - Navigate the tree to Computer Configuration ➤ Administrative Templates ➤ Windows Components ➤ Remote Desktop Services ➤ Remote Desktop Session Host ➤ Remote Session Environment.

  - Choose the policy Use hardware graphics adapters for all RDS sessions and set this policy to enable GPU rendering in the remote session.

  - For instance, choose the policy Prioritize H.264/AVC 444 Graphics mode for remote desktop connections and enable this policy to enable to force H.264/AVC 444 codec in the remote session.

  - Either perform a group policy update or reboot the machine.

- Validate GPU existence in your AVD machine via Task Manager.

- Verify GPU-accelerated application rendering via nvidia-smi for Azure VMs with an NVIDIA GPU.

With this now, let us focus on the image management layer of the resource layer.

AVD Image Management

The idea of image management is that you create a master image that contains all the necessary software and OS to deliver that image to numerous target AVD VMs. Using image management, AVD administrators can provide users with appropriate OS and a set of applications they need based on their requirements because reusability and simplified management are vital concepts.

A master image can be used a preconfigured template for all AVD end users. A master image is also called a golden image or base image. The AVD master image provides needed consistency and ease of deployment. A master image provides enterprise deployment with easy management of personal and pooled desktop experience or a remote app experience; the master image streamlines AVD deployment's build and BAU management.

The following are three of the main benefits of using a master image.

1. **Saves Time and Effort**

    Master images enable AVD administrators to deploy several remote desktops, remote applications, and VMs based on a single base image. As a result, they are all consistent whether you deploy 5, 10, or 1,000 session hosts.

2. **Reduces Errors**

    Microsoft AVD allows you to have a single instance image management of your host pool. Every update to a master image creates a new version of the vDisk, providing version control. Having versioned vDisks allows changes to be rolled back as quickly as they were rolled out. When the AVD administrator manually configures two or more session hosts with identical applications and patches, managing individuals' AVD VMs could cause errors.

3. **Ensures Consistency**

    In addition to saving time, master images can also ensure consistency by eliminating the need for repetitive configuration changes and performance tweaks.

Figure 4-59 depicts building block around Azure AVD resource layer – image management.

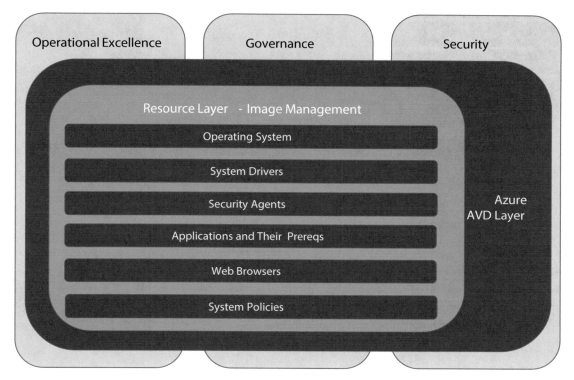

Figure 4-59. *Design elements of resource layer – image management*

Microsoft recommends AVD architects and administrators use an image from the Azure image gallery. However, if you as an AVD architect and administrator need to use a customized image, make sure you don't already have the AVD Agent installed on your VM.

Any virtual desktop failures can often be traced back to the golden image file, so you must be pristine with the golden image. Pay close attention to preinstalled applications, OS, security settings, and user access as you create a golden image. A virtual deployment of Azure begins with creating and distributing an Azure virtual disk image file that contains the VM, its OS, apps, preferences, and other settings. AVD images are built by first deciding what kinds of images you need in your design.

All session hosts in a collection need to be at the same level for the host session pool, but you can have multiple groups. You can have a group of Microsoft Windows Server 2016 session and Microsoft Windows Server 2019 session hosts. If your AVD administrator plans to upgrade your RD session host to Windows Server 2019, upgrade the license server. See Figure 4-60.

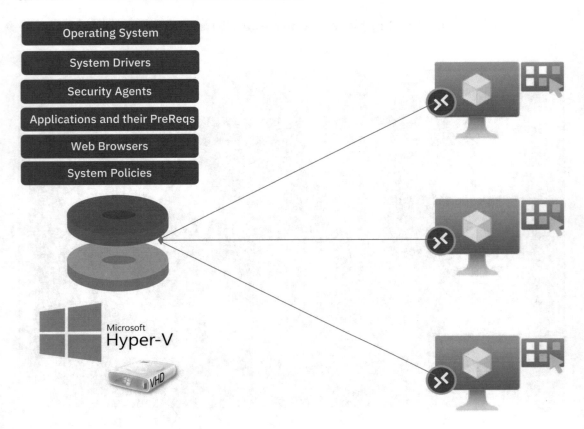

Figure 4-60. *Image management*

OS: For the golden image, think first about what OS/patching level you want to use. In most AVD implementations, it is probably best to start with the current state of end users. Therefore, the end user will have a stable starting point with fewer changes.

Deploy the server OS or client OS, perform OS updates, add to AD, enable RDS if it is server OS, activate Windows OS licenses, Create a snapshot (optional), and perform OS optimization as agreed with cloud consumers.

System Drivers: For the golden image, think next about what drivers are required in the image. In most AVD implementations, it is probably best to start with the printers, scanners & imaging devices, USB storage drives, smartcards, webcams, microphones, virtual card reader, signature pads, barcode scanners, credit card readers, speech mics, dictation foot pedals, fingerprint readers, pin pads, and so on.

Security Agents: For the golden image, think next about what security agents are required in the image. In most AVD implementations, it is probably best to start with endpoint protection, data loss protection, and gradually test rollout all cloud consumer security policy guidelines.

Applications and Their PreReqs: The golden image would benefit from the addition of preinstalled applications. It is a good idea to start with the applications most frequently used by end users. Applications such as Microsoft Office, Teams, One Drive, and so forth are safe bets to include in a golden image virtual disk. Also, consider installing base build applications such as Microsoft.Net, Java run time, Microsoft VC++, and so on required for your business-critical application.

Web Browser: The golden image would benefit from the web browser preinstalled in the golden image. It is a good idea to start with Microsoft Edge, Google Chrome, and on a demand basis, you can provision Mozilla Firefox ESR after completing your internal vulnerability assessment.

System Policies: The organizational unit structure for AVD computers will probably look something like the image picture. AVD administrators must duplicate some settings in your standard workstation GPOs when using this method, but it keeps the OU structure relatively flat. Preferably have system/computer policies applied via GPO. Take user policies into a profile management solution.

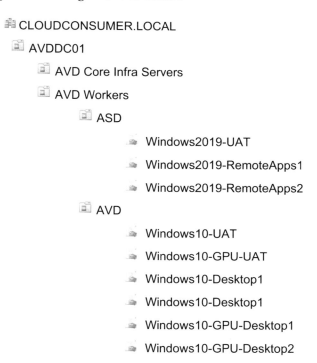

Image Management Release Process

AVD image management practices can deliver high speed and reliability of AVD functions using release management. Release management in AVD golden image is about discipline to follow from planning to building to testing and go-live. AVD golden image management should promote collaboration and distinctness everywhere in the complete delivery process by decreasing feedback circles and allowing simpler, agile release management.

AVD image management release process should focus on compile, verify, quality of control, merging different sources, removing duplicate features, and end the release with quality.

In AVD image management, running a reliable golden image aspires to reliable release methods. The AVD administrator needs to understand that the system's software installation and configurations are reproducible and automated so that instances of release engineering are repeatable.

The objective of AVD Image management release engineering is to expedite the rollout of new features or new propaganda as much as possible. AVD image management release engineering should also focus on applications to convert into packages with fully integrated, compiled, tested, and signed by product owners for enthusiastic release.

AVD image management release engineering is a phrase used to catch all the processes and artifacts related to preparing a closet into a running production IT function. Automating releases can avoid problems typical of the traditional meshes associated with release engineering:

- The toil of repeated and hand-operated tasks.

- The paradox of a nonautomated process.

- The inadequacy of grasping the exact position of a rollout.

- The pressure of rolling back.

AVD image management release deployment models are to be used for high velocities such as canary and blue-green. See Figure 4-61.

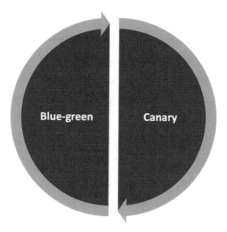

Figure 4-61. *Image deployment model*

Canary Release: Canary release is a release engineering method utilized to diminish the risk of opening new golden image features. It achieves this by deliberately rolling out the features to a small subset of end users, driving it out to the entire infrastructure, and delivering it to all end users.

Canary release key benefits:

- Limits permissible errors from any AVD administrator problems when there is a progressive deployment of the new features or functionality.

- Diminishes the risk of disadvantageous outcomes influencing a large percentage of the end-user base when publishing new features or functionality to end user. See Figure 4-62.

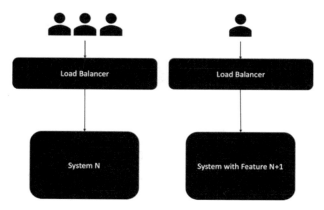

Figure 4-62. *Canary release deployment model*

Blue-Green: The blue-green release is moderately manageable. It is nothing about running two identical AVD golden images. Green is about live production load. Blue is parallel production in sync with green. Deploying the change first in blue and end to end testing happens in blue, and once blue is signed off by the product owner, it is ready to go. Change the routing and update load balancer and reverse proxy to the blue environment.

AVD image management can use blue-green deployments as conventional canaries by appropriating both blue and green deployments concurrently. In this method, the AVD administrator can deploy the canary to the blue (standby) instance and slowly split traffic between green and blue environments.

Blue and green benefits include enhancing availability and diminishing risk. For example, consider that the golden image to the blue environment disappoints because of concerns with the updated golden image. While the golden image attaining amended and recommitted to the closet, the green climate assists the live traffic, and there is no downtime. See Figure 4-63.

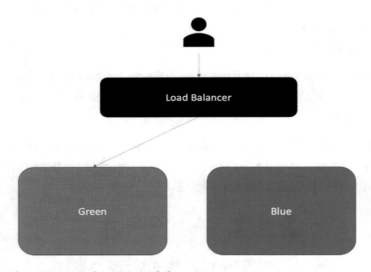

Figure 4-63. *Blue-green release model*

Reversible change should be agile to minimize downtime as much as attainable. The blue-green build reaches this by guaranteeing the two production environments are as indistinguishable as understandable, minus the product version. So, in a nutshell, release engineering has frequently been a reconsideration, and this way of thinking must change as golden images continue to grow in size and complexity.

In the digital workplace, AVD golden image release management makes reliability engineering more agile, improving efficiency. Release management contributes an enormous opportunity to improve the AVD image management practices. Systematic golden image release practices can enhance workflow across the AVD pool and assure that each process's coordination is attained high. The AVD administrator team can deploy best practices to meet needs adhering to the release policies. The approach suggests steps like plan, program, perform, workflow control, arrangement, production across varied environments.

Golden Image Update Process

This section aims to provide the overall process and guidelines necessary to update/release an existing golden image so that the image contains the most recent software and configuration changes. Each time the golden image is updated, the AVD administrator should create a new version to capture the changes without changing the golden base image.

A golden image update is a five-stage fully integrated process. See Figure 4-64.

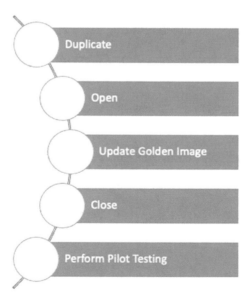

Figure 4-64. *Image release process*

Stage 1: Duplicate Golden Image – Make a snapshot of the current golden image.

Stage 2: Open Golden Image - Prepare for the changes

Stage 3: Update Golden Image Implementation of Approved Change - Perform for the changes

Stage 4: Close Golden Image – Use an automated script to perform closure activities

Stage 5: Perform Pilot Testing – Before massive rollout, perform pilot testing with a few limited users so that it will be easy to identify defects and fix them before any impact on wider audiences

In the next step, let us explore how to set up the Azure custom golden image for AVD, and the following are various method to provision. Generally said, you can use the following versions of Windows for your AVD in the Microsoft Azure cloud:

- Windows 10 Enterprise multisession, Version 1909

- Windows 10 Enterprise multisession, Version 1909 (GEN2)

- Windows 10 Enterprise multisession, Version 1909 + Microsoft 365 Apps

- Windows 10 Enterprise multisession, Version 1909 + Microsoft 365 Apps (GEN2)

- Windows 10 Enterprise multisession, Version 2004

- Windows 10 Enterprise multisession, Version 2004 (GEN2)

- Windows 10 Enterprise multisession, Version 2004 + Microsoft 365 Apps

- Windows 10 Enterprise multisession, Version 2004 + Microsoft 365 Apps (GEN2)

- Windows 10 Enterprise multisession, Version 20H2

- Windows 10 Enterprise multisession, Version 20H2 (GEN2)

- Windows 10 Enterprise multisession, Version 20H2+ Microsoft 365 Apps

- Windows 10 Enterprise multisession, Version 20H2+ Microsoft 365 Apps (GEN2)

- Windows 7 Enterprise

- Windows Server 2019

- Windows Server 2016

- Windows Server 2012 R2

To use the full capabilities of AVD in this book, we are going to use the Windows 10 Enterprise Template, multisession 20H2 Windows 10 Enterprise multisession along with Microsoft 365 Apps when possible in the Azure image gallery.

There are two possibilities for customizing this golden image.

- The primary choice is to provision a VM in Azure by following the wizard in Build a VM from a managed image and then skip ahead to Software preparation and installation.

- The secondary choice is to build the golden/master image locally by downloading it, provisioning a Hyper-V VM, and customizing it to suit your needs.

Step 1: Log in to personal or business account into Azure portal

- The following is the link: `https://portal.azure.com/`.

Step 2: Go to "Create a new Resource" and under get started search for "Windows 10". See Figure 4-65.

Figure 4-65. *Workflow of golden image creation*

Step 3: In the next step, provide the following details in the **Basics tab**

- Resource Group – Provide your resource group.

- Region - Location of AVD Master VM to be deployed.

- Availability Options - Availability zones are unique physical locations within an Azure region (typically at least three places).

- Availability Set - Automatically distribute your master VMs across multiple fault domains. Fault domain would be a rack that shares a power source.

- Image – Choose specific image version.

- Gen1 vs. Gen2 (new feature Q1 2021) – Gen 2 uses more recent hardware, supports unified extensible firmware interface (UEFI) boot instead of BIOS, and newer images, sizes, and capabilities.

- Spot Instance – Set the maximum bid for unused Azure to compute capacity. At any point in time when Azure needs the capacity back, the Azure infrastructure will evict Azure spot VMs. Therefore, Azure spot VMs are great for workloads that can handle interruptions like AVD master machine.

- Size - Choose VM size based on workload type and requirements. Select the smallest VM size to save costs for the AVD environment, shut down when not used, and delete when not required. See Figure 4-66.

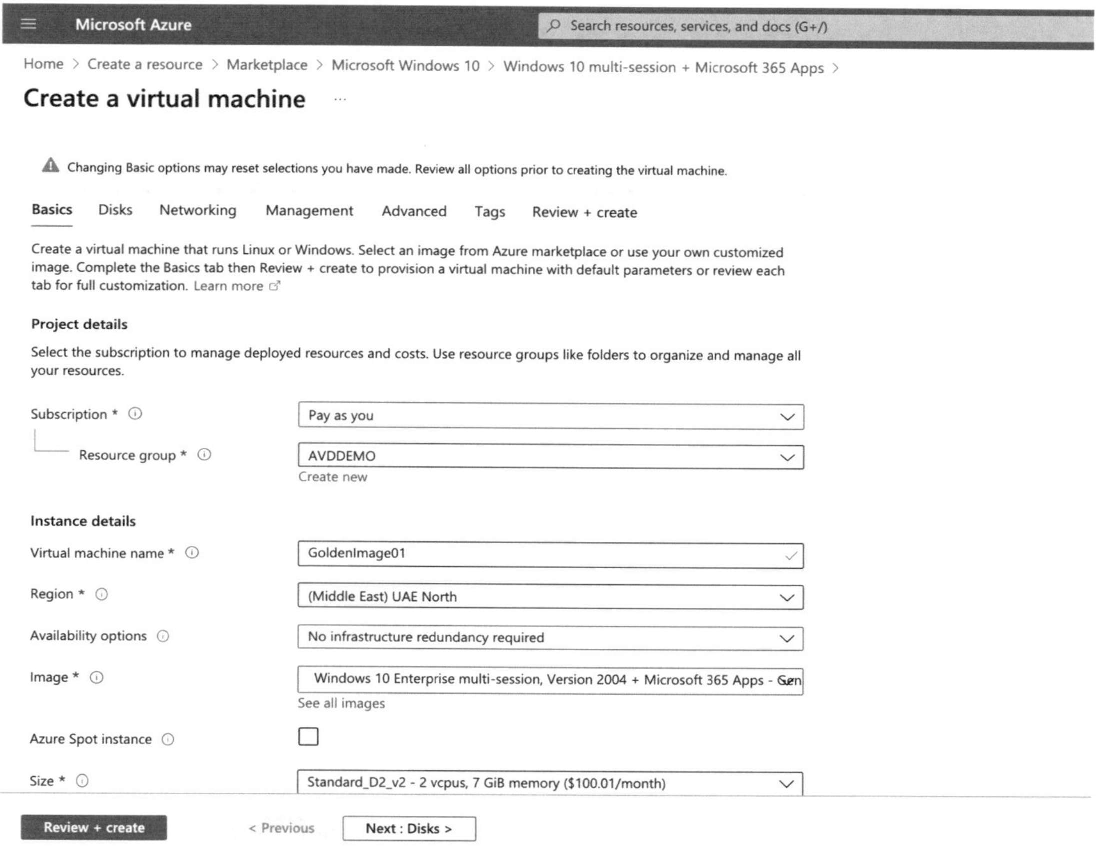

Figure 4-66. *Workflow of golden image creation*

- Administrator Account – Select administrator username and password.

- Inbound Port – Ports that need to be opened from the public Internet (for Windows RDP- 3389, for Linux SSH -22) For remote access, you could also implement a Bastion host.

Bastion provides secure RDP and SSH access to all VMs in the virtual network in which it is provisioned.

Azure Bastion lets you connect using a web browser to a VM through the Azure portal. You can provision this PaaS platform inside your virtual network. The Azure portal allows seamless access to your VMs over TLS using RDP/SSH. With Azure Bastion, your VMs do not need an IP address, agent, or special software to connect. See Figure 4-67.

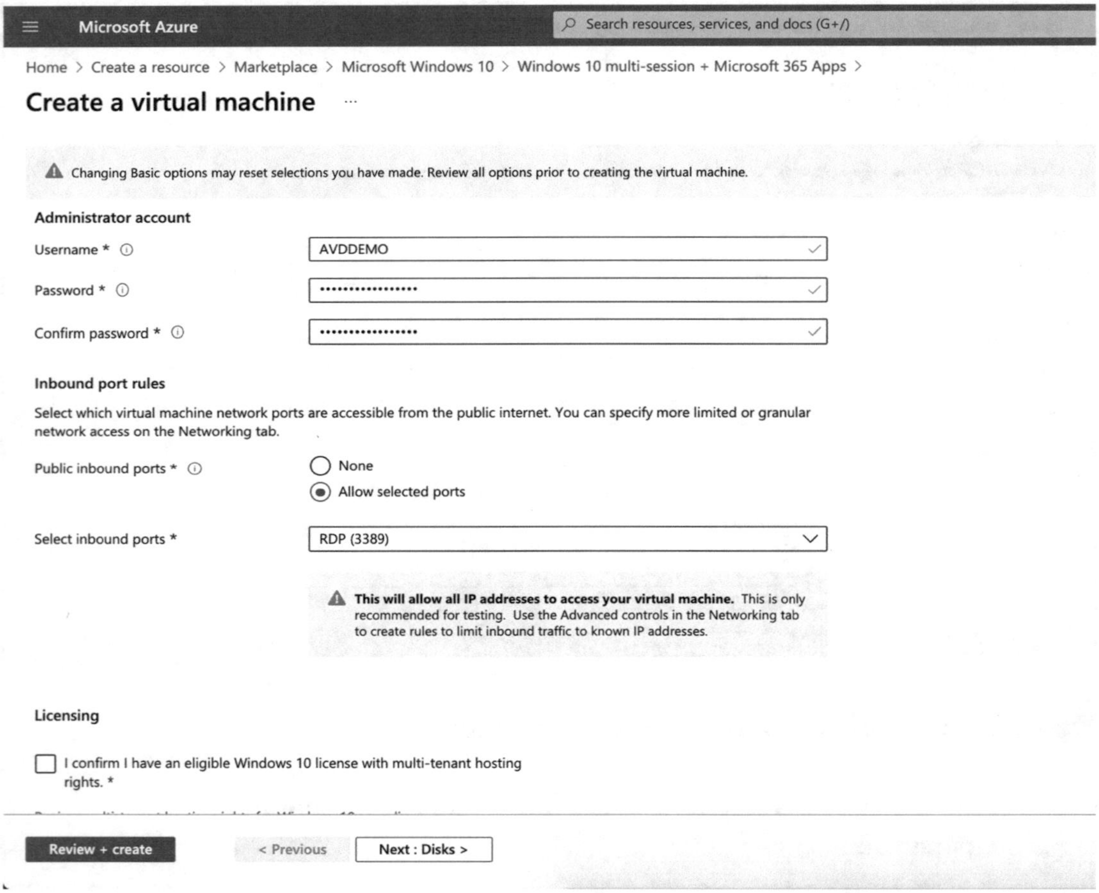

Figure 4-67. *Workflow of golden image creation*

Step 3: In the next step, provide the following details in **Disks** tab

- OS Disk Type: Choose disk type, standard HDD, standard SSD, premium SSD.

- Data Disks: Create or add an existing disk. For a new disk, the following will be required: disk name, size, source type (snapshot, storage blob, none/empty), encryption type, enable shared disk. See Figure 4-68.

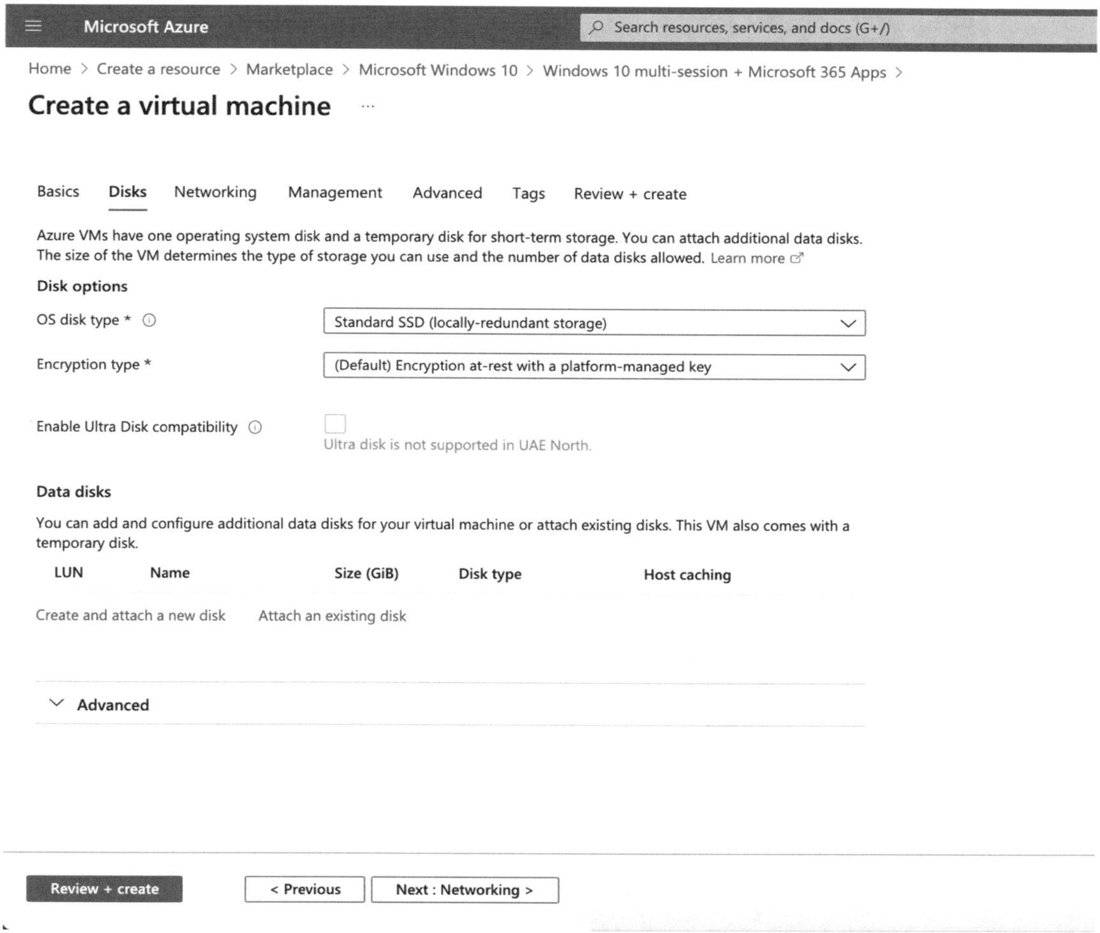

Figure 4-68. *Workflow of golden image creation*

Step 4: In the next step, provide the following details in the **Networking** tab

- Virtual Network: Network border in your subscription.

- Subnet: This is a range of IP addresses to divide up the vNETs.

- Public IP (assigned by default): For AVD master machine purposes, do not use a public IP address since there will be additional costs.

- NIC Network Security Group (NSG): Contains security rules that allow or deny inbound network traffic to the master machine or outbound network traffic.

- Load Balancing: Will the VM be behind a load balancer? Will need to select the name and type of load balancer (external or internal Azure load balancer or application gateway). See Figure 4-69.

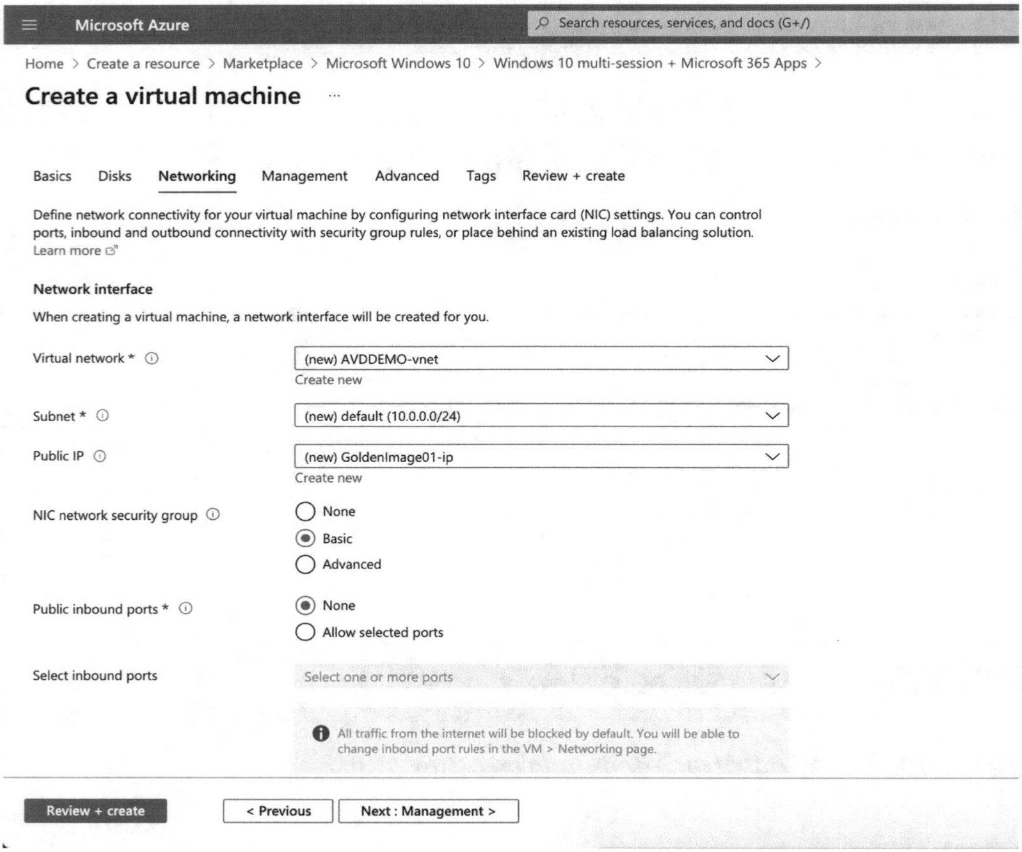

Figure 4-69. *Workflow of golden image creation*

Step 5: In the next step, provide the following details in **Management** tab

- Boot Diagnostics: Disable

- Identity, Azure AD, Auto Shutdown, Site Recovery: Do not enable.

- Guest OS Update: Choose manual update. See Figure 4-70.

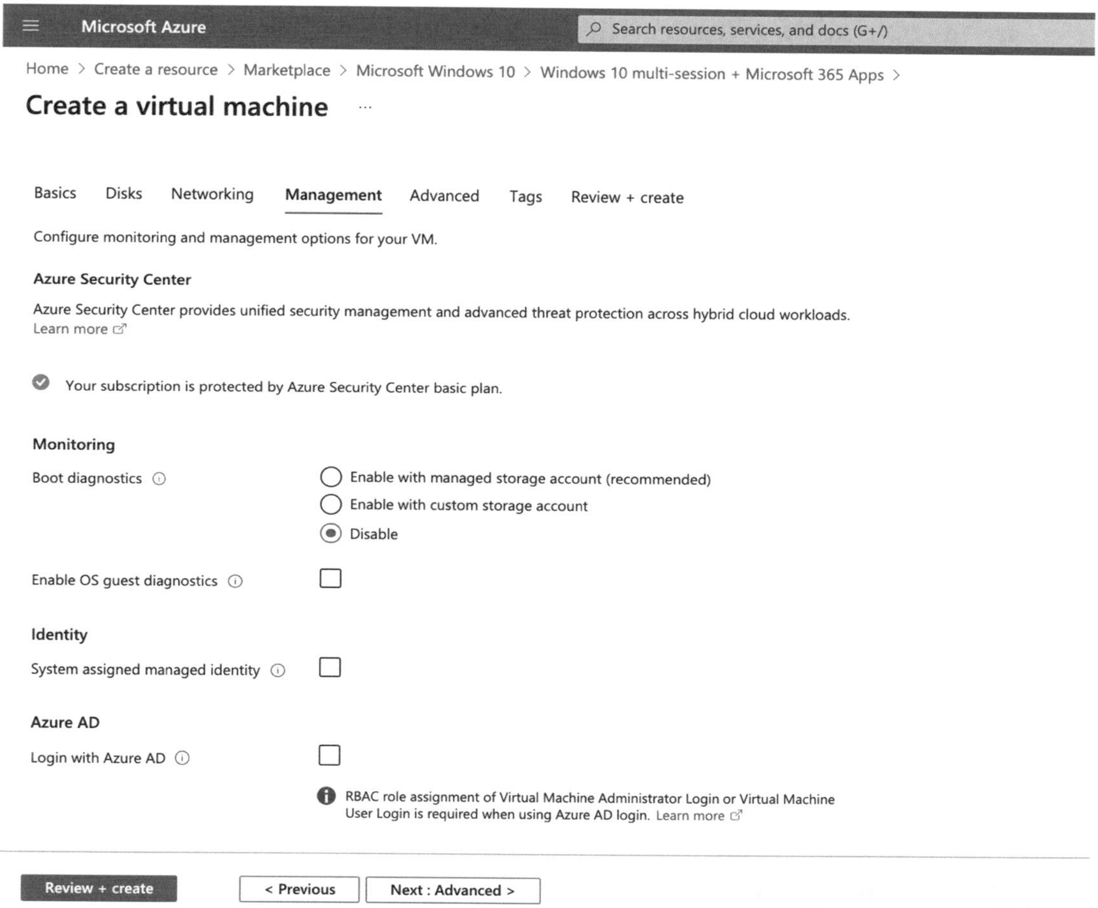

Figure 4-70. *Workflow of golden image creation*

Step 6: Provide the following details in **Advanced** tab

- Extensions: Using extensions, add new features, like configuration management or antivirus protection, to your master machine.

- Custom Data: Pass a script, configuration file, or other data into the VM.

- Host Group: Azure dedicated hosts allow you to provision and manage a physical server within our data centers dedicated to your Azure subscription.

Step 7: Perform Windows OS update

Step 8: Remove preinstalled AppxPackage applications

We should observe the preinstalled Windows 10 AppxPackages. To see the list of package names of currently enabled AppxPackages for all users, open an elevated PowerShell, and then enter this PowerShell command:

```
Get-AppxPackage -AllUsers | ft Name
```

All preinstalled apps can be removed from all user accounts. Start a PowerShell session with elevated privileges and type. Then enter this PowerShell command:

```
Get-AppxPackage -allusers PackageFullName | Remove-AppxPackage
```

Step 9: Disable all nonrequired Windows services from the golden image. The following list provides examples of services that can be disabled.

- Windows Update

- Background Intelligent Transfer Service

- Diagnostic Policy Services

- Windows Update

- WWAN AutoConfig

- All Xbox Services

- Themes

Step 10: Disable all nonrequired scheduled tasks from the golden image. The following list provides examples of services that can be disabled.

- AD RMS Rights Policy Template Management (Manual)
- EDP Policy Manager
- SmartScreenSpecific
- Microsoft Compatibility Appraiser
- ProgramDataUpdater
- StartupAppTask
- CleanupTemporaryState
- DsSvcCleanup
- Proxy
- UninstallDeviceTask
- AikCertEnrollTask
- CryptoPolicyTask
- KeyPreGenTask
- ProactiveScan
- CreateObjectTask

Step 11: Install all the application, agent, and business-critical application prereqs.

- Set up user profile container (i.e., FSLogix)
- Set up collaboration (i.e., MS teams)
- Setup security agent (i.e., configure Windows defender, antivirus, endpoint detection and response)

Step 12: Optimize all registry key and set up any local policies.

Step 13: Once image is completed, make a snapshot.

Snapshots can be used to duplicate a golden image relatively quickly since it is faster than copying a blob. AVD administrators still must shut down the master machine to ensure consistency, but creating the snapshot only takes a few seconds. The Sysprep tool can run up to 1001 times in Windows 10. Taking a snapshot before running Sysprep is not necessary; however, having the option to revert to a previous image is recommended.

Step 14: Create a golden image capture

Once creating the disk snapshot, start the master machine, run Sysprep. (C:\Windows\System32\Sysprep\sysprep.exe).

Choose Generalize and to set the Shutdown Option to Shut down; once the snapshot is created, automatically delete this master machine after creating the image

Step 15: Create a shared image gallery (SIG) and add an image to SIG

Step 16: Deploy AVD host pool with golden image

Step 17: Version management is key: In the SIG, give the image a version

With this taken care of now, let us focus on the application management layer of the resource layer.

AVD Application Management

AVD application management is the process of managing the maintenance and upgrading of an application over its lifecycle. Application management layer in your design AVD should provide cloud consumers with a suite of management tools that let your AVD administrator publish, push, configure, monitor, and update cloud consumer client applications. As a cloud consumer, it's essential to understand the available capabilities and choose the correct application delivery method for AVD consumers.

MSIX is a modern application packaging format, and the MSIX app attaches a delivery system that the AVD administrator can use when performing an AVD. The MSIX app connect presents AVD administrators to follow applications to AVD end users dynamically, although of their session host. AVD administrators can also use enduring Microsoft management tools to manage cloud consumer AVD applications.

MSIX is a new Windows application packaging form and development structure, and when connected with MSIX app attach, the AVD–specific service, it presents a delivery mechanism. MSIX offers a modern application packaging encounter for cloud consumer Windows applications, interpreting the application installation process for users and the AVD administrator.

Client applications that are packaged utilizing MSIX run in a lightweight app container. The MSIX application and child processes run inside this container and are isolated using the filesystem and registry virtualization. Client MSIX application can register the global registry. An MSIX app writes to its virtual registry and application data folder, and this data will be deleted when the app is uninstalled. Other apps do not have access to the virtual registry or virtual filesystem of an MSIX app.

Applications can be repackaged or converted into MSIX packages using the MSIX packaging tool implemented; it provides a simplistic user interface and command-line interface to convert and package Windows applications into MSIX packages.

With MSIX, files are eliminated from duplicating across applications, while Windows manages files shared between apps. The client applications are still autonomous, so updates will not change other applications sharing the file. A clean uninstall is assured even if the platform runs shared files beyond application.

The AVD administrator can package and distribute Win32 applications using the MSIX by using the Microsoft Store, enabling the AVD administrator to offer self-service solutions to AVD users.

The MSIX application attaches a way for VMs within AVD to run MSIX applications. Today, AVD offers MSIX app attach capabilities that can be managed and delivered across Azure regions.

An MSIX app writes to its virtual registry and application data folder, and all MSIX app methods run inside that container. Applications packaged in MSIX form are deployed in the "c:\Program Files\WindowsApps" folder. Each package folder involves a set of regulated files wanted for the MSIX package to work. See Figure 4-71.

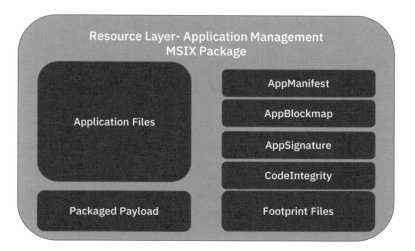

Figure 4-71. *Resource layer-application management*

App payload: The payload files are the application code files and assets that are built when building the package.

AppxBlockMap.xml: The package block map file is an XML document containing the app's files, indexes, and cryptographic hashes for each data block stored in the package. In signing the package, a digital signature is used to verify and secure the block map file. It supports incremental download and validation of MSIX packages and differential updating of app files after installation via the block map file.

AppxManifest.xml: As a package manifest, an MSIX application provides the system with information about deploying, displaying, and updating it. Identify the package, list its dependencies, the capabilities required, and describe its visual elements.

AppxSignature.p7x: The AppxSignature.p7x is created when the package is signed. All MSIX packages are expected to be signed before install. AppxBlockmap.xml allows the platform to validate the package and install it.

With MSIX app attached, application data is isolated from the user and the OS using a lightweight container. By leveraging the MSIX packaging format, MSIX app attach removes the need for repackaging.

Benefit of using MSIX app attach over other technologies include

- Predictable and safe deployment.

- Clean removal without leftovers.

- Disk space optimization techniques such as single-instance storage of files.

- Managed by Windows (install, update, remove).

- Differential updates support to minimize network usage.

- Tamper protection.

- A way for MSIX to deliver applications that won't delay user login.

- Significantly reduces the AVD administrator's management to perform in installing and maintaining silos of session hosts that host a pool of applications for different sets of user groups within a business.

In the next step, let us explore how to configure MSXI app and attach AVD, and the following are prerequisites.

- There must be at least one active session host in the AVD host pool.

- Microsoft's packaging tool for MSIX.

- Uploading an MSIX-packaged application into a file share.

- Software repository to MSIX package.

- All VMs in the host pool must access the file share where you uploaded the MSIX image. Access to the image will be restricted to readers.

Under Azure Virtual Desktop> Host Pools> Host Pool Portal, the AVD administrator can locate MSIX packages under the Manage option within the Azure portal. AVD administrators can add MSIX packages to the AVD host pool using the following steps. Choose the MSIX package tab and enter the following values:

1. For the MSIX image path, provide a valid UNC path pointing to the MSIX image on the file share.

2. For the MSIX package, choose the proper MSIX package name from the drop-down menu.

3. For package applications, create a list that contains all MSIX applications required for AVD end users.

4. Alternatively, enter a display name if you want your package to be more user-friendly in AVD user deployments and ensure that your version has the exact version number.

5. Choose the registration type; on-demand registration postpones the complete registration of the MSIX application until the user starts the application. This is the registration type Microsoft recommends using.

6. For State, using the active status lets AVD end users interact with the package.

7. Finally, Add.

Next, we see the method to publish the apps into the package. AVD administrators need to do this for both desktop and remote app application groups..

1. Select the Application groups tab in the AVD resource provider and choose the application group you want to publish the apps to.

2. Choose the Applications tab. The Applications grid will display all apps within the app group and choose + Add to open the Add application tab.

3. For the Application source, prefer the source for your application. If you're using a remote app group, then the following choices exist:

   - Start menu

   - App path

   - MSIX package

4. Provide application name, display name, description and click Add

With this now completed, let us focus on the Profile management layer of the resource layer.

AVD Profile Management

Microsoft Azure service recommends FSLogix profile containers as user profile solutions for AVD. FSLogix is designed to roam profiles in virtual desktop and application environments, such as AVD. It stores a complete user profile in a single container. Virtual hard disks (VHD) and Hyper-V Virtual hard disks (VHDX) are natively supported by this container and are dynamically attached to the computing environment at sign-in. An instant user profile appears in the system just like a native profile. In this section, let us explore how FSLogix profile containers work along with the Azure files function in AVD. User profiles contain data about individuals, including configuration information such as desktop settings, persistent network connections, and application settings. When Windows is first launched, a local user profile is created by default. A remote user profile partitions an OS and user data. Users' data is not affected when the OS is changed or replaced. In virtual apps and virtual desktop infrastructures (AVD), the OS may be replaced for the following reasons:

- An upgrade of an OS

- replacing an existing VM

- A user being part of a pooled or personal desktop

A variety of technologies enable Microsoft products to work with remote user profiles, including these technologies:

- Roaming user profiles

- User profile disks

- Enterprise state roaming

User profile disks and roaming user profiles are the most widely used technologies in personal and pooled legacy VDI environments. However, it comes with the following set of challenges.

Technology	User Profile Disks	Roaming User Profile
OS user system-level configuration	Yes	Yes
OS user data-level configuration	Yes	Yes
Modern configuration	Yes	No
Win32 configuration	Yes	Yes
Back-end storage on Azure	No	No
Back-end storage on-premises	Yes	Yes
Version support	Win 7+	Win 7+
Subsequent log-in time	Yes	No

Windows remote computing environments can be enhanced and facilitated with FSLogix user profiles. You can also use FSLogix to make physical devices more portable when using it.

FSLogix includes the following benefits in your design and deployment.

- User Profile Container

- Microsoft Office Container

- Client Application Masking

- Java Run Time Environment Version Control

FSLogix allows your AVD administrator to perform the following:

- Roam user data among AVD session hosts.

- Lessen sign-in times for AVD environments.

- Optimize file I/O among AVD session host/ AVD end-user client and remote profile store.

- Implement a local profile experience, dropping the requirement for roaming profiles.

- Simplify the management of client applications in golden images.

- Define the version of Java to be utilized by specific URL and applications.

Microsoft FSLogix provides network access to user profiles. In contrast to solutions that copy profiles from and to the network location, mounting and using the profiles over the network eliminates delays typically associated with them.

Microsoft FSLogix only redirects Office data from the profile by using the Office container. By using Office container, companies that use alternate profile solutions can use Office with pooled desktops.

Cloud cache and profile container can be used to create resilient and highly available environments. Cloud cache copies a portion of the profile VHD to a local drive. An AVD administrator can specify more than one remote profile location in cloud cache. The local cache, with numerous remote profile containers, protects AVD users from network and storage failures.

Microsoft FSLogix provides that user profiles are treated as local drives by applications. Applications are not aware that FSLogix profiles are on the network, as their filter drivers redirect the profiles. Because many applications will not work correctly if the profile is saved on remote storage, blocking the redirection is essential.

Microsoft FSLogix provides a masking application capability, and manages access to applications, fonts, printers, or other items. AVD end-user access can be controlled by the user, IP address range, and other end-user KPIs. Many golden images can be managed more accessible by applying application masking.

The following licenses are automatically eligible for FSLogix entitlement.

- Microsoft 365 E3/E5

- Microsoft 365 A3/A5/ Student Use Benefits

- Microsoft 365 F1/F3

- Microsoft 365 Business

- Windows 10 Enterprise E3/E5

- Windows 10 Education A3/A5

- Windows 10 VDA per user

- RDS CAL

- RDS Subscriber Access License (SAL)

- AVD Per-User Access License

Profile Container

FSLogix is a set of solutions that improve, enable, and analyze nonpersistent Windows computing environments. FSLogix solutions are suited for virtual desktop environments in the Azure cloud.

For connecting FSLogix with AVD as a desktop virtualization solution on Azure, store AVD end-user profiles on both Azure files and Azure NetApp files for FSLogix profile containers in AVD.

The user profile container VHD will include the complete AVD end-user Windows profile, excluding the TEMP (TMP) folder and IE cache folder locations.

The Microsoft Windows AVD end-user profile is composed of a specific folder location and any registry data. The AVD administrator can specify that parts of the AVD end-user profile are persisted in the profile container. Exclusions can be performed via redirections.xml file. FSLogix and the redirections.xml file control how specific folders within the profile container are directed into the local C: drive.

Exclusions should be the exemption and should never be used unless the explicit exclusion is completely understood by the AVD administrator configuring the exclusion.

Exclusions should constantly be required to be tested in the AVD environment where they are intended to be implemented. Configuring omissions may impact reliability, functionality, stability, and performance.

FSLogix's internal architecture is based on a filter driver. It's common in virtual desktop scenarios to copy a profile to and from the network when an AVD end user logs in and out of a remote environment. Since some AVD end-user profiles can often be extensive, log in and log out times often became unacceptable.

Several concurrent sessions and concurrent access are made possible in the profile container to merge changes into the primary container. When numerous concurrent sessions are simultaneously running, you will need to consider in your design an additional storage capacity as well as last-write-wins. It does not allow merging read-write copies back into a primary container once the Outlook cached mode has been enabled. Microsoft Office container also supports concurrent access and multiple sessions.

If concurrent session access per-session containers are enabled, in your design, kindly plan for storage capacity to handle multiple Office containers, recognizing the number of containers that will be kept.

FSLogix containers redirect user profiles to a network location. Profiles are placed in VHDx files and fixed at run time. Setting and using a user profile on the network drops delays often connected with solutions that copy files.

The Windows service agent needs to be installed in the golden image. The agent installs two filter drivers, and that gets injected into the OS. After that, the AVD administrator can set a proper registry or via group policy entries to place a VHDx container on a file share or SMB share location as per your design.

Key Design Consideration of Resource Layer

Designing the best resource pool for AVD end-user consumption starts with identifying the solution for the following design thinking.

- A formula for better performance when implementing an AVD environment

- Where can I get the best value for my money with AVD?

- Identify that GPUs are a prerequisite for the best possible experience, even if there is no need for graphics applications

Sizing the pooled and personal host pool is a vital success factor for your design. Analysis test results are used to obtain the optimal Azure VM configuration for your AVD environment based on your workload and end-user profile. The following guidelines help determine a structure that can be considered your domain's whole AVD solution building block.

- Avoid converting existing physical datacenter to cloud sizing. Field engagements testing has determined that scaling out (recommended for more, smaller VMs) improves performance over deploying larger devices in AVD environments.

- All pool types should have more than two cores, which should not have more than 32. Windows 10 and its UI elements use at least two parallel threads for heavier rendering operations. When the UI and applications are unstable due to multiple users using a dual-core VM, the quality of the user experience will be lowered. Multiuser VMs can have up to four cores, which is the lowest possible amount.

- Microsoft recommends at least two physical CPU cores per VM (typically four vCPUs with hyperthreading). Ask the software vendors specific to your AVD cloud consumer workload if your business needs more precise VM sizing suggestions for single-session scenarios. AVD VM sizing for single-session VMs will suitably align with physical device guidelines.

- AVD users can run various workloads on the VMs managed by
  AVD. Balance your design and deployment depending on the
  proposed need of the different types of AVD end users. The following
  table provides examples of a range of workload types to help you
  estimate what size your VMs need to be in your design estimation.

Workload Type	Example Users	Example Apps
Light	Employee marks attends, email only or call center similar type	Browser-based webapp internal or external
Medium	Third-party consultant or task worker	Browser-based webapp internal or external, Microsoft Word, Excel PowerPoint, One Drive and Teams
Heavy	Software engineers and content creators	Browser-based webapp internal or external, Microsoft Word, Excel PowerPoint, One Drive and Teams, Adobe Cloud Suite
Power	Graphic designers, 3D model makers, machine learning researchers	Browser-based webapp internal or external, Microsoft Word, Excel PowerPoint, One Drive and Teams, Adobe Cloud Suite, Photoshop or graphics extensive apps

After setting up your VMs, you should continually monitor their actual usage and adjust their size accordingly. You can quickly scale up or down your Azure deployment if you need a larger or smaller VM.

Microsoft recommendations in this section are nonexclusive guidelines, and in your design, you should only use them for preliminary performance evaluations. The following tables list the highest proposed number of AVD users per virtual central processing unit (vCPU) and vRAM and the minimum VM configuration for each workload category.

The following table shows a baseline proof-of-concept scenario with fewer than 20 users per Microsoft's recommendation.

Workload Type	Maximum Users per vCPU	vCPU/RAM/OS Storage Minimum	Example Azure Instances	Profile Container Storage Minimum
Light	4	4 vCPUs, 16 GB RAM, 32 GB storage	D4s_v4, F4s_v2, D4as_v4	30 GB
Medium	4	4 vCPUs, 16 GB RAM, 32 GB storage	D4s_v4, F4s_v2, D4as_v4	30 GB
Heavy	2	4 vCPUs, 16 GB RAM, 32 GB storage	D8s_v4, F8s_v2, D8as_v4, D16s_v4, F16s_v2, D16as_v4	30 GB
Power	1	6 vCPUs, 56 GB RAM, 340 GB storage	D4s_v4, F4s_v2, D4as_v4, NV12, NVv4	30 GB

The following table shows a baseline standard or larger user workloads with 20 or more users per Microsoft's recommendation.

Workload Type	Maximum Users per vCPU	vCPU/RAM/OS Storage Minimum	Example Azure Instances	Profile Container Storage Minimum
Light	6	8 vCPUs, 16 GB RAM, 16 GB storage	D8s_v4, F8s_v2, D8as_v4, D16s_v4, F16s_v2, D16as_v4	30 GB
Medium	4	8 vCPUs, 16 GB RAM, 32 GB storage	D8s_v4, F8s_v2, D8as_v4, D16s_v4, F16s_v2, D16as_v4	30 GB
Heavy	2	8 vCPUs, 16 GB RAM, 32 GB storage	D8s_v4, F8s_v2, D8as_v4, D16s_v4, F16s_v2, D16as_v4	30 GB
Power	1	6 vCPUs, 56 GB RAM, 340 GB storage	D8s_v4, F8s_v2, D8as_v4, D16s_v4, F16s_v2, D16as_v4, NV12, NVv4	30 GB

Finally, Microsoft recommends you use simulation tools like Login VSI to test your design and deployment with stress tests and real-life production workload simulations. Ensure your AVD solution is responding and resilient adequate to meet AVD user needs and learn to vary the load size to avoid wonderments.

Virtual desktop in Azure utilizes GPU acceleration to enhance the performance and scalability of apps. Applications that require graphics acceleration are critical.

Choose one of Azure's NV-series, NVv3-series, or NVv4-series VM sizes. Most applications and the Windows user interface are accelerated GPU, tailored for app and desktop virtualization. There are many factors to consider when choosing your host pool, including the application workload, user experience, and price. At a given density of users, a larger GPU provides a better user experience. Smaller and fractional GPUs enable more precise control of cost and quality at the same time.

For the following OS, AVD offers GPU-accelerated rendering and encoding:

- Windows 10 version 1511 or newer

- Windows Server 2016 or newer

You must configure Azure AVD with the appropriate graphics drivers to make use of Azure N-series VMs' GPU. Consider in your design the following from driver upfront.

- Neither NVIDIA CUDA nor NVIDIA GRID drivers are supported for GPU acceleration on Azure NV-series or NVv3-series VMs. If you choose to install drivers manually, be sure to install GRID drivers. If you install drivers using the Azure VM extension, GRID drivers will automatically be installed for these VM sizes.

- VMs running on Azure NVv4 should be installed with AMD drivers provided by Azure. You may install them automatically using the Azure VM extension, or you may install them manually.

Choosing the correct display protocol defines the state of static images, video, and text within the AVD end user's session and prepares the impression on single-server scalability.

Every time a user logs onto an AVD session, they must finish the login process, including the following

- Session startup,

- User profile loading,

- Group policy preferences execution,

- Drive mapping,

- Printer mapping,

- Logon script execution,

- Desktop initialization.

An AVD end user's profile is critical in performing a consistently positive user experience within a virtual desktop or remote application. A well-designed AVD solution can break if the AVD end users are disappointed due to long logon times or misplaced settings. So having an appropriate user profile is critical for your design success.

The following are standard best practices for printing.

- Amidst AVD, printing is offered differently than it is in conventional cloud desktops. The printing choices are varied based on how you access your AVD session.

- A remote desktop virtual printer will be displayed within an HTML5 web session. The AVD end user downloads PDF files to a local machine. After that, the end user of the AVD will publish it (PDF from their local printer).

- Your AVD end user can access their local printers from their AVD remote desktop session while using remote desktop. The local printer will be used as usual. As in AVD, the name of their local printer will be (Redirected-When a user logs on to a session, this setting controls whether client printers are mapped to a VM hosted in Azure.), followed by their local printer's name.

- The printing solution involves designing and deploying and includes the following provisioning printers, managing print drivers and print job routing. If your cloud consumer demands extended use cases like secure print, consider a third-party printing solution.

The following are standard best practices for MSIX-based application management.

- Exclude VHD(x)'s and CimFS files from profile containers and antivirus scanning.

- For production, don't place MSIX packages on the identical storage as FSLogix profiles.

- For the DR purpose for AVD session hosts, consider extending that to add the storage location hosting the MSIX packages.

- Any application dependencies should be put in the golden image. At the same time, they can be put into the package.

- Microsoft does not recommend it, as there is no guarantee that the dependency will be delivered before the application.

- Place the storage service in the same Azure region as the AVD session hosts.

The following are standard best practices for FSLogix-based user profile management.

- For optimal performance, the storage solution and the FSLogix profile container should be in the same Azure DC location.

- Exclude the VHD(X) files for profile containers from antivirus scanning to avoid execution threshold.

- Microsoft recommends using a separate profile container per host pool while having two active sessions.

- FSXLogix required all host pool VMs have the same type and size VM with the same master golden image.

- It is necessary to place all pooled server VMs in the same logical resource group to aid management, scaling, and updating.

- FSLogix profile containers should be located within the Azure data center for optimal performance.

- Master images must be in the same region and subscription as the VMs.

- Azure files storage account necessity be in the corresponding Azure region as the session host VMs.

- Kindly have a well-defined approach, including considerations for capacity planning, monitoring, and maintenance for FSLogix profile containers and Office containers.

Building Block 4: Design of Hosting layer

A fourth layer of the design methodology is the AVD hosting layer; AVD design and deployment are typically accountable for the reliability of an end-user computing (EUC) function end-to-end across technical realms and towers. Hence, an AVD architect/consultant needs to apply system reliability thinking against each AVD function. Cloud computing grants AVD administrators the ability to swiftly generate heterogeneous systems and deploy them continuously at a large global scale. This approach comes with built-in unique reliability risks.

AVD architects/consultants should not consider the Azure cloud hosting layer to be reliable by default.

Reliability and availability have always been a significant concern in the spread systems' IT function. Providing highly available and reliable cloud computing services is essential for preserving consumer prosperity and preventing revenue losses. Although numerous solutions have been aimed at cloud availability and reliability, no thorough libraries cover all intricate aspects of the difficulty.

The reputation and regulation of cloud computing have expanded manifold in the last few years. From commanding tech companies worldwide to brand-new startups, every IT service provider wants to endeavor this space. While it is the cloud service provider's commitment to take responsibility for their infrastructure and ensure security and refuge at all ends, sometimes it doesn't quite happen. So it is helpful to have an AVD architect. You can fill the gap by following system thinking and applying reliability patterns at the hosting layer level.

The ultimate objective of system thinking against reliability is to avoid single-point failure in your AVD design and deployment. Every AVD function element can fail but applying system thinking against reliability should build a robust system to tolerate an individual component failure.

As cloud operations become more pervasive, AVD functions become further conditioned; failures such as hardware failure, natural disasters, and data corruption should not disrupt or stop AVD function activities. The AVD function should enable the business capability of operating on alternative information performance systems. Any AVD architect/consultant must consider such systems' reliability throughout their hosting design and use.

By identifying and agreeing on the KPIs for the AVD function, AVD architects/administrators can trigger automation tasks whenever a breached threshold is reported. Identified KPIs should measure business value, not the technical aspects of the service's operation. This allows intuitive intelligence, tracking failures, and programmed recovery methods that work around or correct the crash. With more advanced automation, it's achievable to intercept and remediate breakdowns before they happen.

In an on-premises data center, dev, UAT, and Prod Pilot testing is performed to settle that the workload accomplishes a specific objective. Testing is not typically used to validate reliability and recovery procedures. AVD administrators can perform end-to-end testing on workload fails in the cloud, and AVD administrators can validate site reliability engineering (SRE) recovery procedures via automation. AVD administrators can use automation to mimic different crashes or to stimulate situations that are escorted to impacts. As mentioned earlier, the system reveals crash pathways that AVD administrators can promote and fix before an actual crash happens. Therefore, it helps the AVD administrator's team in reducing risk and increasing reliability. See Figure 4-72.

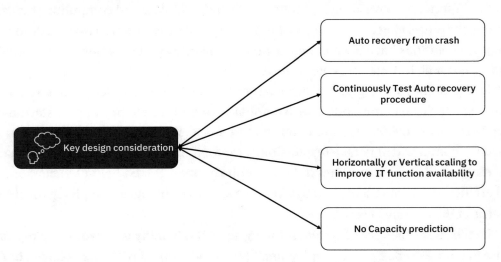

Figure 4-72. *Key design considerations for reliability system thinking*

Reinstate one AVD session workload with many small workloads to reduce a single point of failure impact on the total solution. Load balance the service requests across many, more diminutive resources to assure the reliability of the system.

A typical cause of a single point of failure in the on-premises data center is VDI function resource congestion. The demands overwhelmed by a workload exceed its allocated capacity, and it is subjective to security constraints. AVD administrators can observe request and workload utilization in the cloud and automate AVD resources' extension or relocation to keep the idle comfort level whenever demand goes beyond the underlying capability. It can create limitations in some scenarios; for those, SLA should be mitigation.

In Microsoft Azure, this is a joint responsibility where AVD cloud consumers should leverage their architecture's platform features to build a resilient AVD landscape. Figure 4-73 presents guidelines around the hosting layer.

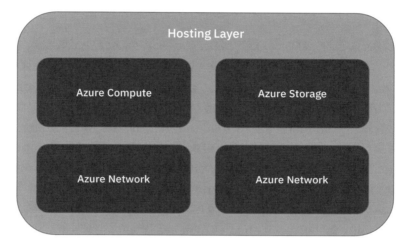

Figure 4-73. *Key design elements for hosting layer*

Guidelines for AVD naming standards: Having consistent naming conventions is critical in any organization with multiple departments, networks, services, and applications. Resource identification and identification can become complicated when inconsistent naming is applied. For these various services to function effectively, we need to establish a common standard.

Guidelines for AVD subscriptions: In Azure, the subscription is the top-level container. Registrations can contain many subscriptions with AVD administrative boundaries. The system works well for separating end-user departments and persona and different workloads such as production, staging, testing, and development. While this is great for setting clean administrative boundaries, centrally directing many subscriptions can create added overhead.

Guidelines for AVD resource group: Essentially, a resource group is a logical container that holds Azure resources that are related. The life expectancy of group resources depends on who will manage them.

Group resources that share the same lifecycle: It is possible to deploy and monitor resources by resource group and track the costs of resources by resource group. In addition, resources can be deleted together, which is extremely convenient for testing. By naming resources appropriately, you can simplify locating and understanding their purpose.

Guidelines for AVD VM provisioning: A VM can be selected from a list of published images, or a custom-managed image or VHD file uploaded to Azure blob storage can be used.

There are several different sizes of VMs in Azure. View Azure VM sizes for more information. Move AVD workloads into Azure by using the VM size closest to the extent of your end-user workloads. You may need to adjust the size based on your actual workload and CPU, memory, and disk input/output operations per second (IOPS).

Commonly, choose an Azure region that is closest to your AVD end users.

Guidelines for AVD storage: The VHDs of AVD VMs should reside in the backend storage, whether they use managed disks or unmanaged disks. For resiliency, managed disks are recommended by Microsoft since underlying storage stamps are handled when implementing availability sets. The AVD VM disks are distributed across fault and update domains like compute instances. It ensures high availability and resiliency at both the compute layer and the storage layer.

With unmanaged disks, AVD VMs to be placed in an availability set, and the disks of unique AVD VMs can be placed in separate storage accounts. By deploying availability sets across multiple fault domains and updated domains, single points of failure are avoided. The storage accounts used for hosting VMs in Azure datacenters are part of a larger storage unit. There is no guarantee that the dedicated storage accounts you use for your architecture are provisioned from a different storage unit.

When using managed disks for AVD VMs, the theory of fault domains is also extended to storage units. The platform manages the storage account used for disks. If AVD VMs are distributed across availability sets, the platform effectively places the disks connected with the VMs across various storage units. It ensures that not all AVD VMs in the availability set are swayed in the case of a failure in one storage unit.

Guidelines for AVD backup: Having a clear backup plan for AVD data is essential for ensuring the reliability of Azure's infrastructure. As a native solution to this issue, Azure backup is available from the first-party vendor. Pay-as-you-go Azure backup offers an alternative to traditional backup solutions without sacrificing enterprise-level security. Here are a few of the critical benefits of the solution.

- Backups are safely stored on Azure cloud storage, so planning and managing capacity on a long-term basis are not required.

- Since Azure cloud storage uses locally redundant storage (LRS), Azure cloud storage used for backup data is resilient by default. Using LRS, your data exists in three copies within a region. A globally redundant storage solution (GRS) can enhance your data's resilience by replicating it in a secondary backup region.

- A restore operation does not incur any charges or result in data egress. Azure does not charge for ingress data. Hence all data transfers for backup are effectively free.

- Security is ensured during transit and while at rest. The AVD cloud consumer manages a passphrase for encrypting data.

Guidelines for AVD network: Azure best practices for network security include placing your VMs on Azure virtual networks to make them accessible to networked devices. Therefore, VNICs can be connected to a virtual network to enable a network-enabled device to communicate using TCP/IP. Azure virtual cloud networks may link to other virtual networks, applications on the Internet, or hardware on-premises with VMs connected to them. So, use strong network controls in your Azure network design.

Azure virtual networks are like on-premises LANs. Virtual networks are based on creating a shared IP address space that is used to create a network on which all your Azure VMs reside. In addition to Class A IP address spaces (10.0.0.0/8), there are Class B IP address spaces (172.16.0.0/12) and Class C IP address spaces (192.168.0.0/16), so use logically segmented subnets in your design.

Legacy perimeter-based networks run on the hypothesis that all internal IT functions within a network can be trusted. In today's digital workplace world, AVD end users can access their organization's resources from anywhere through various devices and apps, which makes perimeter security controls irrelevant. It is not enough to restrict access only to those who have access to a resource. When balancing safety and productivity, security administrators must also consider how resources are accessed, so adopt zero-trust architecture in your design.

Building Block 5: Design of User Layer

A final layer of the design methodology is the AVD user layer, which each unique user group determines. The AVD user layer suitably sets the overall trend for each AVD end-user group's environment. The user layer incorporates the evaluation criteria for business preferences, and the AVD end-user group wants to define adequate endpoints and AVD client strategies. Your design decisions affect the versatility and functionality of each AVD end-user group.

Four essential design factors of user layer are devices, peripherals, security and management. See Figure 4-74.

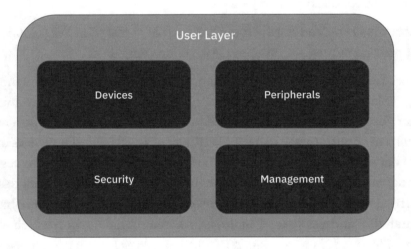

Figure 4-74. *Key design elements for user layer*

Devices, corporate-wide endpoint determination is a key step in your design. All endpoints have their capabilities, including:

- Laptop (BYOD and enterprise owned)

- Desktop PC

- Thin client

- Tablet-based (BYOD and enterprise held)

- Smartphone (BYOD and enterprise held)

AVD clients are deployed to maintain AVD resources on Windows 10, Windows 10 IoT Enterprise, and Windows 7 using the Windows desktop client.

The web client lets an AVD end user access their AVD resources from a web browser without the long deployment process.

The AVD end user can access AVD resources from their iOS and Android device. AVD end users use the Android client on Chromebook devices that support the Google Play Store. AVD end users also use the Apple store on devices that support it.

The AVD end user can access AVD resources from their macOS devices with the Microsoft AVD client.

The AVD end user can access AVD resources from the corporate-owned thin client. AVD supports a majority of partners, including 10ZiG, Dell, HP, IGEL, NComputing, and Stratodesk.

In your design, make sure user endpoint devices align with AVD cloud consumer business objectives and each user's role and requirements. The use of multiple endpoints may be appropriate in many circumstances, each offering different capabilities.

In many businesses, endpoint devices are corporate-owned and controlled. However, more and more companies are organizing supports for BYOD to improve remote employee working, decrease costs, and simplify device management.

Peripherals: Azure virtual support for peripherals attached to an AVD end-user client device is a fundamental functionality. Support for many client-side peripherals exists. Therefore, AVD users can use their peripheral devices seamlessly with applications that have been published remotely.

Client-side peripherals are supported in one of two primary methods:

- Device-Level Redirection – This method involves the high-level device's redirection (a.k.a. "mapping") known by the OS, such as keyboards, mice, or printers. The OS does not identify such devices by the hardware ports they connect but preferably by the device itself. The following tables examine the support matrix for the device and other redirections across the various clients. These tables cover the redirections that AVD end users can access once in an AVD remote session.

Redirection/ Mapping	Windows Desktop Client	Microsoft Store client	Android	iOS	macOS	Web client
Keyboard	Yes	Yes	Yes	Yes	Yes	Yes
Mouse	Yes	Yes	Yes	Yes	Yes	Yes
Touch	Yes	Yes	Yes	Yes		Yes
Local drive/storage	Yes	Yes	Yes	Yes	Yes	Yes
Microphones	Yes	Yes	Yes	Yes	Yes	Yes
Speakers	Yes	Yes	Yes	Yes	Yes	Yes
Scanners	Yes					
Smart cards	Yes					

- Port-Level Redirection: This method means the redirection of the low-level port itself. It involves communication port (COM), line printer terminal (LPT), and USB ports. The OS knows these ports, and traffic is redirected between the AVD session host and the AVD client. When the AVD administrator enables USB port redirection, any USB devices attached to the USB port are automatically recognized in the AVD session.

Redirection/ Mapping	Windows Desktop Client	Microsoft Store client	Android	iOS	macOS	Web client
Serial Port	Yes					
USB	Yes					

Security: An AVD administrator must control access to the applications and data in the AVD environment when distributed workers access it from multiple devices. The protection of AVD resources accessed from personal devices is generally essential. A few design things to think about when presenting AVD resources to mobile devices:

- What help can a jailbroken device access?

- Can AVD end users copy/paste between personal apps and AVD apps?

- Can AVD end-user devices with no configured passcode get access to AVD resources?

- Can mobile device users access Intranet sites with a browser optimized for mobile devices or a pooled desktop browser?

Management: Endpoint management solution should offer complete asset visibility, reporting & monitoring, and comprehensive management of your corporate-owned device. You need comprehensive management because of AVD client updates and much more.

AVD client updates: Microsoft is actively developing the AVD client. The software is regularly updated with new features or fixes to address user issues. With any actively developed product, the latest version should be deployed to endpoints so that users can take advantage of the newest functionality and maintain compliance with product support lifecycles. The AVD administrator can update AVD client and associated plug-ins using a variety of methods.

- **Auto-Update** via Internet

- **Enterprise software deployment** – ESD tools provide a business with direct control over the time/frequency of AVD client updates to managed devices. Additional design thinking must be given to updating unmanaged devices and endpoints outside of the corporate firewall.

- **Manual updates** – When no automated solution is open, manual methods that can be used to update AVD client are the final choice. Whether deployed on an AVD client for a Web site or an external site, these options will require user involvement in updating the AVD client. Manual updates have a dynamic nature that can lead to user error.

Summary

In this chapter, you read about designing and deployment essentials of each building block of the AVD solution DaaS, a list of design principles, best practices to be considered in your design and deployment for Azure virtual, desktop.

In the final chapter of the book, you will read about AVD management and security.

CHAPTER 5

Managing and Securing AVD Solution

In the last chapters, we have read about design essentials and deploying Azure Virtual Desktop (AVD). Now you're ready to manage day 2 operations of AVD.

AVD enables its end users to be productive and stay connected with a desktop and application virtualization experience identical to what AVD end users used to have after moving to Windows Server 10 and Windows 10 Enterprise. Latency concerns about cloud-hosted desktops worry many businesses. Microsoft Azure supports over 60 regions worldwide, so you can get a virtual desktop and applications close to any user's location and establish a fast connection. Thus, users are able to remain productive during long loading times.

To understand distributed systems operations for AVD, as a reader of this book, you must first know how it is different from typical enterprise datacenter management. One must also understand the source of tension between procedures and basic techniques for scaling operations. System administration is a continuum. On one end is a regular IT department, firm for traditional desktop and client-server computing infrastructure, often called IT Ops. On the other end, a site reliability engineering (SRE) or comparable team is accountable for a cloud computing environment, generally connected with the cloud-hosted solution and services. While this may be a comprehensive generalization, it assists in illustrating some notable differences.

So, managing and securing AVD cloud-native solutions for day 2 operation needs a broader skill set than regular on-prem VDI management. In this chapter, let us read about it.

© Puthiyavan Udayakumar 2022
P. Udayakumar, *Design and Deploy Microsoft Azure Virtual Desktop*,
https://doi.org/10.1007/978-1-4842-7796-6_5

By the end of this chapter, you should be able to understand the following:

- Managing AVD Solution

- Securing AVD Solution

- Resiliency for AVD Solution

Managing AVD Solution

Managing AVDs based on the Microsoft Azure platform is done in the SRE way. In this chapter, let us get started by understanding what SRE is.

Reliability represents an AVD capability to function under declared circumstances for a specified period. Reliability engineering is a subprocess of systems engineering that maintains AVD's ability to run without a crash. Reliability is closely associated with availability, typically defined as an AVD's capability to run at an itemized moment or time interval as agreed between service provided and service consumer.

Traditionally, VDI support functions enable system & security administrators to run complex on-premises infrastructure in line with security standards and compliance demands. However, on-prem infrastructure started to evolve as a cloud offering. In the digital workplace, private and public are current and hybrid cloud is the future. The way of working is demanding adoption of an agile approach. Agile methodology demands features that remove unnecessary burns on time, effort, and cost. It is time for VDI administrators to develop the skills from site reliability engineers (SREs) to fulfill the digital workplace needs.

SRE is fundamentally changing the way of work done by infra and security ops teams. Changing the position involves using infrastructure-as-code (IaC) skills and pressuring IT administrators to put automation into place for manual, repetitive tasks. Let us look at the critical skills needed to become a successful AVD specialized site reliability engineer. Skills include software engineering, design thinking, analysis, business needs, functional and nonfunctional, business requirements gathering, design, deployment, testing, implementing changes, and maintenance of a well-engineered AVD system.

Success in SRE means to progress efficiently and securely, offering a flawless AVD system of services for AVD end users. When you work as a team, the SRE AVD team is responsible for automation, reliability, availability, latency, performance, efficiency, change management, monitoring, emergency response, capacity planning, compliance, and security of services. At a glance, SRE is an approach to operations that ensures continuous integration and delivery of applications that run very efficiently and reliably using software engineering, automation, and orchestration solutions. The critical concept is engineering, which includes a science-driven approach to operations, a culture of automation to deliver efficiency and reduce toil, and structured and unstructured data-driven methodology in incident, performance, and capacity tasks. Figure 5-1 depicts the transition from conventional methodology to an SRE-based approach.

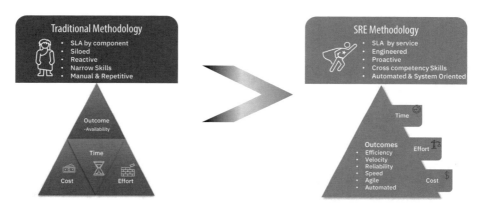

Figure 5-1. *Traditional methodology transition to SRE methodology*

SRE is in a stable position to become much more than that because it focuses more on the people and process of improvement towards AVD functions than on the software and technology components underneath them. Nevertheless, if you ask SREs who are on the organizations' jobs, they may give us different SRE descriptions. As the next step, let us read about why SREs demand the modern digital workplace. Traditionally, companies have employed system administrators L1 to L4 to manage complex VDI traditional environments.

With an ever-going continuous shift in IT digital services aimed at delivering business requirements, changes are constant. A new business strategy approach is essential and requires a new set of principles and guidelines to support the best practices in achieving end users' desired outcomes. The SRE-built and driven solution enables hybrid cloud operations to provide reliability, availability, velocity, flexibility, quality, recoverability, and performance essential for modern-day business.

As enterprises redeploy themselves and adopt a cloud-native hybrid, they must deliver more incredible speed than ever before with more system and site reliability. Traditionally, VDI systems were managed and controlled via numerous processes, methodology, and tools. Often reliability is left at the application, product, or infrastructure component design level, and critical nonfunctional requirements are given less priority at the operational level.

Figure 5-2 illustrates the traditional system engineer vs. SRE key change in the digital era approach.

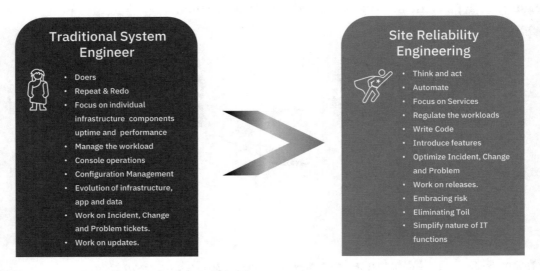

Figure 5-2. *Key characteristics of SRE*

The essential list of characterizes is expected by the global markets from every individual SRE.

- SREs specialize in reliability and resiliency with knowledge & skills in software and systems.

- SREs should build their skills around DevOps, DevSecOps, and AI-Ops.

- SREs should focus on the system reliability that delivers IT services without disruptions despite location and network connectivity.

- SREs should focus on service availability that should withhold any failures, and IT services should remain working from a user's perspective.

- SREs should create, modify, and update code and use software engineering methodologies to develop, deploy, upgrade, and maintain Agile features meaningful to business users and on-demand write code to gain better visibility into the IT functions.

- SREs should deal with operations like system engineering issues and ease deployments and configuration via IaC.

- SREs should engage with core product/developer teams to find and apply the fix for production outages.

- SREs should actively participate in the release of new features as per Agile methodologies.

- SREs should focus on reducing tasks that are human dependent, repetitive, automatable, tactical, devoid of enduring value, and that scale linearly as a service grows through automation.

- SREs should use a scientific approach to find facts and conclude driving factors based on data.

SRE is a methodology for AVD functions that ensures that functions are regularly delivered and run efficiently with reliability, founded in the use of system thinking, software engineering, automation, and artificial intelligence capabilities.

The way of working is going to change for IT administrators. IT administrators need to gain critical skills to be SREs. The essential skills are systems and software engineering. SRE extends existing skills, including 50% in managing, monitoring via Azure monitor or third-party solution, resolving the incidents, and performing root causes analysis. The remaining 45% of the time is spent overperforming blameless post-mortems, developing new features that reduce toil via automation, embracing the risk, preparing for disaster recovery (DR), and improving reliability via AVD service improvement actions. See Figure 5-3.

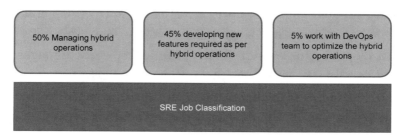

Figure 5-3. *Day of life as SRE*

The AVD SRE job in a day has many moving parts and needs to balance the system's velocity, change, and reliability with the art of creating. As an approach to understanding the foundation for any solution, the IT industry believes it starts with understanding the basic success criteria as a reader. The following are the essential success criteria for SRE. Successful deliverables of the AVD SRE role will be evaluated via service-level agreement (SLA), SLI, SLO, and the definition of slowness and outages. You have already read about SLA, SLI, and SLO in this chapter's previous section. I am sure that you know what SLA all is about, and let us get directly into SLO. Setting a measurable engineering objective that maps towards the service-level objective (SLO) is critical to define the success criteria. Measuring the quality of service-level indicator (SLI) for every AVD function within an IT organization is a must criterion. SLO should always be defined, measured, and governed. Applying an SLO is something new to smaller organizations. SLO aims to offer the mathematical definition of what happy users are seeking.

In the SRE world, defining an outage is another critical parameter. An outage can also be slowness reported by the AVD users and not necessarily be in the system. To summarize the success criteria of an SRE, start with SLA, SLO, SLI, and the definition of an outage, inclusive of slowness. You need to understand that system thinking is an essential foundation that should be applied on demand. Figure 5-4 depicts the reliability system thinking.

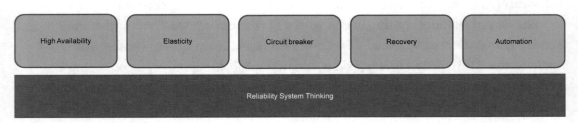

Figure 5-4. *Foundation for system thinking*

AVD SREs should also work on identifying actionable tasks and improving the velocity at the same time. AVD SREs should discover the use case and failure points covering broad areas of AVD function such as single point of failure, high availability (HA), scale-out and in, circuit breaker and resiliency monitoring, event management, logging, business continuity, and DR. AVD SREs can improve the velocity of automating the build test, and Deployment scenario that focus on immutable and mutable deployment models and intensely focus on zero downtime deployments can be achieved through Agile mechanisms such as continuous integration and continuous deployment.

AVD SREs should focus on redundant AVD cloud resources to handle the components that are expected to fail, and they must provide a solution: for example, bike application notetaking over a workload executed by a failure system. AVD SREs should have the capability to scale to handle the change in the workload according to volume or complexity needs.

AVD SREs should continuously apply various best practices to prevent the AVD solution from attempting an action known to fail. SREs should always keep an eye open towards every AVD function that is expected to die. In failure, AVD SREs should be prepared to recover the failed IT function as quickly as possible with the required agility. AVD SREs should be equipped themselves with infrastructure automation capability. They should apply software engineering thinking to fix the operational problem, and this indeed will help reduce the toil, improve the accuracy, and automate the process.

The following essential foundation is that SREs also need to restore failed AVD functions. Their job is to make sure that issues do not reoccur. A blameless post-mortem needs to identify the root cause of an incident and result in a balanced action plan to address them. Figure 5-5 represents the service management specific to SRE.

Figure 5-5. *Foundation for service management with respect to SRE*

Traditional VDI administrators are typically not required to mitigate the risk, whereas AVD site reliability engineers embrace risk in a controlled manner. They follow the error budget method to identify agreeable risks and make formal decisions about when major or minor change requests are to be implemented. The error budget lets AVD SREs limit the amount of time the system is allowed to be down, as agreed by service providers and service consumers as per SLA or the highlighted SLO. The majority of the service consumers stop new releases made by service providers whenever service providers are predicted to be missing the SLA.

Error budget removes the barriers, moves forward with a step ahead, and allows us to perform required modern testing and release if downtime is acceptable as per contract agreement between the service provider and service consumer.

In AVD functions reported to be unreliable, service consumers have a total obligation to restrict any change implementation. If no reliability issues are reported to the EUC service management organization, SREs will use the opportunity to innovate or upgrade features as required to bring additional reliability to AVD functions.

The following essential foundation of AVD site reliability engineers should be writing code in line with automation principles to build, provision, update, upgrade, decommission, rollback, and rebuild using the desired state configuration. Foremost, system administrators need to be AVD SREs. AVD SREs should write code, apply policies per context, and integrate/reuse the existing code from Github with an automation environment. See Figure 5-6.

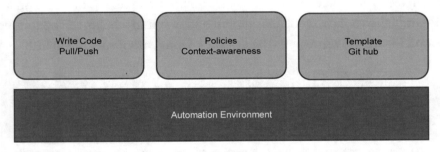

Figure 5-6. *Foundation for automation environment with respect to SRE*

In the digital workplace, automation environments for infrastructure are managed via IaC. Software development practices are applied to infrastructure automation in IaC. It emphasizes consistent, repeatable routines for provisioning and changing AVD solutions and their configuration. You make changes to code, then use automation to test and apply those changes to your plans.

In this book, we show example code to perform day 2 operations using IaC.

The AVD SRE modern workplace management practices demand concept exploits the changing nature of the contemporary workplace, whereas infrastructure and application platform changes are frequent. IaC is an approach to building an AVD solution that embraces continuous change for high reliability and quality.

A successful IT function leads to growth over some time. More individuals consume it; as the IT function grows, changes become more dangerous and more complicated. It frequently becomes a more challenging and time-consuming approach for handling changes; it can be either a bug fix or a service improvement to the IT function. This can significantly create a negative view of the ITSM cycle instead of driving better quality and required results. The industry follows three core practices of IaC to build positive views as in the following.

- Determining all infrastructure components via code,

- Applying continuous testing and delivering,

- Developing small form factors.

IaC is the process of managing and provisioning virtual machines (VMs), containers, and serverless platforms, either on-prem or on the cloud, via machine-readable definition files rather than via interaction tools. As an SRE, you should clarify the difference between "configuration orchestration" and "configuration management" tools, both of which are considered tools. Configuration orchestration systems, such as Terraform and Azure Resource Manager (ARM templates), are designed to automate infrastructure components' deployment.

Actually, before probing into that, let me set the display and explain the notion of IaC for those just beginning their journey. Realizing this is key to the recognition of Terraform.

Refactoring physical datacenter to software-defined thus opened the doors and generated the concept of IaC, determining and providing a complete infrastructure architecture based on lines of code.

So what is Terraform? Terraform is an open-source tool developed by HashiCorp that allows you to provide IaC.

IaC @ AVD SRE infrastructure has unfolded from maintaining VM to engineering the complete stacks; let us quickly recall the foundation. Most AVD functions face mounting infrastructure volume and complexity. The AVD SRE team often strives to keep up with this increase with inadequate time and engineers, resulting in the slowed provision, release, updates, patching, and resource commitment. Automation can be used for everyday SRE management tasks such as provisioning, adding, removing, configuring, deploying, and de-provisioning. Automation elucidates AVD SRE at scale, allowing AVD SRE to reacquire limitation over and clarity into infrastructure.

As both infrastructure and networks expand in volume and complexity, it is frequently challenging to manage risk, security, and compliance manually. Manual processes can result in slower exposure and remediation of effects, resource configuration failures, and inconsistent policy application, leaving end-user/

downstream systems vulnerable to compliance concerns, threats, and attacks. Automation can help SREs streamline daily runs and integrate security into processes, apps, and infra/cloud from the beginning.

In the digital workplace, automation environments for infrastructure are managed via IaC. It is the process of collecting and provisioning VMs, containers, and serverless platforms, either on-prem or on the cloud, via machine-readable definition files rather than via interaction tools.

As an AVD SRE, you should clarify the difference between "configuration orchestration" and "configuration management" tools, both of which are considered tools. Configuration orchestration systems, such as Terraform and AWS CloudFormation, are designed to automate the deployment of infrastructure components. Configuration management systems like Chef, Puppet, and many others may help configure the software and services running either on-prem or cloud infrastructure that has already been provisioned.

The following shows the differences between provisioning and configuration tools.

Terraform is a provisioning tool. It is used to provision the infrastructure such as the VMs, networks, and storage where you need to host an application; strictly speaking, it does not deploy the application. I say strictly speaking, as Terraform can deploy custom server images that contain preinstalled applications, but it is just semantics. Products like Chef, Puppet, and Ansible are configuration management tools; they deploy and manage software on existing servers and don't provide the infrastructure components themselves. So, it makes sense that AVD architects often combine provisioning tools such as Terraform with configuration management tools such as Chef, Puppet, and Ansible to gain complete control over their infrastructure and application stacks.

As a reader, just in case if you're new to IaC as a theory, IaC is the method of maintaining infrastructure in a code file willingly rather than the system administrator configuring IT function underlying resources in a console. Resource, in this case, is any part of the infrastructure, either on-prem or cloud, such as a bare metal, VM, containers, storage, backup, security group, network interface, and so on. In the big picture, IaC enables SRE to use command-line interface (CLI) to scope, author, plan, bootstrap, initialize, and apply code files to complete the desired target via an automated process of installing, building, changing, updating, releasing, restoring, and destroying the infrastructure component.

While many of the current tools for IAC exist in the AVD digital workplace world, as an AVD SRE, you have to make sure it is fit for purpose aligning to your AVD environment and make sure the solution you implement can function platform & vendor agnostic, desire state management along with SRE. This produces confidence in the tool, showing that you can orchestrate, manage configuration, perform the application platform, provision, implement continuous delivery, and control security and compliance via the automation.

The method of building your automation works with the workflow depicted in Figure 5-7.

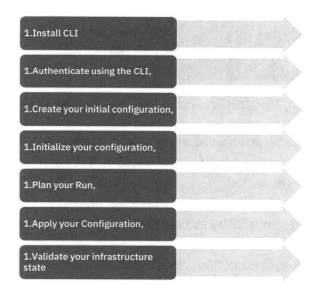

Figure 5-7. *Method of technical enablement*

Method of performing a change in your automation works with the workflow depicted in Figure 5-8.

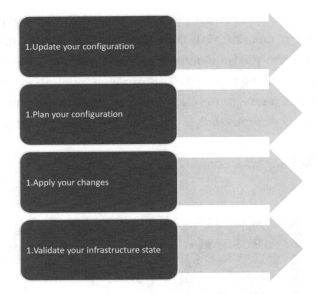

Figure 5-8. *Method of performing change in technical enablement*

Some areas are possible to automate yet not found on the following list; these areas can expand as you work more with different use cases. But the following list shows areas where SREs frequently get started.

Progress application resiliency with chaotic testing: Chaos testing intends to purposefully fail a production AVD function to lessen the time from mean time to failure (MTTF) and mean time to recovery (MTTR). In the big picture, chaotic testing builds the ability to constantly and randomly create various system failure scenarios. SRE practice is expected to inquire about the resiliency of the AVD function and helps to plan MTTR. You can visualize AVD SRE as continuous; stochastic failures are injected into the production AVD function. As service improvements are continuously made into AVD function, the overall production system will become much more reliable and recovery times will be reduced.

Automate alert notifications for first responders: As an SRE, you can visualize the best method to communicate with first responders: combining alert notification solutions into SRE monitoring solutions to create alerts when an issue is identified automatically.

Notification solution you can implement and the following capabilities include sending notifications via various channels, including email, SMS, messages, and integration with enterprise collaboration platforms such as Slack, MS Teams, and so on. Also, you can choose to configure how each responder accepts information.

Centrally control security to reduce sprawl: The problem is that security for infrastructure and application needs to be centralized. Moreover, static IP-based solutions don't scale in the hybrid cloud with ever-varying applications and platforms. As SRE, you can apply the solution to manage, control, and enforce access to security based on trusted sources of application, user identity, and context awareness.

Protect sensitive data in rest and transit in hybrid clouds: All AVD function data should be encrypted for both data in rest and transit; however, implementing cryptography and key management infrastructure is costly and troublesome to execute against.

Key Principles for IaC

Idempotence is a key principle of IaC. Idempotency means whatever the situation arises, SREs run the IAC code. As an SRE, you will end up with the same business agreed and defined state, whatever the current state is. It simplifies the method of provisioning the infrastructure and lessens the uncertainties of variable results. Idempotency can be accomplished via a stateful tool with declarative language.

Immutable infrastructure is a key principle of IaC. Immutable infrastructure means replacing existing infrastructure; as an SRE, you can replace it with new infrastructure components by provisioning new infrastructure every time. As an SRE, you have to make sure it is reproducible and doesn't afford configuration drift across time. Immutable infrastructure also empowers scalability when provisioning infrastructure in a hybrid cloud.

A Terraform cloud infrastructure can be defined, previewed, and deployed. Terraform uses HCL syntax to create configuration files.

In the HCL syntax, AVD SRE can designate Azure and the components of the AVD solution. After creating AVD configuration files, as AVD SRE, you make an execution plan that allows you to preview your infrastructure changes before deploying. Once you verify the changes, you can apply the execution plan to deploy the AVD end to end.

The Azure CLIs are used to build and operate AVD resources. You can use the Azure CLI to work with Azure across all services, emphasizing automation. So Azure CLIs become prerequisites for Terraform. Using an Azure cloud shell environment is the easiest way to learn how to use the Azure CLI. Now let us explore various Microsoft Azure PowerShell virtual desktop command lines: the following command list shows commands used to build a new environment.

Command-Line Syntax	General Description
New-AzWvdApplication	Create an application
New-AzWvdApplicationGroup	Create an applicationGroup
New-AzWvdHostPool	Create a host pool
New-AzWvdMsixPackage	Create an MSIX package
New-AzWvdRegistrationInfo	Create AVD registration info
New-AzWvdScalingPlan	Create a scaling plan
New-AzWvdWorkspace	Create a workspace

The following list shows commands used to get information about your AVD environment.

Command-Line Syntax	General Description
Get-AzWvdApplication	Information of an application
Get-AzWvdApplicationGroup	Information of an application group
Get-AzWvdDesktop	Information of a desktop
Get-AzWvdHostPool	Information of a host pool
Get-AzWvdHostPoolRegistrationToken	Registration token of the host pool
Get-AzWvdMsixPackage	Information of an MSIX package
Get-AzWvdRegistrationInfo	Information of AVD registration info
Get-AzWvdScalingPlan	Information of a scaling plan
Get-AzWvdSessionHost	Information of a session host
Get-AzWvdStartMenuItem	List start menu items in the provided application group
Get-AzWvdUserSession	Information of a userSession
Get-AzWvdWorkspace	Information of a workspace

The following list shows commands used to remove components from your AVD environment.

Command-Line Syntax	General Description
Remove-AzWvdApplication	Delete an application
Remove-AzWvdApplicationGroup	Delete an applicationGroup
Remove-AzWvdHostPool	Delete a host pool
Remove-AzWvdMsixPackage	Delete an MSIX package
Remove-AzWvdRegistrationInfo	Delete the Windows virtual desktop registration info
Remove-AzWvdScalingPlan	Delete a scaling plan
Remove-AzWvdSessionHost	Delete a SessionHost
Remove-AzWvdUserSession	Delete a userSession
Remove-AzWvdWorkspace	Delete a workspace

The following list shows commands used to update components on your AVD environment.

Command-Line Syntax	General Description
Update-AzWvdApplication	Update an application
Update-AzWvdApplicationGroup	Update an applicationGroup
Update-AzWvdDesktop	Update a desktop
Update-AzWvdHostPool	Update a host pool
Update-AzWvdMsixPackage	Update an MSIX package
Update-AzWvdScalingPlan	Update a scaling plan
Update-AzWvdSessionHost	Update a session host
Update-AzWvdWorkspace	Update a workspace

The following list shows misc commands used to manage components on your AVD environment.

Command-Line Syntax	General Description
Disconnect-AzWvdUserSession	Disconnect an AVD user session
Expand-AzWvdMsixImage	Expand and list MSIX packages in an image, provide the image path
Send-AzWvdUserSessionMessage	Send a notification/message to a user

The following list shows register and unregisters commands used on your AVD environment.

Command-Line Syntax	General Description
Register-AzWvdApplicationGroup	Register an AVD application group
Unregister-AzWvdApplicationGroup	Unregister the AVD application group

The following shows the validation of Terraform; using Azure cloud shell, you can deploy Terraform. Upon release of Terraform's new version, cloud shell automatically updates to this version. Nevertheless, if you want to install Terraform immediately, the following steps will show you how to do so.

Validate the version of Terraform using the following:

```
terraform version
```

Terraform is a declarative language. It only acknowledges the desired end-state. If AVD SRE needs to change the size of a Terraform-created AVD VM from Ds4_v4 to Ds8_V4, Terraform will not simply scale as like management tools such as Azure Portal, via PowerShell or Azure CLI; instead, it will destroy and deploy it from the start using the new size.

The Azure provider is to configure the AVD solution in Microsoft Azure using the ARM APIs. The principles of cloud-based AVD infrastructure embody the differences between traditional, static VDI infrastructure and modern, dynamic infrastructure:

- Assume cloud-based systems are unreliable

- Make everything reproducible

- Actualize disposable things

    - to minimize variations

    - so that any task can be repeated

AVD SREs can write infrastructure code more quickly with the human-readable configuration language. Terraform's state will help AVD SRE track changes to resources throughout AVD deployment. AVD SRE can commit their configurations to version control to safely collaborate on infrastructure.

Historical changes made in the AVD environment can be managed via the Terraform state.

Terraform records its state in a custom JSON form in the same folder as the main Terraform files are produced from, saving it as terraform.tfstate.

There are currently five types of AVD resources now available in the Terraform Azure:

- azurerm_virtual_desktop_application

- azurerm_virtual_desktop_workspace

- azurerm_virtual_desktop_application_group

- azurerm_virtual_desktop_host_pool

- azurerm_virtual_desktop_workspace_application_group_association

Terraform providers automatically measure mandates between resources to build or destroy them in exact order.

The following list syntax option used against virtual desktops.

```
azurerm_ virtual_desktop_application
```

The following is the reference link: `https://registry.terraform.io/providers/`
`hashicorp/azurerm/latest/docs/resources/virtual_desktop_workspace`

Terraform Resource	Type	General Description
name	Required	The name of the AVD application. Changing the title requires a new resource to be produced.
application_group_id	Required	Resource ID for an AVD application group to associate with the AVD application. Changing the ID strengths a new resource to be produced.
path	Required	The file path location of the application on the virtual desktop operating system.
command_line_argument_ policy	Required	Defines whether this published application can be launched with command-line arguments presented by the client, command-line arguments specified at publishing time, or no command-line arguments at all. Possible values include: DoNotAllow, Allow, Require.
friendly_name	Optional	Set a friendly name for the remote application.
description	Optional	Set a description for the remote application.
command_line_arguments	Optional	Command-line arguments for remote application.
show_in_portal	Optional	Defines whether to show the remote application program in the RD Web Access server.
icon_path	Optional	Defines the path for an icon which will be used for this AVD application.
icon_index	Optional	The index of the icon the AVD administrator wishes to use.

The following list syntax option used against virtual workspace.

`azurerm_virtual_desktop_workspace`

Terraform Resource	Type	General Description
name	Required	The name of the AVD workspace. Changing the name forces a new resource to be created.
resource_group_name	Required	The name of the resource group in which to create the virtual desktop workspace. Changing the resource group name forces a new resource to be created.
location	Required	The location or region where the AVD workspace is located. Changing the location or region forces a new resource to be created.
friendly_name	Optional	A friendly name for the AVD workspace.
description	Optional	A description for the AVD workspace.
tags	Optional	A mapping of tags to assign to the resource.

The following list syntax option used against Application Group.

`azurerm_virtual_desktop_workspace_application_group_association.`

Terraform Resource	Type	General Description
workspace_id	Required	The resource ID for the virtual desktop workspace.
application_group_id	Required	The resource ID for the virtual desktop application group.

The following list syntax option used against Application Group.

`azurerm_virtual_desktop_application_group.`

Terraform Resource	Type	General Description
name	Required	The name of the virtual desktop application group. Changing the name forces a new resource to be created.
resource_group_name	Required	The name of the resource group in which to create the virtual desktop application group. Changing the resource group name forces a new resource to be created.
location	Required	The location/region where the virtual desktop application group is located. Changing the location/region forces a new resource to be created.
type	Required	Type of virtual desktop application group. Valid options are RemoteApp or desktop application groups.
host_pool_id	Required	Resource ID for a virtual desktop host pool to associate with the virtual desktop application group.
friendly_name	Optional	Option to set a friendly name for the virtual desktop application group.
description	Optional	Option to set a description for the virtual desktop application group.
tags	Optional	A mapping of tags to assign to the resource.

The following list syntax option used against Host Pool.

`azurerm_virtual_desktop_host_pools`

Terraform Resource	Type	General Description
name	Required	The name of the virtual desktop host pool. Changing the name forces a new resource to be created.
resource_group_name	Required	The name of the resource group in which to create the virtual desktop host pool. Changing the resource group name forces a new resource to be created.
location	Required	The location/region where the virtual desktop host pool is located. Changing the location/region forces a new resource to be created.
type	Required	The type of the virtual desktop host pool. Valid options are personal or pooled. Changing the type forces a new resource to be created.
load_balancer_type	Optional	BreadthFirst load balancing distributes new user sessions across all available session hosts in the host pool. DepthFirst load balancing distributes new user sessions to an available session host with the highest number of connections but which has not reached its maximum session limit threshold. Persistent should be used if the host pool type is personal.
friendly_name	Optional	A friendly name for the virtual desktop host pool.
description	Optional	A description for the virtual desktop host pool.
validate_environment	Optional	Allows you to test service changes before they are deployed to production. Defaults to false.
start_vm_on_connect	Optional	Enables or disables the start VM on connection feature. Defaults to false.
custom_rdp_properties	Optional	A valid custom RDP properties string for the virtual desktop host pool; available properties can be found in this article.

(continued)

Terraform Resource	Type	General Description
personal_desktop_assignment_type	Optional	Automatic assignment – The service will select an available host and assign it to an user. Direct assignment – Admin selects a specific host to assign to an user.
maximum_sessions_allowed	Optional	A valid integer value from 0 to 999999 for the maximum number of users that have concurrent sessions on a session host. Should only be set if the type of your virtual desktop host pool is pooled.
preferred_app_group_type	Optional	Option to specify the preferred application group type for the virtual desktop host pool. Valid options are none, desktop or RailApplications. Default is none.
registration_info	Optional	A registration_info block which is documented in the following. Specifies configuration on the registration information of the virtual desktop host pool.
tags	Optional	A mapping of tags to assign to the resource.

Alright! We've built the backbone of the AVD solution in previous chapters, but how do we make it work? This chapter will discuss these and other topics of interest, focusing on the hands-on administration and delivery of the AVD to serve AVD end users. The AVD cloud-hosted solution provides us with two main methods of delivering these applications to AVD end users under Windows/0365 licensing terms: remote applications or pooled/dedicated desktops. Remote applications are installed and run on the pooled RDS server but through the AVD. In the previous chapter, you have seen a method to create a host pool using the Azure portal and assign VM.

In this section, now let us explore the top 10 administrative tasks required to be performed from day 2 operation of your AVD.

You have created a host pool in the previous chapter and workspace that we can utilize to deploy a remote app. Let's build a RemoteApp application group to experience an application with a different user in the business.

Task 1: Create and Publish Applications

- Review the type of application groups

- Prereqs for publishing applications

- Create and publish applications from the Azure portal

- Create and publish applications via AVD PowerShell module

- Create and publish applications via Terraform.

Type of Application Groups

- RemoteApp, wherever AVD end users access the RemoteApps, you independently select and publish to the application group.

- Desktop, wherever AVD end users access the complete desktop.

Prereqs for publishing applications are the following:

- AVD administrator with Azure AD account with subscription owner rights.

- AVD end user accounts in different AD groups for UAT and production.

  - It is essential to validate the published application.

Let us explore how to set up and assign remote applications via Azure Portal (see Figures 5-9 and 5-10).

Step 1: Log in to personal or business account into Azure portal

The following is the link: `https://portal.azure.com/`.

Step 2: Use the search box to discover AVD.

Step 3: Choose Application Groups ➤ Create.

Step 4: Choose the subscription, resource group, host pool, application group type, and application group name.

Subscription	Subscription where you need the application group to run
Resource group	Resource group you've deployed for AVD resources

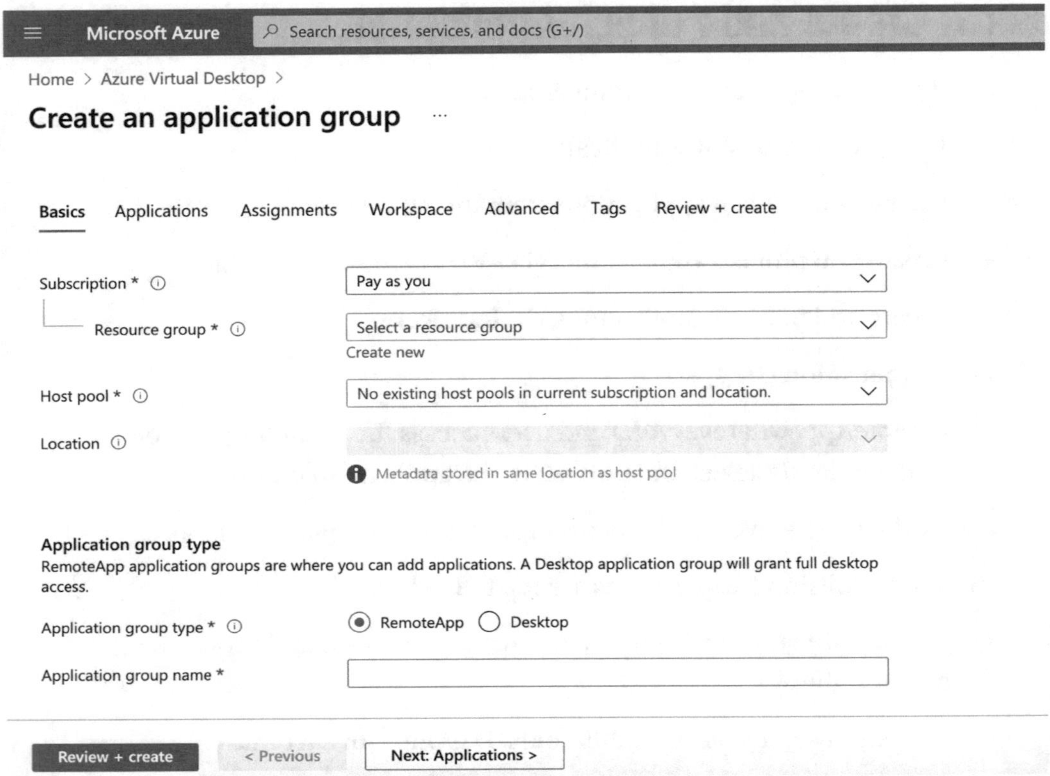

Figure 5-9. *Workflow to create a host pool*

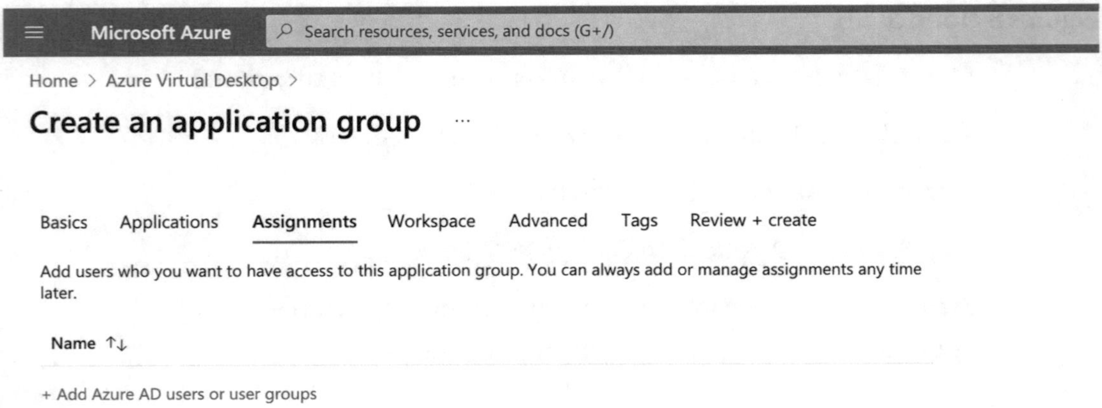

Figure 5-10. *Workflow of create an application group*

Step 5: Choose **Add applications**, Application source (Start menu), Application Name, Display name Application name, icon path, and icon index.

Step 6: Choose Add Azure AD users or user groups; you can choose single or multiple users or AD groups.

Step 7: Next, **register application group**, choose **Yes**, and then **Review + create**.

Upon successful publishing you can validate the application.

Step 1: Go to the AVD web client.

Step 2: Log in using the AVD end-user credentials for the user you assigned to the RemoteApp application group.

Step 3: AVD end users should see the application in the AVD workspace.

Let us explore how to set up and assign remote applications via Azure AZ PowerShell.

All versions of PowerShell 7.x and later work with Azure Az PowerShell. When PowerShell 7.x or later is used, Azure PowerShell needs no additional requirements.

The following is the command used to verify the PowerShell version:

```
$PSVersionTable.PSVersion
```

PowerShell script execution policy needs remote signed or less restrictive.

```
Set-ExecutionPolicy -ExecutionPolicy RemoteSigned -Scope CurrentUser
```

AZ PowerShell module installation is preferred. AZ module will be installed for the current user only.

```
Install-Module -Name Az -Scope CurrentUser -Repository PSGallery -Force
```

The following is the command used to connect to Azure account:

```
Connect-AzAccount
```

The following is the command used to verify the AVD module is installed:

```
Get-InstalledModule -Name Az.Desk*
```

The following is the command used to install the AVD module:

```
Install-Module -Name Az.DesktopVirtualization
```

The following is the command used to update the AVD module:

```
Update-Module Az.DesktopVirtualization
```

The following is the command used to find and configure the host pool ARM path:

```
Get-AzWvdHostPool -ResourceGroupName AVDDEMO -HostPoolName AVDDEMOHP1
$hostPoolArmPath = (Get-AzWvdHostPool -ResourceGroupName AVDDEMO
-HostPoolName AVDDEMOHP1).Id
```

The following is the AZ PowerShell command used to create an application group:

```
New-AzWvdApplicationGroup -Name "PowerShellLabAG" `
    -FriendlyName "PowerShellLabAG" `
    -ResourceGroupName "AVDDEMO" `
    -ApplicationGroupType "RemoteApp" `
    -HostPoolArmPath $hostPoolArmPath `
    -Location CentralUS
```

The following is the AZ PowerShell command line used to publish built-in apps:

```
New-AzWvdApplication -Name <appname> -ResourceGroupName
<Azresourcegroupname> -ApplicationGroupName <appgroupname> -FilePath
"shell:appsFolder\<PackageFamilyName>!App" -CommandLineSetting
<Allow|Require|DoNotAllow> -IconIndex 0 -IconPath <iconpath>
-ShowInPortal:$true
```

The following is the command used to verify an application group:

```
Get-AzWvdApplicationGroup
```

The following is the command line used to publish Microsoft Edge built-in apps:

```
New-AzWvdApplication -Name -ResourceGroupName -ApplicationGroupName -FilePath
"shell:Appsfolder\Microsoft.MicrosoftEdge_8wekyb3d8bbwe!
MicrosoftEdge" -CommandLineSetting <Allow|Require|DoNotAllow> -iconPath
"C:\Windows\SystemApps\Microsoft.MicrosoftEdge_8wekyb3d8bbwe\
microsoftedge.exe" -iconIndex 0 -ShowInPortal:$true
```

As for the next method, let us explore how to set up and assign remote applications via Terraform.

The following shows the installation of Terraform; using Azure cloud shell, you can deploy Terraform. Upon release of Terraform's new version, cloud shell automatically updates to this version. Nevertheless, if you want to install Terraform immediately, the following steps will show you how to do so.

Validate the version of Terraform using the following:

```
terraform version
```

The following sample code shows the method to create a remote application group:

```
Create RemoteApp Application Group resource
"azurerm_virtual_desktop_application_group" "AVDRemoteApp"
{
    name = var.pooledhpremoteappname
    location = var.region
    resource_group_name = azurerm_resource_group.default.name
    type = "AVDRemoteApp"
    host_pool_id = azurerm_virtual_desktop_host_pool.pooleddepthfirst.id
    friendly_name = var.pooledhpremoteappfriendlyname
    description = var.pooledhpremoteappdescription
}
```

The following sample code shows the method to publish a remote application (i.e., Google Chrome):

```
resource "azurerm_virtual_desktop_application" "chrome" {
  name                          = "googlechrome"
  application_group_id          = azurerm_virtual_desktop_application_group.
                                    remoteapp.id
  friendly_name                 = "Google Chrome"
  description                   = "Chromium based web browser"
  path                          = "C:\\Program Files\\Google\\Chrome\\
                                    Application\\chrome.exe"
  command_line_argument_policy = "DoNotAllow"
  command_line_arguments       = "--incognito"
```

```
show_in_portal              = false
icon_path                   = "C:\\Program Files\\Google\\Chrome\\
                              Application\\chrome.exe"
icon_index                  = 0
}
```

The following sample code shows the method to associate a remote application group with workspace resource:

```
"azurerm_virtual_desktop_workspace_application_group_association"
"AVDRemoteapp"
{
workspace_id = azurerm_virtual_desktop_workspace.workspace.id
application_group_id = azurerm_virtual_desktop_application_group.
pooledremoteapp.id
}
```

Task 2: Set Drain Mode Enable and Disable

The AVD administrator applies patches and performs maintenance; the drain mode separates a session host from other users. If the session host is isolated, new sessions will not be accepted. Sessions will continue to run until a user logs out or the AVD administrator terminates it. AVD administrators can also connect directly to the server without using the AVD service when the session host is in drain mode. AVD administrators can implement this setting to both pooled and personal desktops.

Drain mode can be turned on via the Azure portal:

1. Open the Azure portal and go to the host pool you want to isolate.

2. Choose Session hosts.

3. Next, choose the hosts you want to turn on drain mode for, then choose Turn drain mode on.

Drain mode can be turned off via the Azure portal:

1. Open the Azure portal and go to the host pool you want to isolate.

2. Choose Session hosts.

3. Next, choose the host pools with drain mode turned on, then choose Turn drain mode off.

Execute the following cmdlet to enable drain mode:

```
Update-AzWvdSessionHost -ResourceGroupName <resourceGroupName>
-HostPoolName <hostpoolname> -Name <hostname> -AllowNewSession:$False
```

Execute the following cmdlet to disable drain mode:

```
Update-AzWvdSessionHost -ResourceGroupName <resourceGroupName>
-HostPoolName <hostpoolname> -Name <hostname> -AllowNewSession:$True
```

Task 3: Create and Publish Desktop

Creating a host pool, specifying the session host VMs, and creating an AVD workspace are the first steps in deploying AVD.

Desktop application groups are created as next. After that, the virtual desktop will be assigned to the appropriate user and enabled in the user's workspace.

Let us explore how to set up and assign personal desktop via Azure Portal.

Step 1: Log in to personal or business account into Azure portal.

- The following is the link: https://portal.azure.com/.

Step 2: Access **Azure Virtual Desktop** via the search bar, then locate and choose **Azure Virtual Desktop** under Services and in the **Azure Virtual Desktop** summary page, choose to **Create a host pool**. See Figure 5-11.

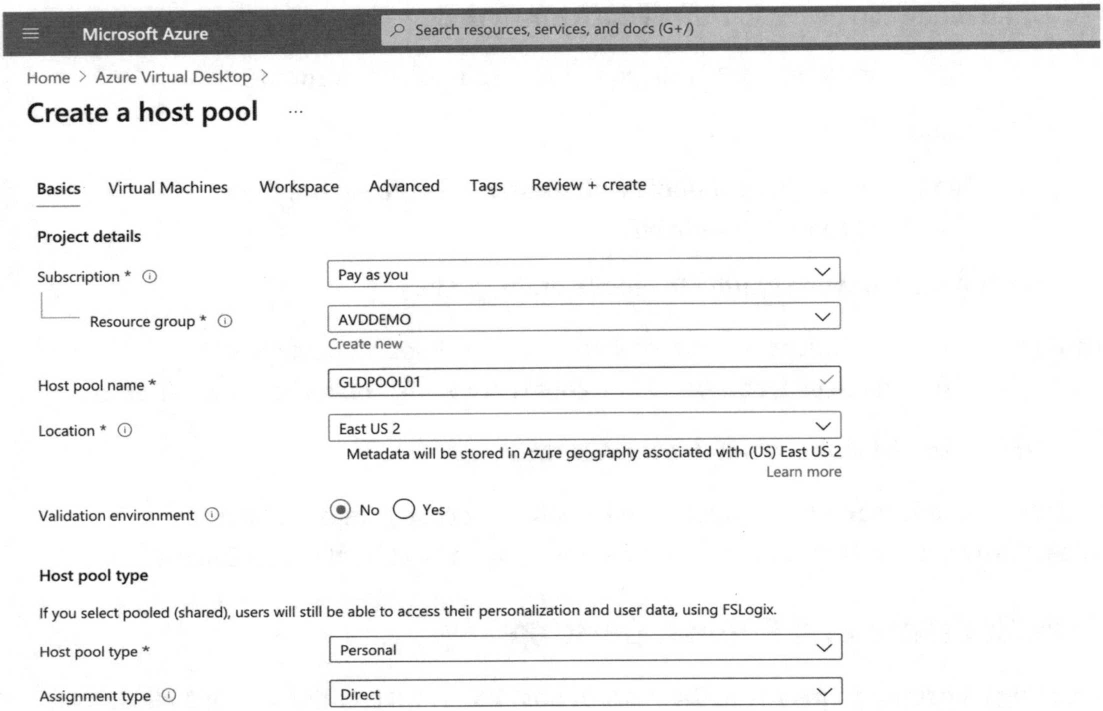

Figure 5-11. *Workflow of create a host pool*

Step 3: In the **Basics** tab, provide the following project details:

1. Choose the exact subscription.

2. Register a unique title for your AVD host pool.

3. Choose the Azure region where the AVD objects are to be deployed. The metadata for the object will be in the geography associated with the territory.

4. The validation host pool allows your AVD instance for dev/UAT service changes before production is set up.

5. Choose host pool type; if your AVD administrator chooses the pooled (shared), AVD end users will still access their personalization and user data using FSLogix.

Under the Host pool type, the AVD administrator chooses whether the host pool will be **Personal** or **Pooled**. If your AVD administrator determines **Personal**, they can select either **Automatic** or **Direct** in the Assignment Type field.

Automatic assignment – AVD service will choose an available desktop and assign it to an AVD end user.

Direct assignment – The AVD administrator will choose a specific host to assign to an AVD end user.

6. Assume as an AVD administrator that you choose personal and direct to meet the requirement for dedicated desktop.

Step 4: In the **Virtual Machines** tab, provide the following project details, and enter the following information against the VM tab as per the table that follows Figure 5-12.

Field	Value
Add VMs	Yes
Resource group	Azure resource group AVD administrator created for AVD resources
VM location	Azure region needs to be on the same location as your virtual network
VM size	Select the VM size you want to use. You can either keep the default size as-is or choose Change size to adjust the size. If you choose Change size in the window that appears, pick the size of the Azure VM suitable for your workload
Number of VMs	1
Name prefix	AVD-Pooled-Direct
Image type	Gallery

(*continued*)

Field	Value
Image	• Windows 10 Enterprise, Version 1909 • Windows 10 Enterprise, Version 1909 (GEN2) • Windows 10 Enterprise, Version 2004 • Windows 10 Enterprise, Version 2004 (GEN2) • Windows 10 Enterprise, Version 20H2 • Windows 10 Enterprise, Version 20H2 (GEN2)
OS disk type	Standard SSD
Use managed disks	Yes
Virtual network	VNet that can communicate to the domain controller
Subnet	Subnet AVD administrator created to dedicated AVD segment VMs
Public IP	No
Network security group	Basic
Public inbound ports	No
Specific domain or unit	Yes
Domain to join	Choose whether you require the AVD VMs to be joined to Active Directory (AD) or Azure AD
AD domain join UPN	User name for the user account that's assigned to the AD Domain administrator role
Password	Password for the AD Domain administrator's account
Confirm password	Confirm the password

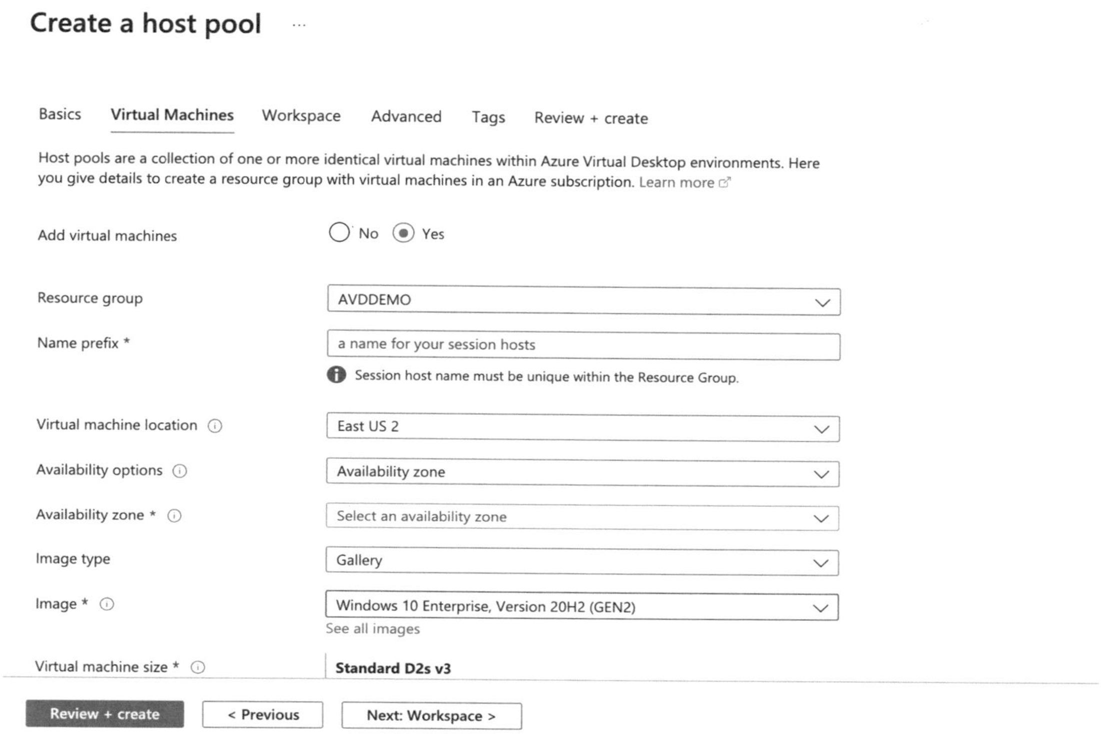

Create a host pool ...

Basics   **Virtual Machines**   Workspace   Advanced   Tags   Review + create

Host pools are a collection of one or more identical virtual machines within Azure Virtual Desktop environments. Here you give details to create a resource group with virtual machines in an Azure subscription. Learn more ⌐

Add virtual machines	○ No ⦿ Yes
Resource group	AVDDEMO ⌄
Name prefix *	a name for your session hosts
	ⓘ Session host name must be unique within the Resource Group.
Virtual machine location ⓘ	East US 2 ⌄
Availability options ⓘ	Availability zone ⌄
Availability zone * ⓘ	Select an availability zone ⌄
Image type	Gallery ⌄
Image * ⓘ	Windows 10 Enterprise, Version 20H2 (GEN2) ⌄
	See all images
Virtual machine size * ⓘ	**Standard D2s v3**

[Review + create]   [< Previous]   [Next: Workspace >]

Figure 5-12. *Workflow of create a host pool*

Step 7: On **Workspace** tab, provide the following registration details to register the desktop app group to a workspace:

1. Choose **Yes**.

   If you select **No**, the AVD administrator can register the app group later. Still, Microsoft recommends that the AVD administrator get the workspace registration done ASAP, so your host pool works appropriately.

2. Next, choose whether you require to set up a brand-new workspace or choose from already existing workspaces. Only workspaces designed in the exact location as the host pool will register the remote application group.

Step 8: On **Tags** tab, provide the following:

- Optionally, the AVD administrator can select **Next: Tags ➤**.

- Here you can add tags to group the objects with metadata to make things easier for your admins.

Step 9: Finally, select Review + **create.**

Step 10: Assign desktop application group to the user.

Assign the desktop application group to an AVD end-user account that's in AD.

1: Choose Application groups.

2: Choose the desktop application group.

3: Choose Access control (IAM) ➤ Add ➤ Add role assignment.

4: For Role, select Desktop Virtualization User.

5: For Select, enter the name of an AVD end-user account that's in AD.

6: Choose Save.

Upon successful publishing you can validate the application.

1: Go to the AVD web client.

2: Log in using the AVD end-user credentials for the user you assigned to the pooled direct desktop application group.

3: AVD end-users should see the AVD pooled direct desktop in the AVD workspace.

Now that you know various methods to deploy a desktop and remote application to a workspace, let's customize the workspace.

Task 4: Set Up and Configure Workspace

Step 1: Log in to personal or business account into Azure portal

- The following is the link: `https://portal.azure.com/`.

Step 2: Use the search box to find Azure Virtual Desktop and choose Workspace.

Step 3: You can create a workspace; configure workspace name and friendly name. See Figure 5-13.

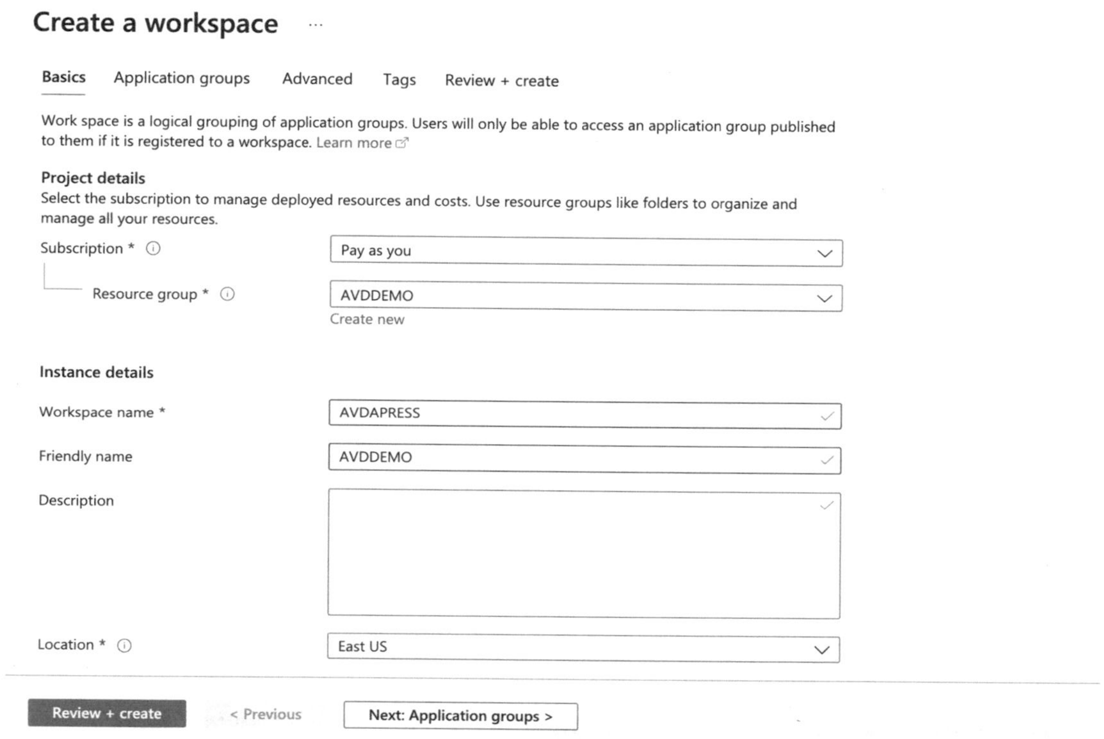

Create a workspace ⋯

Basics   Application groups   Advanced   Tags   Review + create

Work space is a logical grouping of application groups. Users will only be able to access an application group published to them if it is registered to a workspace. Learn more ⃞

Project details
Select the subscription to manage deployed resources and costs. Use resource groups like folders to organize and manage all your resources.

Subscription * ⓘ	Pay as you ⌄
Resource group * ⓘ	AVDDEMO ⌄
	Create new

Instance details

Workspace name *	AVDAPRESS ✓
Friendly name	AVDDEMO ✓
Description	✓
Location * ⓘ	East US ⌄

Review + create   < Previous   Next: Application groups >

Figure 5-13. *Workflow of create a workspace*

Step 4: You can customize a workspace; update workspace name and friendly name post creation if required. See Figure 5-14.

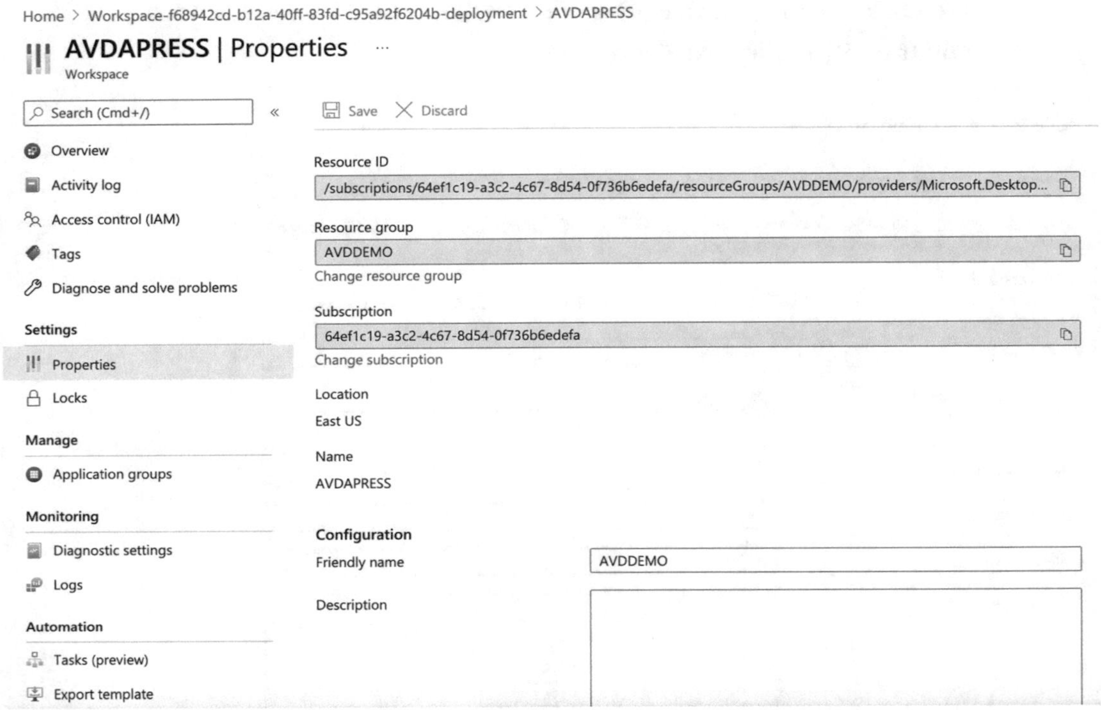

Home > Workspace-f68942cd-b12a-40ff-83fd-c95a92f6204b-deployment > AVDAPRESS

AVDAPRESS | Properties ...
Workspace

Search (Cmd+/) «	🖫 Save ✕ Discard

- 🌐 Overview
- ▤ Activity log
- 🔒 Access control (IAM)
- 🏷 Tags
- 🔧 Diagnose and solve problems

Settings
- ⋮⋮ Properties
- 🔒 Locks

Manage
- 📦 Application groups

Monitoring
- 📊 Diagnostic settings
- 📈 Logs

Automation
- 🔩 Tasks (preview)
- 📤 Export template

Resource ID
/subscriptions/64ef1c19-a3c2-4c67-8d54-0f736b6edefa/resourceGroups/AVDDEMO/providers/Microsoft.Desktop... 📋

Resource group
AVDDEMO 📋
Change resource group

Subscription
64ef1c19-a3c2-4c67-8d54-0f736b6edefa 📋
Change subscription

Location
East US

Name
AVDAPRESS

Configuration
Friendly name
AVDDEMO

Description

Figure 5-14. *Workflow to update workspace*

The following is the AZ PowerShell command used to create a desktop pool.

```
az desktopvirtualization hostpool create --host-pool-type
{Personal, Pooled}
                                --load-balancer-type
                                {BreadthFirst, DepthFirst,
                                Persistent}
                                --location
                                --name
                                --personal-desktop-assignment-type
                                {Automatic, Direct}
                                --resource-group
```

The following is the sample code.

```
az desktopvirtualization hostpool create --location "eastus"
--description "Dedicated" --friendly-name "My Desktop" --host-pool-type
"Personal"  --personal-desktop-assignment-type "Direct" --registration-
info expiration-time="2020-10-01T14:01:54.9571247Z" registration-token-
operation="Update" --sso-context "KeyVaultPath" --tags tag1="value1"
tag2="value2" --name "MyClientOSPool" --resource-group "AVDDEMO"
```

The following is the AZ PowerShell command used to assign a single user to a direct desktop pool.

```
New-AzRoleAssignment -SignInName "AVDEMO@apress.com" `
    -RoleDefinitionName "Desktop Virtualization User" `
    -ResourceName "AVDEMODIRECT" `
    -ResourceGroupName "DIRECTPOOL" `
    -ResourceType "Microsoft.DesktopVirtualization/applicationGroups"
```

The following is the AZ PowerShell command used to verify role assignment.

```
Get-AzRoleAssignment -ResourceGroupName " DIRECTPOOL" `
    -ResourceName " AVDEMODIRECT" `
    -ResourceType "Microsoft.DesktopVirtualization/applicationGroups" `
    -RoleDefinitionName "Desktop Virtualization User"
```

In the next method, let us explore how to set up and assign desktop via Terraform. Validate the version of Terraform using the following in Azure cloud shell or CLI.

```
terraform version
```

The following sample Terraform code shows the method to create a desktop.

```
resource "azurerm_resource_group" "example"
{
  name     = "AVDDEMO"
  location = " Europe"
}

resource "azurerm_virtual_desktop_host_pool" "example" {
  location            = azurerm_resource_group.example.location
  resource_group_name = azurerm_resource_group.example.name
```

```
name                     = "pooleddepthfirst"
friendly_name            = "pooleddepthfirst"
validate_environment     = true
start_vm_on_connect      = true
custom_rdp_properties    = "audiocapturemode:i:1;audiomode:i:0;"
description              = "Acceptance Test: A pooled host pool -
                             pooleddepthfirst"
type                     = "Personal"
personal_desktop_assignment_type = "Direct"
}
```

Task 5: Install and Configure AVD Agent

The AVD service topology has three central elements: remote desktop client, the AVD service, and the AVD session host pool.

The session host lives in the cloud customer subscription where the AVD agent and agent bootloader are deployed. The AVD agent acts as the common integration point between the AVD service and the AVD session machines, facilitating connectivity. Accordingly, if the AVD administrator is experiencing issues with the agent deployment, update, or configuration, the AVD session host won't connect to the AVD service. The agent bootloader is the binaries that load the agent.

A Geneva monitoring agent is deployed as soon as the agent is installed. It is required for AVD and AVD end users to establish a secure server-to-client reverse connection. The health of the Geneva monitoring agent is monitored. To ensure correct end-to-end connectivity, each of these components is necessary.

The Microsoft-recommended way to deploy AVD VMs is using the Azure portal creation template. The template carries automated deployment of the AVD agent. Confirm that the two components are deployed by checking in Control Panel ➤ Programs ➤ Programs and Features. If AVD agent and AVD agent boot loader aren't visible, they aren't deployed on the VM. Deploying the following are prerequisites to prepare your AVD session host VMs. Make sure to register the VMs to your AVD host pool:

- AVD administrator must domain-join the machine. It allows incoming AVD end users to be assigned from their Azure AD account to their AD account and successfully access the virtual desktop and applications.

- The session host VM runs a Windows server OS; AVD must install the remote desktop session host (RDSH) role. The RDSH position allots the AVD agents to install correctly.

To support a secure AVD environment in Azure, Microsoft recommends that the AVD administrator not open inbound port 3389 on AVD VMs. AVD doesn't need an open inbound port 3389 for AVD end users to access the session host pool.

Download and run the installer. During the time of writing this book, the latest version was Microsoft.RDInfra.RDAgent.Installer-x64-1.0.3130.2900.

Click Next (Figure 5-15).

Figure 5-15. *Workflow to RDS infrastructure agent setup*

Review and accept the license agreement (Figure 5-16) and click Next. If you are asked for the registration token by the installer, enter the value returned by Get-AzWvdRegistrationInfo (Figure 5-17).

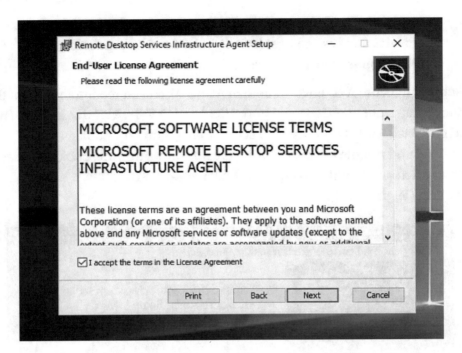

Figure 5-16. *Workflow to RDS infrastructure agent setup*

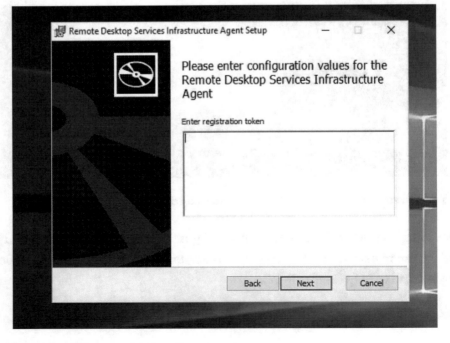

Figure 5-17. *Workflow to RDS infrastructure agent setup*

As an alternate option, the package administrator can use the Super ORCA application source to modify the .msi file and attach the generated token value.

Complete the deployment. And as the next step, download and run the installer Microsoft.RDInfra.RDAgentBootLoader.Installer-x64.msi.

Review and accept the license agreement and click Next (Figure 5-18).

Figure 5-18. *Workflow to agent boot loader setup*

Click Next (Figure 5-19).

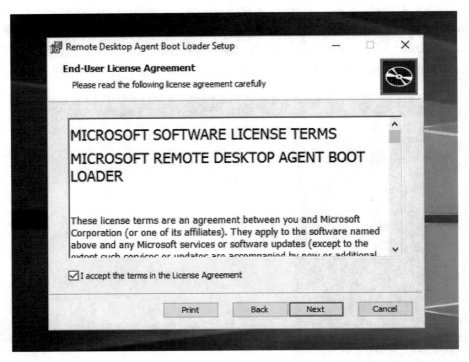

Figure 5-19. *Workflow to agent boot loader setup*

Complete the installation and reboot your AVD VM (Figure 5-20).

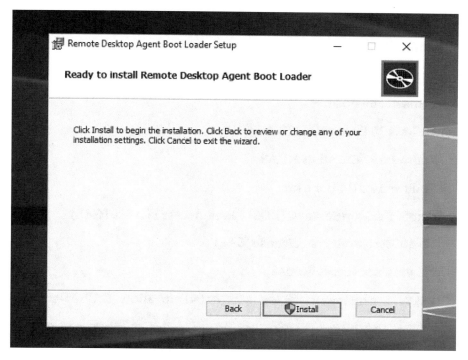

Figure 5-20. *Workflow to agent boot loader setup*

Task 6: Install and Configure FsLogix Client

Microsoft has enlarged its capacity to produce essential endpoint abilities to AVD users from anywhere. Designed to change the standard AVD capabilities, installing FSLogix on AVD can improve nonpersistent environment needs. The following are the key benefits.

- Manage user context and consistent log-in times for nonpersistent environments

- Optimize file I/O between host/client and remote profile store

- Simplify the management of applications and golden images

- Specify the version of Java to be utilized by specific URL and applications

As per Microsoft, the following license holders are eligible to use FSLogix.

- Microsoft 365 E3/E5

- Microsoft 365 A3/A5/ Student Use Benefits

- Microsoft 365 F1/F3

- Microsoft 365 Business

- Windows 10 Enterprise E3/E5

- Windows 10 Education A3/A5

- Windows 10 VDA per user

- Remote Desktop Services (RDS) Client Access License (CAL)

- RDS Subscriber Access License (SAL)

- AVD per-user access license

The FSLogix setup installs in the following default location: 'C:\Program Files\FSLogix\Apps'

- FrxTray.exe offers FSLogix Profile system tray status utility

- ConfigurationTool.exe offers FSLogix Profile configuration tool

- FrxContext.exe offers FSLogix vhd(x) context manager

The FSLogix setup includes three installers that are utilized to deploy the specific elements needed for AVD use.

- FSLogixAppsSetup.exe for FSLogix Apps Agent installer

- FSLogixAppsRuleEditorSetup.exe for FSLogix Apps Rule Editor installer

- FSLogixAppsJavaRuleEditorSetup.exe for FSLogix Apps Java Rule Editor installer

Download and run the installer FSXLogixAppSetup.exe, review and accept the license agreement, and click Install (Figure 5-21).

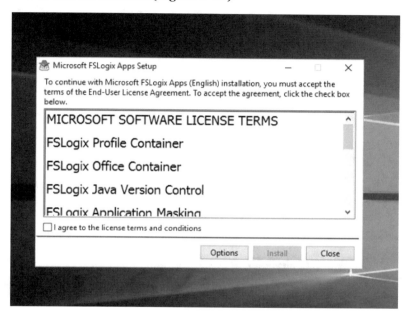

Figure 5-21. *Workflow to FSLogix app setup*

Click Options to modify default installation path (Figure 5-22).

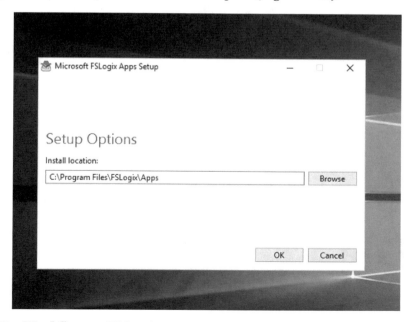

Figure 5-22. *Workflow to FSLogix app setup*

Click OK, and click Install (Figure 5-23).

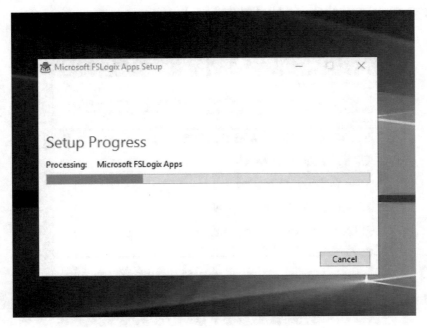

Figure 5-23. *Workflow to FSLogix app setup*

Click Finish to complete the installation (Figure 5-24).

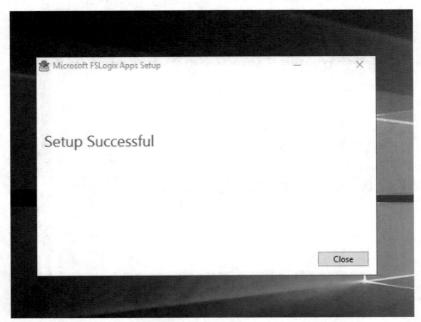

Figure 5-24. *Workflow to FSLogix app setup*

As the next step, download and run the installer FSLogixAppsRuleEditorSetup.exe. Review and accept the license agreement and click Install (Figure 5-25).

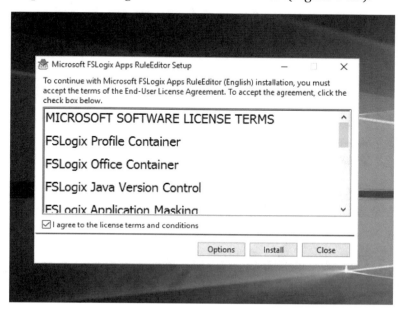

Figure 5-25. *Workflow to FSLogix app rule editor setup*

Click Options, to modify default installation path (Figure 5-26).

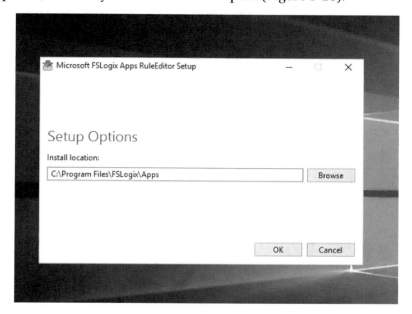

Figure 5-26. *Workflow to FSLogix app rule editor setup*

Click OK, and click Install (Figure 5-27).

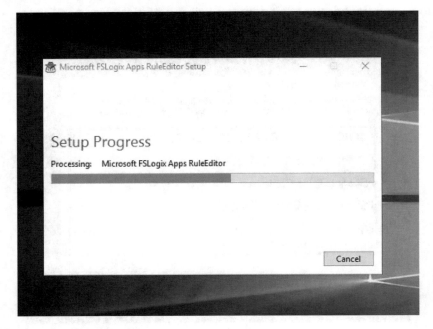

Figure 5-27. *Workflow to FSLogix app rule editor setup*

Click Finish to complete the installation (Figure 5-28).

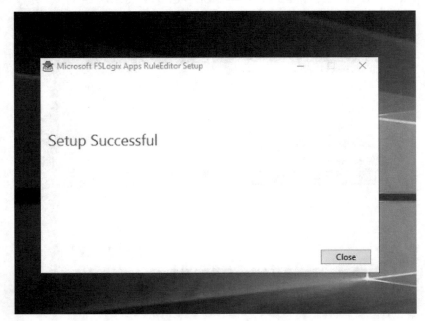

Figure 5-28. *Workflow to FSLogix app rule editor setup*

Download and run the installer FSLogixAppsJavaRuleEditorSetup.exe, Review and accept the license agreement and click Install (Figure 5-29).

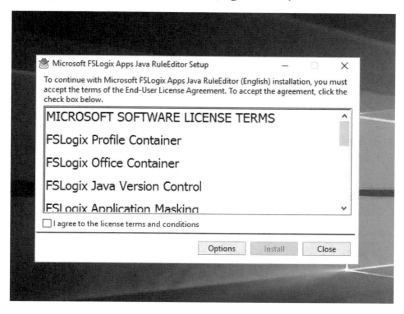

Figure 5-29. *Workflow to FSLogix apps Java rule editor setup*

Click OK, and click Install (Figure 5-30).

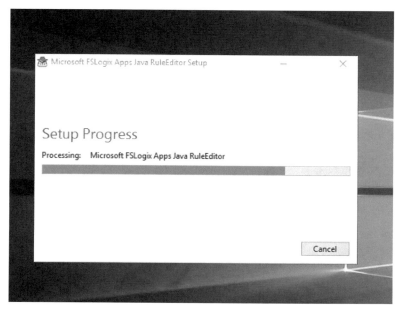

Figure 5-30. *Workflow to FSLogix apps Java rule editor setup*

Click Finish to complete the installation (Figure 5-31).

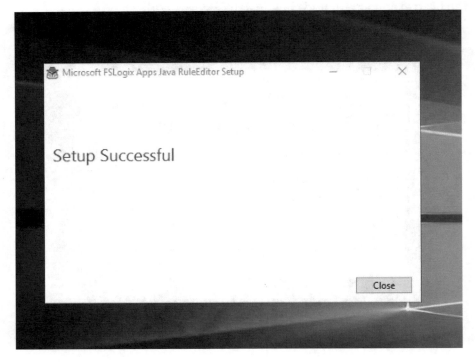

Figure 5-31. *Workflow to FSLogix apps Java rule editor setup*

Alternate method of deployment using unattended installation

Silent Install Switch	Description
/install	Product installation
/repair	Supports repair
/uninstall	Command for uninstall
/quiet	Hides the installation wizard
/norestart	Suppresses restart after deployment

Task 7: Install and Configure Microsoft 365 Proplus

There are several versions of Microsoft Office available through many Office 365 (and Microsoft 365) plans. It includes familiar applications such as Access, Excel, OneNote, Outlook, PowerPoint, Publisher, Skype for Business, One Drive, Teams, and Word. These applications can connect to Microsoft 365 services like SharePoint Online, Exchange Online, and Skype for Business Online via Office 365 (or Microsoft 365).

Shared computer activation lets an AVD administrator install Microsoft 365 Apps for enterprise to an AVD golden image that is obtained by multiple session hosts and users.

Use the Office O365 deployment tool to deploy Office. Office versions supported by Windows 10 Enterprise multisession are:

- Microsoft 365 Apps for enterprise

- Microsoft 365 Apps for business along with Business Premium subscription

You can download and install Microsoft 365 apps on the golden image with the Office Deployment Tool (ODT). The ODT gives AVD administrators more control over an Office installation: AVD administrator can determine a set of products and languages to be installed, preferred update method, location, and whether or not to display the install experience to your users. ODT requires an XML configuration file.

After downloading the file, run the self-extracting executable file containing the ODT executable (setup.exe) and a sample configuration file (configuration.xml).

Before using the ODT to download or install Office, we recommend ensuring you have the latest version.

The ODT consists of two files: setup.exe and configuration.xml. To work with the ODT, you can edit the configuration file to define what options the AVD administrator wants and then run setup.exe from the command line. For instance, the AVD administrator can edit the configuration file to install the 64-bit English edition of Office with the EULA automatically accepted.

Prepare officeConfig.XML

```
Configuration>
  <Add SourcePath="\\DFS\AVDShare"
       OfficeClientEdition="32"
       Channel="SemiAnnual" >
```

```
    <Product ID="O365ProPlusRetail">
      <Language ID="en-us" />
      <Language ID="ja-jp" />
    </Product>
    <Product ID="VisioProRetail">
      <Language ID="en-us" />
    </Product>
  </Add>
  <Updates Enabled="TRUE"
          UpdatePath="\\Server\Share" />
    <Display Level="None" AcceptEULA="TRUE" />
</Configuration>
```

Parameters	Description
Add SourcePath="\\DFS\AVDShare"	Office will be downloaded to "\\server\share" on AVD network and deployed using installation files at that location
Add OfficeClientEdition="64"	Downloads and installs the 64-bit edition of Office
Add Channel="SemiAnnual"	Microsoft Office will be deployed using Semi-Annual Enterprise Channel
Product ID="O365ProPlusRetail"	Downloads and installs Microsoft 365 Apps for enterprise
Language ID="en-us"	Downloads and installs US English versions
Updates Enabled="TRUE"	Microsoft Office will check for updates
Updates UpdatePath="\\DFS\ AVDShare\Update"	Microsoft Office checks for updates at "\\DFS\AVDShare\ Update " on AVD network
Display Level="None" AcceptEULA="TRUE"	During installation of Office, no user interface is displayed and licenses are accepted silently

The following shows the overall steps involved in the installation.

Step 1: Download

> To download Microsoft 365 Apps products and languages, use **download** mode.

```
For instant, setup.exe /download officeconfig.xml
```

Step 2: Direct deploy

> To deploy the downloaded Microsoft 365 Apps products and languages on a session host. Syntax **configure** mode is used to install, remove and update Office products and languages.

```
For an instant, setup.exe /configure officeconfig.xml
```

> **(Optional) - Prepare the package (AppV)**

> To create an App-V package for Microsoft 365 Apps. Syntax **packager** mode is used for App-V sequencing.

```
For an instant, setup.exe /packager officeconfig.xml
```

Step 4: Customized installation

> To apply new O365 preferences to AVD session hosts that already have Microsoft 365 Apps installed. Syntax **customize** mode is used to apply only application preferences without altering any other deployment configurations.

```
For instant, setup.exe /customize officeconfig.xml
```

Task 8: Install and Configure Microsoft Teams

AVDs with Microsoft teams support chat and collaboration. With media optimizations, it also helps to call and to meet functionality.

With media optimization for Microsoft teams, the Azure desktop client controls audio and video locally for team calls and meetings. AVD end users can use Microsoft teams on AVD with other clients without optimized calling and meetings like Cisco Webex or Zoom.

Microsoft Teams integrate with SharePoint and Outlook and offer messaging, wiki pages, and storage functionality. Teams also permit to run virtual meetings amongst AVD end users in your AVD world from anywhere. Facilitating meetings in teams requires thoughtful planning and preparation.

Microsoft teams can be installed on a machine or a user basis. There are two versions of teams installation. Currently, VDI with audio/video optimization is certified with AVD.

An AVD administrator must at the very least open the following common ports and locations, for all locations, for media in teams, in addition to the normal web traffic.

- TCP ports 80 and 443 outgoing from clients that will use teams

- UDP ports 3478 through 3481 outgoings from clients that will use teams

- IP address ranges:

  - 13.107.64.0/18

  - 52.112.0.0/14

  - 52.120.0.0/14

Here is the process of the per-user default installation

```
msiexec /i <path_to_msi>/Teams_windows_x64.msi /l*v <install_logfile_name>
```

Microsoft uses this to install teams to the %AppData% of every user folder. Teams won't work appropriately with per-user installation on a nonpersistent setup.

Here is the process of the per-machine default installation:

```
msiexec /i <path_to_msi>/Teams_windows_x64.msi /l*v <install_logfile_name>
ALLUSER=1
```

Microsoft installs teams to the program files (x86) folder on a 32-bit and the program files folder on a 64-bit operating system of the golden image. Deploying Microsoft teams per machine is recommended for nonpersistent setups.

Two different parameters are possible:

```
ALLUSER=1 and ALLUSERS=1.
```

It is essential to know the difference between them. The ALLUSER=1 parameter is used only in VDI settings to specify a per-machine installation. The ALLUSERS=1 parameter can be used in non-VDI. The AVD administrator can find the machine-wide installer in Control Panel/Programs and Features and Windows Settings/Apps and Features. To prepare the golden image for teams, run RegEdit as an administrator. Navigate to `HKEY_LOCAL_MACHINE\SOFTWARE\Microsoft\Teams`.

Set `IsWVDEnvironment – DWORD 1`.

Deploy the teams key if it doesn't previously exist.

Task 9: Create MSIX Package to the Host Pool

All Windows apps can be packaged with MSIX, a modern package format for Windows apps. In addition to enabling modern packaging and deployment features to Win32, Windows forms, and Windows presentation foundation apps, the MSIX package format preserves the functionality of existing app packages and install files. The following are the key benefits.

- Reduce the complexity of traditional software packaging and deployment.

- Rather than delegating the packaging and distribution of software to specific teams, empower software developers to own the entire process from design to deployment.

- With pipelines, existing manual processes can be automated.

- Through the new self-service approach, Windows desktop apps will be deployed faster and easier, resulting in significant cost savings.

- Compared to other container formats, MSIX is fast and straightforward. The Microsoft Store provides applications packaged using MSIX.

With MSIX, AVD cloud consumer organizations can ensure their applications are always up-to-date and current. By reducing repackaging, it allows IT pros and developers to deliver a user-centric solution while still reducing the cost of ownership.

At the time of writing this book. MSIX supported on the following versions of Windows:

- Windows 10, version 1709, and later.

- Windows Server 2019 LTSC and later.

- Windows Enterprise 2019 LTSC and later.

Applications packaged with MSIX run inside a lightweight app container. With the help of virtualization, MSIX app processes and their children are segregated and isolated in the container. The global registry is accessible to all MSIX applications. MSIX apps write to their virtual registry and application data folder, all deleted after uninstalling or resetting the app. The virtual registry and file system of an MSIX app aren't accessible to other apps. To maintain compatibility with existing applications, an MSIX package must separate the application state as much as possible from the system state. Microsoft Windows 10 achieves this by placing the application inside an MSIX package, then detecting and redirecting some changes it makes to the system's file system and registry at runtime.

AVD administrators create packages of desktop applications that are desktop-only applications that have full-trust authorization to interact with other desktop applications the same way that classic desktop applications do. In MSIX App packages, the executable is named application_name.exe, and is placed at C:/Program Files/WindowsApps/ MSIX_Package_Name. A file (AppxManifest.xml) in each package folder contains the XML namespace for each packaged app. There is an <EntryPoint> element in that manifest file, indicating a full-trust app. It runs as the user instead of inside an app container when that application is launched. Once deployment is completed, MSIX package files are read-only and locked down by the guest operating system. Microsoft Windows stops apps from launching if these files have been tampered with.

The following are critical steps in preparing the MSIX Packaging environment.

- MSIX Packaging Tool requires Windows 10 1809 as the minimum OS version.

- Microsoft recommends using a clean VM that is preconfigured for the minimum version of support for the MSIX packaging tool.

- The MSIX packaging tool can create an MSIX application package from any of the following options: current package methods such as MSI, EXE, ClickOnce, Microsoft App-V, Script, and manual installation.

AVD Packager will first want to understand what will happen with the installer you wish to convert. AVD Packager can specify them here to interpret workflow with any of the following installers, or AVD Packager can manually operate it at the moment of installation later in the workflow. It is most commonly used to create an application package. To build an MSIX package, AVD packagers use installers or manually deploy client applications to develop MSIX packages (Figure 5-32).

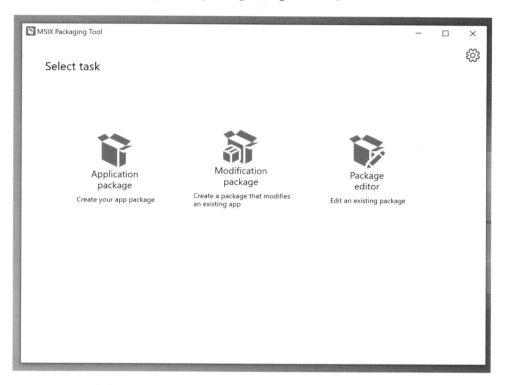

Figure 5-32. *Workflow to MSIX packaging*

The MSIX packaging tool offers three choices: let us choose Create package on this computer (Figure 5-33).

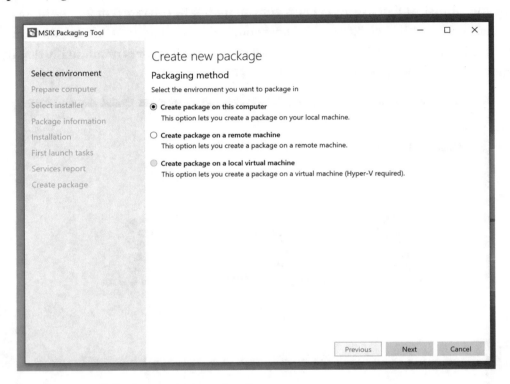

Figure 5-33. *Workflow to MSIX packaging*

For the MSIX packaging tool driver to be deployed, Windows updates must be disabled and there must be no pending reboot.

The **MSIX Packaging Tool Driver** is required, and the MSIX packaging tool will automatically try to enable it if it is not allowed. The MSIX packaging tool will first check with deployment image servicing and management (DISM) to see if the driver is deployed. Our AVD packagers will temporarily disable Windows update during packaging to prevent the collection of unnecessary data (Figure 5-34).

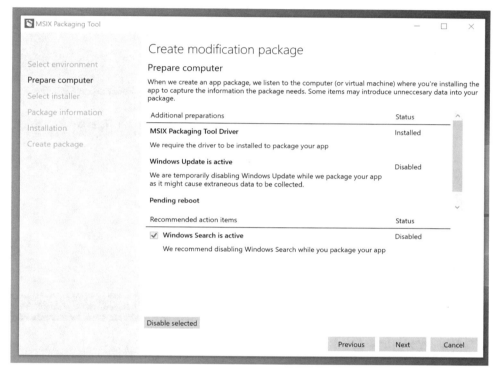

Figure 5-34. *Workflow to MSIX packaging*

For this book's purpose, let us use notepad.exe to demonstrate MSIX packaging creation (Figure 5-35).

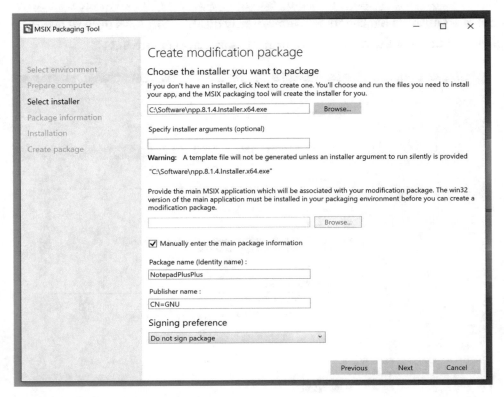

Figure 5-35. *Workflow to MSIX packaging*

Choose a signing preference under Signing preference. If AVD Packager sets this up in MSIX settings, AVD packages save a few steps whenever they convert. See Figure 5-36.

- Sign with Device Guard signing

- Sign with a certificate(.pfx)

- Specify a .cer file (does not sign)

- Do not sign package

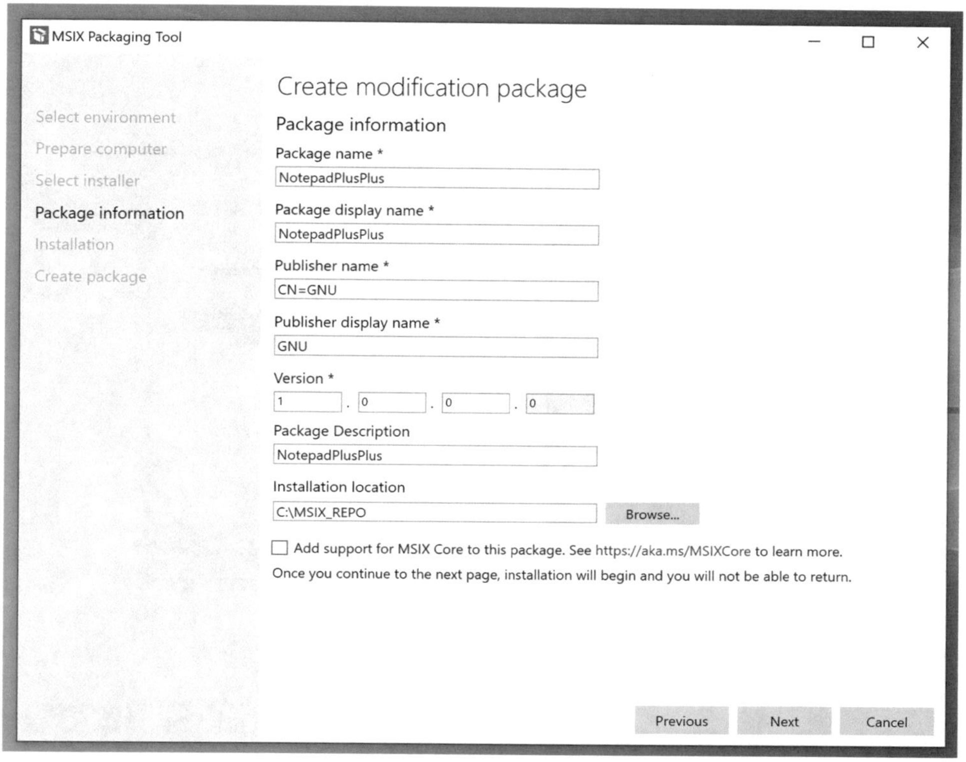

Figure 5-36. *Workflow to MSIX packaging*

Upon choosing to package your application, you must provide details about the application. In order to fill in these fields, the tool will use the installer's information. Whenever necessary, you can update the entries. When a field has an asterisk*, it is required. The entry is provided with inline help if it is not valid.

Click Next. This is the phase of applying software packages, when MSIX packaging tools monitor and record the installation process. The MSIX packaging tool will launch the installer in the environment that was previously specified, and AVD Packager will have to go through the installation wizard to install the application.

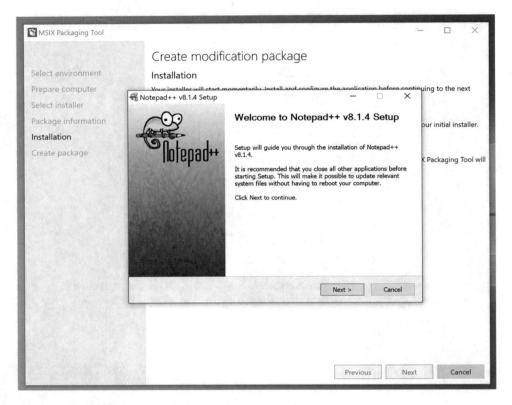

Figure 5-37. *Workflow to MSIX packaging*

When the packager has completed the deployment of the application, click **Next**
(Figure 5-37).

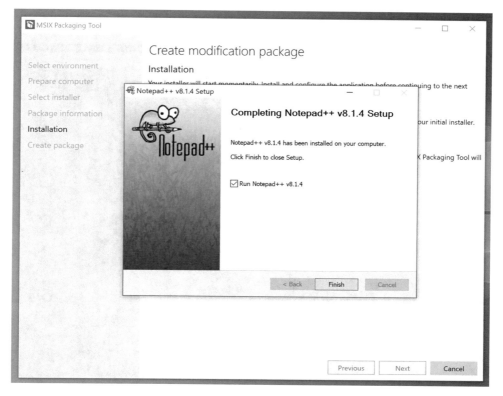

Figure 5-38. *Workflow to MSIX packaging*

Click Next. You'll be prompted with a pop-up asking for confirmation that you're finished with application installation and managing first launch tasks (Figure 5-38).

- If you're done, click Yes and move on.

Click Create Package and save the package in your preferred location (Figure 5-39).

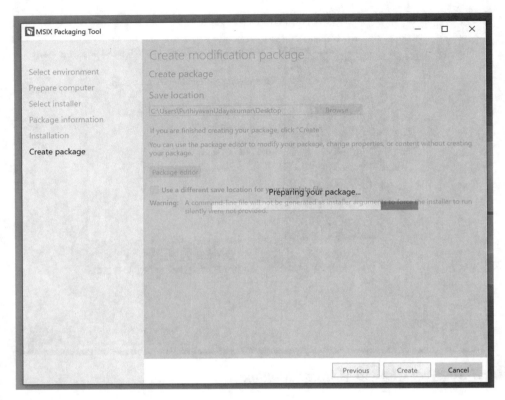

Figure 5-39. *Workflow to MSIX packaging*

This completes the MSIX packaging process.

Task 10: Add and Publish MSIX Package to the Host Pool

In this task, we will add the MSIX image to the AVD host pool.To add the MSIX image:

Step 1: Log in to personal or business account into Azure portal

The following is the link: https://portal.azure.com/.

Step 2: Enter **Azure Virtual Desktop** into the search bar, then select the AVD service name.

Step 3: Choose the AVD host pool where you intend to place the MSIX apps.

Step 4: Choose **MSIX packages** to open the data grid with all **MSIX packages** currently added to the host pool.

Step 5: Choose **+ Add** to open the **Add MSIX package** tab.

Step 6: In the **Add MSIX package** tab, enter the following values:

> For **the MSIX image path**, enter a valid UNC path pointing to the MSIX image on the file share and interrogate the MSIX container to check if the path is correct.

> For **the MSIX package**, choose the appropriate MSIX package name from the drop-down menu.

> For **Package applications**, make sure the list contains all MSIX applications you want to be available to users in your MSIX package.

> Optionally, enter a **Display name** if you require your MSIX package to be more user-friendly in AVD end-user deployments.

> Make sure the **Version** has the exact version number.

> Choose the **Registration type** you require to utilize.

> **On-demand registration** postpones the full registration of the MSIX application till the AVD end user starts the apps. This is the registration model Microsoft recommends using.

> **Log on blocking** only registers while the user is signing in.

Step 7: Toward State, choose your preferred State.

> The Active status allows AVD end users to interact with the MSIX package.

> The Inactive status does not allow AVD end users to interact with the MSIX package.

When you're completed, Choose **Add**.

In this task, we will publish the MSIX image to the AVD host pool. To publish the MSIX image, perform the following tasks.

Step 1: Log in to personal or business account into Azure portal

> The following is the link: `https://portal.azure.com/`.

Step 2: Search Azure Virtual Desktop using the search bar, then select the AVD service name.

Step 3: Choose the Application groups tab.

Step 4: Choose the application group you want to publish the applications to.

Step 5: Once you're in the application group, select the Applications tab. The Applications grid will reveal all existing applications within the application group.

Step 6: Choose + Add to open the Add application tab.

Step 7: For the application source, choose the preferred type for your application.

> If you're using a desktop application group, choose the MSIX package.
>
> For the Application name, enter a definitive name for the application.
>
> An AVD administrator can also set up optional pieces such as Display Name and Description.
>
> If you're using a remote app group, you can also configure these options:
>
> Icon path, Icon index, and Show in the web feed.

When you're finished, choose Save.

Securing AVD Solution

Microsoft manages the AVD infrastructure and brokering components, while enterprise customers manage their desktop VMs, data, and clients. This approach allows an enterprise to focus on what's essential to it, such as user experience.

Microsoft security baseline applies to AVD. The Microsoft Azure Security Benchmark provides recommendations on how to secure and use compliance. The security controls are shown in the following table as per Microsoft Azure Security Benchmark. A significant difference between desktop-as-a-service (DaaS) and traditional on-premises VDIs lies in how security is managed. Traditionally, the customer is responsible for all aspects of security in an on-premises VDI. Most DaaS providers and their clients share these responsibilities. AVD cloud users should be aware that while some components come configured for AVD, other areas need to be configured to meet their organization's security needs.

The following table illustrates the AVD cloud consumer responsibility.

AVD Components	Responsibility
Physical Datacenter inclusive of Host, Storage and its networks	Microsoft Managed
AVD Control Plane	Microsoft Managed
AVD Control Plane MFA and Conditional Access	AVD Cloud Consumer responsibility
User Apps, Data, Device, and Identity	AVD Cloud Consumer responsibility
AVD Session Host – End Point Protection	AVD Cloud Consumer responsibility
AVD Session Host – Threat and Vulnerability Assessment	AVD Cloud Consumer responsibility
AVD Session Host – Patch Management	AVD Cloud Consumer responsibility
AVD – Secure Boot, vTPM, Virtualization-based security, Windows Defender Guard, Hypervisor-Protect Code integrity	AVD Cloud Consumer responsibility

Figure 5-40 shows the various AVD security pillars applicable for AVD solutions.

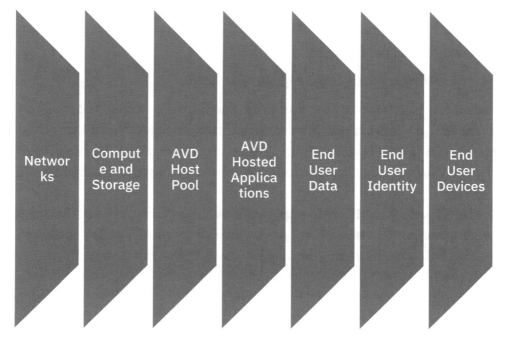

Figure 5-40. *AVD security pillars*

Networking - Network security covers controls to achieve and shield Azure networks. Secure virtual networks, establish private connections, prevent and mitigate external attacks, and secure DNS are included. All Azure virtual networks should be segmented according to the company's risk appetite. Having a network security group (NSG) and a firewall within the virtual network will be sufficient to adequately secure any system that may incur a higher risk for the company. Try to avoid direct RDP connections to session hosts in your environment. Direct RDP access is required for administration or troubleshooting. Connect from an internal network or enable just-in-time access to limit the potential attack surface on the session host. Use Azure firewall to configure your AVD session host pool subnet user established route to route all transactions via Azure firewall.

Compute and Storage - An AVD VM gives you the flexibility of virtualization without buying and maintaining the physical hardware that runs the VM. AVD administrators can build and deploy your applications to ensure that your data is protected and safe in highly secure data centers. With Azure, AVD administrators can build security-enhanced, compliant solutions that:

- Protect AVD VMs from viruses and malware.

- Encrypt AVD sensitive data.

- Provide reliable network traffic.

- Identify and detect threats.

- Meet industry-standard compliance demands.

Have backup and recovery programs to ensure that data backups and configurations at different AVD service tiers are performed, validated, and protected. Plan and implement the following as a minimum: Ensure regular automated backups, Encrypt backup data, Validate all backups, including customer-managed keys, and Mitigate the risk of lost keys.

AVD Host Pool and AVD Hosted Applications - To help secure your AVD hosts and applications, you can take several actions and use various tools. Configuring Microsoft Defender for Endpoint, formerly known as Microsoft Defender Advanced Threat Protection, can help protect your endpoints against malware and advanced threats. For creating and checking compliance with policies, Microsoft Intune is used. Additionally, you can use it to install apps, features, and settings on your device that runs on Azure. Unapproved software can be prevented from running by using AppLocker. AppLocker control policies restrict a file's access based on its attributes, product name, or version. The AppLocker rule collection includes default rules to ensure that Windows-required files are included in the AppLocker rule collection.

Securing End-User Data - As part of your AVD environment, you allow users to access and store their data. Azure Disk Encryption: As the solution for profile containers, Azure Files supports on-premises AD DS with Azure AD DS identity-based authentication using the server message block protocol (SMB). Azure Files uses Kerberos protocols for authenticating with either AD DS or Azure AD DS. Through Azure NetApp Files, all files used by Windows virtual desktop are encrypted according to the Federal Information Processing Standards Publication (FIPS PUBS) 140-2 standard. A unique XTS-AES-256 key is generated for each volume by Azure NetApp Files.

Securing End-User Identity - Microsoft's Windows client for AVD is an excellent option for connecting AVD to local machines to help you keep AVD end users safe when you configure your AVD. By using Azure AD, Azure AD draws together signals, makes decisions, and enforces company policies. The identity-driven control plane is built on conditional access. Policies for conditional access can be viewed as if-then statements: users must perform one or more actions if they want to access a resource.

Securing End-User Devices - Detection and response are core elements of endpoint security. For Azure environments, this includes using the endpoint detection and response (EDR) service and anti-malware service, using centrally managed modern anti-malware software, and ensuring that anti-malware software and signatures are updated. You can design and deploy infrastructure and endpoint security, threat intelligence, security compliance management as per AVD cloud consumer in-country demands, and posture management.

AVD Components	Description
Network Security	Security for Azure networks includes: -Securing and protecting virtual internal networks. -Setting up private connections. -Preventing and mitigating external attacks. -Simply network security tags and rules-Securing DNS.
Identity Management	Using Azure AD, Identity Management covers the control of how identities are created; authentications are strengthened, managed identities and service principles for applications, conditional access, and monitoring of account anomalies.
Privileged Access	The Protected Access control set protects Azure tenants and resources against deliberate and accidental risk by shielding privileged access to your tenant. It includes tools to protect your administrative model, accounts, and workstations against intentional and accidental danger.
Data Protection	Azure Data Protection enables Azure customers to control their data protection at rest, in transit, and through authorized access mechanisms. The controls allow customers to discover, classify, protect, and monitor sensitive data assets through access control, encryption, and logging.
Asset Management	The Asset Management controls provide security visibility and governance over Azure resources, including granting the correct permissions to security personnel, controlling access to asset inventory, and managing approvals for services and resources (list, track, and right).
Logging and Threat Detection	Describes controls to detect threats using Azure services and to enable, collect, and store audit logs for Azure services, including capabilities to generate high-quality alerts for Azure services using native threat detection.It also includes collecting logs with Azure Monitor, centralizing security analysis with Azure Sentinel, time synchronization, and log retention.

(continued)

AVD Components	Description
Incident Response	Azure Security Center and Sentinel automate the incident response process with Azure services known as Incident Response, including preparation, detection and analysis, containment, and post-incident activities.
Posture and Vulnerability Management	Managing security posture and vulnerabilities, or managing posture and exposures, involves controlling the assessment and improvement of Azure security posture in various ways, such as vulnerability scanning, penetration testing, remediation, and tracking security configurations and reporting.
Endpoint Security	Endpoint Security covers EDR controls, including EDR and anti-malware service for endpoints in Azure environments.
Backup and Recovery	Backup and Recovery covers controls to ensure that data and configuration backups are performed, validated, and protected at different service tiers.
Governance and Strategy	Develop a coherent security strategy and documented governance process to ensure security assurance, including roles and responsibilities for different cloud security functions, unified technical design, and policies and standards supporting them.

Resiliency for AVD Solution

To ensure data security and increase the availability of AVDs for cloud consumer organizations, AVD architects should deploy a DR strategy. A good DR strategy keeps your applications and workloads available when a service or Azure outage occurs.

DR is an essential topic in the breadth of scope in and of itself. We consider only crucial aspects of DR and take a more layman's terms perspective on various DR concepts. DR is available as part of AVD in case of an outage. The Azure service infrastructure components continue functioning as expected when there is an outage in an Azure region.

If your Azure region fails, you will need to replicate your VMs to another Azure region (the secondary location) so that your users can still connect. A secondary site is used to failover primary region resources in case of an outage. The second location will not interrupt access to apps for users. The secondary location must also access user identities, in addition to the VM replication. It can be achieved by using profile containers. Alternatively, you could use multiple pools of VMs with automated provisioning across regions instead of VM replication.

Gathering precise business requirements and known constraints for service recovery is based on the "Business Layer" of AVD design methodology. Documenting these items is the first step in the development of any AVD recovery plan.

The following steps help gain clarity on scope and provide direction on the DR strategy most suitable to meet the business and functional requirements and constraints.

Business continuity and DR architecture planning and considerations for Azure virtual apps and desktops are vital to achieving desired recovery time objective (RTO) and recovery point objective (RPO).

The RTO is a KPI that defines the time to recover your AVD services heeding a disaster to assure business continuity.

1. What backup strategy is used today for AVD components?

2. What is the AVD components backup frequency?

3. What is the AVD components retention period?

4. Where is AVD components offsite storage?

5. Are AVD components DR drill/tested?

6. Do AVD components have to be made available right away or within a certain period in a disaster?

The RPO measures the maximum amount of data an AVD end user can tolerate losing during a disaster. Additionally, architects can estimate the time that must pass between the last backup and a disaster without seriously altering end-user business operations.

1. DR can result in varying degrees of data loss, which is determined by the infrastructure component or data classification.

2. Is it possible for a service to recover data that is older than a year old?

3. In terms of 0 minutes? Or an hour? Or a month?

4. As AVD components are concerned with database changes and changes to user data (MSIX packages, User profiles, folder redirections, etc.), this consideration can apply only to the AVD components.

5. As with RTO, the downstream application system for AVD-hosted apps should be considered in your design thinking discussion.

Application readiness, geography, data residency or data classification, regulatory or corporate policy, network bandwidth, network connectivity, and scope of recovery are crucial elements that need significant attention in your design and deployment.

To maintain the integrity of the solution, DR components must also be kept up to date with production. Many customers overlook this activity when designing and deploying such a solution, then start consuming more platform resources in production and forget to increase available capacity to preserve the solution's DR integrity.

For organizations to align with DR needs and achieve recovery objectives, it is critical to understand HA vs. DR. While HA and DR are not synonymous, DR can utilize HA. The following is a description of HA and DR.

Fault tolerance is provided by HA. AVD end users will experience minimal disruption when a service fails over to another system. The solution can be as simple as a clustered application or load-balanced architecture to a more complex environment that is always available and mirrors the production configuration. Typically, failover is automated in these configurations, or you might refer to it as a "geo-redundant" deployment.

The primary goal of DR is to recover service to another location after a system failure at either the app level or the service level. Automatic and manual recovery processes are typically involved in DR. Steps and procedures are documented to orchestrate recovery. Redundancy and fault tolerance are not concerns in this strategy, and it is, in general, a broader scope approach designed to withstand multiple different types of failures. Planning personnel and resources to restore service is the defining concern of DR instead of HA, which is embedded into design and deployment specifications and solutions.

The AVD service is a Microsoft-managed service that provides a control plane for desktop virtualization. As far as I know, Microsoft does not offer an SLA. No SLA is in place for AVD, but we strive for 99.9% uptime. AVD retains customer metadata during breakdowns of a region to ensure business continuity. A failure of the primary location causes the secondary site to resume functioning as expected in case of an outage.

BCDR policies keep your apps and workload available during planned and unplanned service or Azure outages.

During outages, AVD preserves customer metadata with BCDR. A region's core infrastructure components will continue functioning as expected in the event of a regional outage. Service-related metadata can still be accessed, and available session hosts can still be reached. All tenant environments and hosts must remain accessible for the end-user connection to work. When a region goes down, make sure your users' VMs are replicated in a different location.

During an outage, primary site VMs fail over to replicated ones on the secondary site. The second location will not interrupt access to apps for users. You must also keep secondary locations accessible to user identities on top of VM replication. It is also necessary to replicate any profile containers you are using. Lastly, ensure that any business apps reliant on the primary location can fail over to the backup. In summary, if your AVD network goes down, you need to act in this order for AVD end users to stay connected to AVD services:

- Create a secondary site for the VMs.

- Use a secondary location for data replication if you are using profile containers.

- Ensure that the primary location and secondary location have the same user identities.

- If there is any line-of-business application that relies on your primary site, make sure it is migrated to the secondary site.

The following are best practices for AVD BCDR design:

- Microsoft recommends using the active-passive design pattern for the AVD host pool if it satisfies your AVD cloud consumer requirements for RPO and RTO.

- Microsoft recommends using Azure site recovery for personal host pools. Design patterns can be evaluated and compared to the deployment of another host pool in the secondary DR region.

- Microsoft recommends using maximum resiliency of the host pool in a single region and using availability zones. Verify the availability of the zones in each area and whether you can access the VM SKU in each zone.

Every organizational AVD design and deployment is different. However, Figure 5-41 shows the five key components essential to designing and deploying a DR solution for AVD.

Figure 5-41. *AVD security building blocks*

Physical and Virtual Networking- This is the first building block of DR; AVD architects should consider AVD cloud consumer network connectivity during an outage. For Azure resources to failover or communicate with a secondary region, an Azure network admin needs to ensure that a VNet has been set up and configured in their secondary region/location.

DR facility network sizing and firewalls must consider the network bandwidth used by AVD traffic. There are limits to the capacity of virtual firewalls and VPN gateways in Azure desktop virtualization environments. Averaging production traffic from the session host for sizing is essential to effectively size networking. Where network constraints exist, businesses must use different network configurations to accommodate the anticipated DR traffic load when invoked.

Consider an AVD cloud consumer end user who wants to access on-premises services and resources. A VNet will need to be configured as well to allow access to these sites via a VPN in the case of the AVD engineers. A virtual WAN connection, an

ExpressRoute, or a VPN can be established on-premises. On-premises environments can also be connected to AVD through a network virtual appliance (NVA).

Azure site recovery keeps business apps and workloads running during outages so business continuity can be ensured. Site recovery replicates workloads running on physical machines and VMs from a primary site to a secondary location. When an outage occurs at your prior site, you failover to the secondary location and access AVD; after the immediate area runs again, you can fall back to it.

As your primary network's settings are preserved, and peering is not required, Azure site recovery can also be used to set up the VNet in a failover region. The simplicity of its setup requirements makes it an ideal fit for smaller AVD deployments.

The peering of Azure VNets connects between two regions. A peering connection is useful for connecting two VNets without requiring the use of a VPN.

Relying on resources' BCDR and AVD plans should be thoroughly reviewed. Services like network connectivity, authentication, applications, and other on-premises and Azure resources are included.

- As part of a hub and spoke or virtual wide area network architecture, the network infrastructure must be prepared in the secondary region.

- Hybrid connectivity must be highly available in both the primary and secondary regions.

- The DR region must support AD authentication or ensure connectivity to the on-premises domain.

AVD Session Host Pool- This is the first building block of DR; design pattern for an AVD host pool can be active-active or active-passive.

Pros and Cons of Active-Active Design Pattern

- It is possible to test the DR location continuously.

- Neither performance nor cost optimization is considered with this configuration.

- An AVD end user doesn't have to reauthenticate when storage outages occur.

- VMs from different regions can be hosted in the same pool of hosts. FSLogix and office containers are replicated between the regions using the cloud cache in this scenario.

- In each region, for VMs, the registry entry for the local cloud cache needs to be inverted to give precedence to the registry entry for the cloud cache.

- Users may be routed to a remote AVD pool VM when load balancing of incoming connections fails to account for proximity; all hosts are equal.

- You can only use this configuration with pooled host pools. The desktops associated with a user on a particular session host VM won't be changed for a personal type even when unavailable.

Pros and Cons of Active-Passive Design Pattern

- Backups can be maintained with Azure site recovery or through a secondary host pool (hot standby).

- In addition to being available for private and pooled pools, Azure site recovery can be implemented per pool.

- In the failover region, you can create a new host pool while keeping all resources disabled. Any AVD end users for the failover region should be assigned to new application groups to use this method. Then you can create a hosted process using a recovery plan in Azure site recovery.

Resiliency of AVD host pools is implemented using an availability set: this guarantees HA at just the datacenter level of a single Azure datacenter only. You do not need to register these VMs manually when using Azure site recovery. The AVD agent configured on the secondary VM will automatically connect to the AVD service instance closest to it using the latest security token. The secondary region's VM (session host) will automatically be included in the pool of hosts. Only during this process will the customer be required to reconnect. There are no other manual processes needed besides the user connecting once.

To ensure the availability of AVD pools in all regions, the artifacts must be available even during a major disaster when using custom images. Azure shared image gallery can be used to replicate images across all regions where a host pool is deployed, with redundant storage, and in multiple copies.

The Microsoft recommendation is to use availability zones. The data centers where the session hosts and VMs are hosted are distributed across different zones. Although the VMs are still inside the same region, they are more resilient and have a formal 99.99% HA SLA. If a zone in the AVD is lost, the architects must consider capacity planning so that the AVD will continue to function.

Now that you understand how to design and implement a DR solution with VMs, the next essential component is configuring user and app data.

Assuming that profile containers are being used, the next step will be to set up data replication to the secondary server. You can collect FSLogix profiles in the following ways:

- Azure Files

- Azure NetApp Files

- Storage Spaces Direct

- Network drives

- Cloud Cache for replication

Deploy the following practices.

- Deploy Native Azure Replication with the following options

    - Azure Files Standard storage account replication,

    - Azure NetApp Files replication

    - Azure Files Sync for file servers

- Deploy FSLogix cloud cache for both application and AVD end-user data.

- For business-critical data access at all times, set up DR only for apps. The following method allows you to retrieve user data after an outage has ended.

Local profiles should be replicated to the second region by Azure site recovery if you use local profiles. The next step for most organizations using profile containers is to set up replication of the profile container to the secondary location. It is possible to reduce the time taken to back up, restore, and replicate data by separating the user profile and the Office container disks in a disaster situation.

FSLogix offers the opportunity and ability to designate them in separate storage locations. A typical Office profile can use a lot more space than the Office disk. Using the cache data will make backups, replications, and restorations far more time-consuming.

The Office disk does not need to be made resilient because it can be downloaded again; the data it contains is already present in Office 365 online.

AVD Hosted Applications and Their Downstream Applications- This is the third building block of DR. Before approaching disaster planning and design for AVD applications, analyze which applications accessed via AVD are most critical. AVD architects must distribute them from noncritical applications to provide multiple host pools with several DR approaches and abilities.

AVD architects should ensure that apps running in the primary region will fail at the secondary location if data is lost. Also, be sure to configure the settings the apps need to work in the new location. For example, if one of the applications is dependent on the SQL backend, make sure to replicate SQL in the secondary location. The application team should configure it to use the second location as either part of the failover processor or its default configuration. AVD architects should consider application dependencies on Azure site recovery plans.

If there is any data or service running in the primary region, it should be failover to prevent business applications from failing. Any business applications that rely on local data should be able to fail over to the secondary location. Depending on the downstream dependencies, it could be a web service, a SQL database, or another downstream component.

End User Data- This is the fourth building block of DR. Azure services are always available because Microsoft strives to ensure this. However, unplanned service outages may occur. If AVD requires resiliency, Microsoft recommends using geo-redundant storage (GRS) to copy your data to a second region. A DR plan for region-based cloud services is also important for AVD customers. A DR plan must prepare for failover to the secondary endpoint if the primary endpoint is unavailable.

Account failover is supported for Azure storage accounts with GRS. If the primary endpoint becomes unavailable with account failover, your AVD administrator may initiate the failover process for your storage account. As a result of the failover, your secondary endpoint becomes your primary endpoint. Once the failover is complete, clients can begin writing to the new primary endpoint. With ARM deployments, account failover is available for general-purpose v1, general-purpose v2, and Blob storage account types.

Storage accounts on Azure are replicated multiple times to ensure HA. The redundancy option you choose for your account depends on the level of resilience you need. Adding GRS to your account with or without the possibility of reading access from the second region will protect you against regional outages.

The GRS or geo-zone-redundant storage (GZRS) copies your data asynchronously in two geographic regions that are at least hundreds of miles apart. If the primary region goes down, the secondary region will provide a redundant source of your data. An endpoint can be failed over to become the primary endpoint.

GRS with read-access (RA-GRS) or GZRS with read access (RA-GZRS) is GRS with read access to a secondary endpoint. Access can be made to the secondary endpoint when the primary endpoint is down by enabling read access. If you want maximum availability and durability for your applications, Microsoft recommends RA-GZRS.

Azure Files offers failover replication for storage accounts against the other region configured in your storage redundancy plan. The GRS account type is the only one that supports this. You can also use AzCopy or any other file copy mechanism, such as Robocopy.

In case of a major disaster, Microsoft may initiate a regional failover. This situation does not require any action from you. You won't have write access to your storage account until the Microsoft-managed failover has been completed. In the case of RA-GRS or RA-GZRS configuration, your applications can read from the secondary region.

End-User Identities- This is the fifth and final building block of DR. In case of a failover, it must be ensured that the domain controller is available at the secondary location/region. In an outage, the domain controller can be kept accessible by the following three methods.

- Choice 1: Deploy an AD domain controller at the secondary location,

- Choice 2: Use on-premises AD domain controller in your location,

- Choice 3: Replicate AD domain controller via Azure site recovery.

Using site recovery, you can protect the domain controller or DNS server on the VM. In test failovers, site recovery replicates the domain controller. It should meet the following requirements:

- As a global catalog server, the domain controller serves as a domain controller.

- Domain controllers should assume Flexible Single Master Operations (FSMO) role ownership when testing failovers. A failover would be needed if these roles were not captured.

The site recovery replication must be set up on at least one VM hosting a domain controller or DNS server. The target site must be configured with an additional domain controller if more than one is in your environment. In addition to Azure, you can have a second data center on-premises. You might want to fail over the entire site if you only have a few applications and one domain controller. In this case, Microsoft recommends using site recovery to replicate the domain controller to the target site, either in Azure or in a secondary on-premises datacenter. For test failover, you can use the same replicated domain controller or DNS VM. Suppose your environment contains many applications and more than one domain controller. Then Microsoft recommends that you set up an additional domain controller on the target site (either in Azure or in a secondary on-premises datacenter). For test failover, you can use a domain controller that's replicated by site recovery. An additional domain controller can be used on the target site to enable failover.

Site-to-Site Protection: The secondary site should have a domain controller. When you promote the server to a domain controller role, specify the name of the same domain used on the primary site. The AD Sites and Services snap-in lets you configure settings on the site link object to which the sites are added. You can configure settings on a site link to control how often replication occurs between two or more locations.

Site-to-Azure protection: In the Azure virtual network, create your domain controller. When you promote the server to a domain controller role, specify the same domain name that's used on the primary site. Change the DNS server in Azure to be used by the virtual network.

Azure-to-Azure protection: You must first create a virtual network for a domain controller. When you promote the server to a domain controller role, specify the same domain name that's used on the primary site. Change the DNS server in Azure to be used by the virtual network.

Microsoft AVD architecture is a modular design that can quickly grow while supporting in-country and out-of-region user demands. AVD DR plans consist of many components, and their goal is to protect cloud consumers in the event of an unexpected event. While human actions can lead to a high risk of disaster – cyber-attacks, hacking, and so on – natural disasters must be planned for, including tornadoes, fires, floods, earthquakes, and more. Your DR plan should verify that users can access resources and services and test it to ensure it works. Planned site-level failover and failback between primary and secondary sites should be managed via technical recovery plan and procedure.

Planned Failover and Failback: A Microsoft AVD application available at the primary site and action performed part of the DR drill.

Forced Failover and Failback: A Microsoft AVD application not available at the primary site needs to be activated at the secondary site, and the action performed needs to be part of actual DR.

So, build the plan for this specific scenario.

Summary

In the final chapter of the book, you read about managing, securing, and resiliency essentials of each building block of the AVD solution DaaS, along with a list of design principles and best practices to consider in managing and securing from day 2 operations.

Thank you for choosing to read this book.

Index

A

© Puthiyavan Udayakumar 2022
P. Udayakumar, *Design and Deploy Microsoft Azure Virtual Desktop*,
https://doi.org/10.1007/978-1-4842-7796-6